TOWARDS A MEASURE OF MAN

INTERNATIONAL LIBRARY OF SOCIOLOGY
AND SOCIAL RECONSTRUCTION

Founded by Karl Mannheim
Editor: W. J. H. Sprott

A catalogue of the books available in the INTERNATIONAL LIBRARY OF SOCIOLOGY AND SOCIAL RECONSTRUCTION and new books in preparation for the Library will be found at the end of this volume.

TOWARDS
A MEASURE OF MAN
THE FRONTIERS
OF NORMAL ADJUSTMENT

BY

PAUL HALMOS

Lecturer in Psychology and Education
University College of North Staffordshire

Author of *Solitude and Privacy*

LONDON
Routledge & Kegan Paul

First published in 1957
by Routledge & Kegan Paul Ltd.
Broadway House, 68–74 Carter Lane
London E.C.4
Printed in Great Britain
by Butler & Tanner Ltd.
Frome and London

To

ELIZABETH AND IMRE HARTMAN

PREFACE

TODAY sociologists file away their facts and findings in unlabelled cabinets which have no alphabetical index. The cabinets are also widely dispersed and no single sociologist is in a position to be familiar with the location of all of them. Having largely inherited the filing cabinets from social sciences which had been established in business a good deal earlier than sociology, sociology was loath to discard them and is still clinging to them in a pennywise fashion.

Alas this clinging is a virtue of thrifty beginnings and not of epoch-making enterprises. The present book certainly does not claim to be epoch-making. If anything it is a gamble with the accumulated small change of modern psychological knowledge in the hope of winning some of the coveted prizes of sociology and perhaps even of moral philosophy. Yet should my book be branded as a rash enterprise it may still have been well worth the adventure of writing it, for, as it is often observed, even those contribute to the exploration of a maze who come back only to report the itinerary of their failures. Furthermore it seems to me that, even if my stake proves unwise, it will be a gamble of this sort which will eventually rescue social science from its present predicament.

This book deals centrally with the concepts of 'normal' and 'abnormal' in human personality and behaviour. It seeks to establish whether one or the other of these can be defined and thereby an absolute measure of man educed. The string of essays which follows opens with a discourse on the first principles upon which the subsequent chapters depend. Here I shall rely on metaphysical, biological, and psychological information. Following this I develop my arguments to a stage when the conditions of defining the human 'norm' or 'abnorm' are within our view. Thereupon the conclusion I shall reach is that, even though 'normality' is indefinable, the minimum area of 'abnormality' is already a subject of substantial agreement. Yet if my definition

v

of abnormal adjustment, my 'abnorm', will stand the test of time it will inevitably work in an indirect manner as a minimum norm as well. Thereafter I shall be obliged to pay special attention to the exceptional performances in creative work where the 'abnorm' may be easily confused with the necessary or even with the meritorious. A chapter is devoted to examining the relationship between artistic, political, and scientific achievement and the concept of the 'abnorm'. After this I shall turn to the problem of insight upon which the whole question of evidence will largely depend. For without sufficient evidence resistance to my conclusions would forestall any impact I may hope to make on sociological theory and eventually on social action. That no striking impact on social science is anticipated by my conclusions is made clear by their very nature. In the concluding chapter the ground is prepared to match my sociology of adjustment with an adjustment of sociology.

Some years ago, when I first composed a brief outline of this work, I had several discussions with Dr. Portia Holman who saved me much labour by giving me valuable criticisms at that early stage. I wish to record my thanks to her. To Professor Aubrey Lewis I am indebted for a timely warning and advice without which my work would have been sidetracked and considerably delayed. I am most grateful to Dr. Mary Wilson for reading my manuscript and correcting some of its errors. I should like to thank my friend George Buchanan for a searching and sympathetic appraisal of my ideas; he too prompted me to think again when complacency had halted reflection. As in the past so now again I could count on Professor T. H. Marshall to size up and review my work. I wish to express to him my warmest appreciation for some must useful suggestions. It gives me pleasure to write here of my great indebtedness to Dr. Eva Ruth Balken without whose generosity I could not have created the conditions of privacy so necessary for scholarly work. And finally I should like to say that Mrs. Irene Davies gave much of her time and her incisive judgment while assisting me with the final revision of this work's form, style, and substance. To her I am particularly grateful.

I am, of course, alone responsible for the outcome.

P. H.

CONTENTS

vii

CONTENTS

'No hypothesis can lay claim to any value unless
it assembles many phenomena under one concept.'
                Goethe in a letter to Sommering,
                        17 Aug. 1795.

'General concepts and great conceit are always
poised to make a terrible mess of things.'
                Goethe: *Maxims and Reflections*,
                        471 (1829).

I

THE EVOLUTIONARY BACKGROUND

OF THE HUMAN NORM

THE basic contention of my book, *Solitude and Privacy*, that social need is a central quality of life and a principal determinant of human life, has been criticized on several grounds. As this contention is essential to the successful development of the following argument, its brief review and a countering of some of its criticisms are indispensable to my reflections in the present essay. Yet this retrospect will not be in the nature of a recapitulation or designed as a vindication. One hopes that the maturing of one's ideas, stimulated and nourished by observations made by others, may lead to a restatement of those ideas in a more coherent and comprehensive form. In that book, when I was writing of a specific social problem, the problem of loneliness in modern mass society, it was neither necessary nor advisable to digress more widely into metapsychology; the subject matter of the present work both permits and justifies such digression.

The social need of man has been labelled from time to time as 'gregarious instinct', 'social instinct', 'phylic force', 'bio-social drive', 'herd instinct', and perhaps others. But as 'instincts', 'forces', and 'drives' are terms which commit one to a vitalistic philosophy, it seemed desirable that the term *Principium Sociale* should be introduced in preference to the various others with their different connotations. This term was disliked by some on account of its erudite lifelessness and indeed it will be superseded here, though for different reasons. Already in that book, I began to perceive that this *Principium* was not at all essentially *social* in the accepted sense of the word. What in fact it was did not elude me but I did not feel that was the right place to enlarge

3

on a systematic analysis of its ancestry and present character. This omission must be made good now. The analysis will be carried out in two instalments; the first will treat the phylogenetic background of the social needs of man, the second will consider the ontogenesis of this need.

1. *The Phylogenesis of Social Need*

The various theories of evolution show certain points of agreement which, however, on account of their 'simplicity' and of the remoteness of the events to which they refer, are easily ignored. Hypotheses concerning the origin of life on earth constitute such a point of agreement. Thus the medieval belief in the spontaneous generation of life was effectively discredited by Pasteur, but if life was to begin at all, even some 3000 million years ago, it had to be spontaneously generated from the inorganic environment of the primeval earth. Professor Bernal rightly observes that '. . . life in its first stages was entirely dependent on the pre-existence of organic molecules'.[1] These living molecules have been called 'aperiodic crystals'[2] which have their atomic components lined up according to a principle as yet unknown, whereas the periodic crystals of inorganic molecules are fairly well mapped. Now underlying these propositions there is an agreement that spontaneous generation of life must have taken place through some sort of union of inorganic substances. This agreement is my starting point. One may, of course, object that any generalizations which I may cull from speculations on the origin of life are bound to be unconvincing. But are they? If the different versions of the evolutionary theory begin with the same or, at any rate, very similar assumptions about the beginning of evolution, the points on which they agree may well reflect the truth and this truth may assist us in understanding less remote matters. After all, the primordial passage from the inorganic to the organic is merely the first instance of a process which may be going on always, establishing a continuity between life and non-life in our time. According to Sherrington, 'when we systematize, the animate falls unconstrainedly into series with the inanimate. The inanimate then

---

[1] *The Physical Basis of Life*, 1951, p. 47.
[2] *What is Life?* by E. Schroedinger, 1944.

becomes merely a special case within the more general.'[1] A. N. Whitehead too included the atomic and molecular aggregates of physics under the general concept of organism. That this continuity is most relevant to my analysis of the social need of man will become apparent from the following important statement by W. M. Wheeler:

There is something fundamentally social in living things, and closer scrutiny shows that this must be characteristic of all life, since every organism is, at least temporarily, associated with other organisms, even if only with members of the opposite sex and with its parents. ... This statement holds good even of such supposedly unsocial creatures as lions, eagles, sharks, tiger-beetles, and spiders. There are, in fact, no truly solitary organisms. We may say, therefore, that the social is a correlate as well as an emergent of all life in the sense in which Morgan speaks of the mind as being both a correlate and emergent of life. ... Indeed, *the correlations of the social—using the term in its general sense—even extend down through the non-living to the very atom with its organization of component electrons.*[2]

It seems, therefore, that the inorganic-organic continuity has a suggestive contribution to make to the interpretation of the concept 'social'. I believe that this contribution may be made clearer by considering the following points:

(*a*) Atomic constituents unite into atoms.

(*b*) Atoms unite into molecules either with a periodicity that is comprehensible to us or through a periodicity which is not. It is a matter of convenience to describe the latter as aperiodicity.

(*c*) The aperiodic (organic) molecules unite into unicellular living beings. Life appears on earth, according to any account of the theory of evolution, as the outcome of coherence or union. No matter how far our mathematical and mechanical interpretation of this union advance, 'the ultimate entelechy of aggregation ... remains metaphysical' (Bernal). It is certain that each of the three levels of union so far mentioned has its own laws, which are sometimes analogous, sometimes not; yet in spite of all differences between the method of union on each level the principle of union, an ultimate principle, or entelechy, is the same.

[1] *Man and his Nature*, 1951, p. 122.
[2] 'Emergent Evolution and the Development of Societies', by W. M. Wheeler, *Essays in Philosophical Biology*, 1939, pp. 158–9.

5

(*d*) The various theories of evolution all derive multicellular life from the unicellular creatures of the primeval slime. When these began to form themselves into multicellular organisms the evolutionary process had got under way already. Until multicellular organisms appeared mitosis (i.e. reproduction through cell-division) involved separation of the individual units of life. The evolutionary process would have come to a standstill had there not been a force powerful enough to oppose the separation and dispersion of life in spite of mitosis. No multicellular organism could have come into being without this rebellion against separation and dispersion. One of two things had to happen: either cell division ceased to involve separation, or a reunion of separated cells into colonies had to take place. Contemporary microbiology strongly supports the evolutionary hypothesis that both of these occurred.[1]

The simplest multicellular organisms betray little or no division of labour; cell-co-operation is a later evolutionary achievement. The irrevocable sharing-out of functions came slowly and the delay can sometimes be observed even in ontogeny. A famous experiment reported by Hans Driesch[2] illustrates this intermediate stage.

I must mention an . . . experiment on the egg of the sea-urchin [writes Driesch] the so-called 'cleavage' of the egg . . . ends in the formation of the blastula, i.e. a hollow sphere built up of about a thousand cells forming an epithelium. If you cut this blastula with a pair of very fine scissors in any direction you like, each part so obtained will go on developing—provided it is not smaller than one quarter of the whole—and will form a *complete* larva of small size.

The random cut produces two perfect individuals which shows that the cells of the blastula are an aggregate of 'equipotential' (Driesch) individuals, that is to say, it is a multicellular union without an irrevocable division of function. Driesch calls such systems as this 'harmonious equipotential systems'. The colonies of bacteria and spores are not dissimilar in this respect, though there are many which have already passed beyond this stage. A

[1] A third variant is suggested by Hadži, 'By internal cellularization polynuclear Protozoa gave rise to Turbellaria.' (Quoted by G. R. de Beer in *Embryos and Ancestors*, 1951, p. 108.) This is, however, a sub-variant of 'mitosis without separation'.
[2] *The Problem of Individuality*, by Hans Driesch, 1914, p. 11.

simple aggregation without division of labour is not yet an 'organism'; the latter is brought into being eventually by each individual renouncing some of its functions and surrendering its individuality. Driesch defines his harmonious equipotential system in the following, '*Every* cell of the original system can play *every* single role in morphogenesis; which role it will play is merely "a function of its position".' The individuals had been self-sufficient originally but they later gave rise to true multi-cellular organisms. No evolution could have taken place without these individuals surrendering their self-sufficiency. If mitosis is compared to the centrifugal effect of a 'life force', reunion or the cessation of separation is its centripetal effect. They are opposites and yet the dual facets of the self-same life function. The first multicellular unit consisted of Siamese twins, but the twins were not siblings: they were parent and offspring. Alternatively the first multicellular unit came about through the reunion of integral cells which abandoned their independence. Here, once again, the same entelechy, the same principle of union, operates. W. Patten recognized the philosophical significance of this principle; W. C. Allee who sympathized with Patten's point of view described it in these words:

... Patten outlined, mainly from philosophical considerations, his conclusions concerning the importance of biological co-operation. He was rightly impressed by the fact that cells were originally separate, as protozoans are to-day. Some, however, evolved the habit of remaining attached to one another after division. This made a beginning from which the many celled higher animals could develop. With each increase in the ability of cells to co-operate there came power to increase the complexity of organization of the cell masses. The highly evolved bodies of men are thus an expression of increasing inter-cellular co-operation that finally reaches a point at which, for many purposes, the individual person becomes the unit rather than the individual cells of which he is composed.[1]

Patten related co-operation *between* animals to the prior co-operation between the cells of their organisms, a co-operation which in its origin was, in fact, a co-operation between initially independent unicellular creatures. The continuity of the same entelechy, the same principle of union, is recognized by Patten

---

[1] *Co-operation Among Animals*, by W. C. Allee, 1951, pp. 12–13.

and Allee though it is not as yet placed by them in a broad metaphysical system.

The fourth level of union is the formation of multicellular organisms. These four levels are essential to any evolutionary hypothesis and are in fact explicitly or implicitly incorporated in all of them.[1] Surveying the last three of the four levels so far mentioned I deduce two basic principles which are universally pertinent to life: (1) *the principle of growth* and (2) *the principle of cohesion*. These two principles do not define life but they are characteristic of it in all circumstances. When a unicellular creature absorbs food and grows, it reaches a saturation point in its development and undergoes mitosis. If separation follows, the procreation of two new individuals is an instance of growth. A whole species is itself the product of such a growth as this. On those levels of life where sexual reproduction does not as yet play any part procreation is manifestly an instance of expansion or growth. Sexual reproduction is a later acquisition of life and phylogenetically sex is not an ultimate principle. At the dawn of life the production of another independent and self-sufficient individual is the product of growth and not that of sex. Yet when the overspill of growth results in separation this is resisted. The second principle, that of cohesion, means that this resistance operates universally in all separation. But were resistance effective on the level on which separation occurs growth would be arrested and life terminated. Resistance manifests itself by seeking restitution for the separation on a level where continued growth of gestator and offspring would not be hampered. The evolutionary hypothesis depends on both of these principles for without them evolution would be incon-

---

[1] Julian Huxley developed a scheme not unlike mine many years ago. In his book *The Individual in the Animal Kingdom*, 1912, pp. 157–8, he sketches the process from the point of view of individuation. It goes something like this: A.1, unicellular creatures are individuals of the first grade; A.2, compound wholes made up of A.1 without division of labour, e.g. the sixteen celled flagellate gonium; A.3, same as A.2 but with division of labour, e.g. volvox globator or the haplozoon; B.1, full individuals of the second grade, e.g. the metazoa including man taken singly; B.2, compounds made up of second grade individuals without division of labour, e.g. sponges, corals; B.3, same as B.2 but with division of labour, e.g. Bougainvillea; C.1, full individuals of the third grade, e.g. ant communities, *human society*. The raising of the latter to the rank of 'individuals' is an interesting suggestion with somewhat ominous ideological and political consequences. Although there are some differences Huxley's scheme is built up with the same logic as I used in mine.

ceivable. On the inorganic level there need be no analogous principles though it may well be that there is such a thing as 'the evolution of the inorganic'. On the macro-organismic level the analogous principles are: (1) individuation and (2) socialization.

From egg-laying and hatching to mammalian birth the range and variability of reproduction is immense. The fact that these procreations are no longer instances of simple mitosis, that in most of these cases macro-organisms separate at birth, does not weaken my hypothesis that whenever there is separation of life there is also a resistance to separation and a seeking of reunion on a new level. This 'new' level is in fact a 'higher' level though, for the time being, I do not propose to examine the moral implications of this epithet. And again the fact that these procreations are complicated from a very early stage onwards— even among some micro-organisms—by the appearance of sex, need not disconcert us. That the autonomy of sex is so striking that it is regarded by our age as an ultimate biological principle will not conceal its origin or its close collateral relationships. On the level of evolution where sex is firmly established, its autonomy is not questioned; but its imperialistic claims for all-inclusiveness contradict the evolutionary theory; of this we shall hear more later. The principles that determine life vary according to the evolutionary level and while once the level of sexual procreation has been reached sex is a determining principle, at the same time the more general principles of growth and cohesion are found on all levels, and even though the form of their manifestation has changed, they have survived the whole evolutionary span.

Resuming the examination of these basic principles I find that the fourth level is followed by a form of cohesion on a 'higher' level especially deserving of our concern. The macro-organisms cannot remain in, or enter into, the inseparable organic bonds accepted by cell-colonies, for instance. Because plants need food and air and animals must move, macro-organisms could not survive in such bonds. Siamese twins have very slight chances of survival and one need not labour a point as obvious as this with further illustrations. The cohesion is now sought on a level which can, at least, be properly described as *social*. Four levels of cohesion have been outlined in my scheme and this may be described as the fifth. It is often argued that a large number of animal species are not social and that comparatively few of them are truly gregarious. There are many weighty reasons why this objection fails to divert me from my conclusions. These reasons taken in their entirety will easily allow me to proceed with my argument.

Growth and cohesion are action-reaction principles and in the many cases where the reaction of cohesion is delayed or completely fails a life-form exists which will be left behind in the evolutionary process either to manifest cohesion belatedly or to become extinct. Furthermore, all life is lived in and by *species*: no life can subsist for any length of time without the context of a species of life. Apart from parthenogenesis—a marginal minority—procreative behaviour, if nothing else, in the so-called solitary animals necessitates temporary togetherness of two or more individuals. Parasitic, symbiotic, and other *inter-species* associations notwithstanding, the continuation of life must be assured by at least some contacts between members of the *same species*.

And since no one has yet demonstrated the existence of truly asocial animals [wrote Allee], it is impossible to define the lower limits of subsocial living. All that can be found is a gradual development of social attributes, suggesting . . . a substratum of social tendencies that extends throughout the entire animal kingdom. From this substratum social life rises by the operation of different mechanisms and with various forms of expression until it reaches its present climax in insects and in vertebrates including man. Always it is based on phases of mass physiology and social biology that taken alone and in simplest development seems to be social by implication only.

If social attributes develop gradually they may remain latent or may have been arrested in the so-called solitary species. Now this may seem an arbitrary assumption but let us consider whether the alternative view to this, i.e. that the social instinct is not universal, is tenable. Is it true that the principle of cohesion is not universal and that social behaviour is the specific quality of *some* species only? (The third view, that there are no 'social instincts' at all, I shall examine below at some length.) In answer to this another of Allee's observations may be quoted:

The insects stand at the apex of one long line of evolution; mammals and birds are at the peak of another line of evolution; the two have been distinct for a very long time. This view of evolution indicates that the ancestral tree of animals is not like that of a pine tree

10

with man at the very top and insects and all other animals arranged as side shoots from one main stem. Rather, there are at least two main branches that start low, as in a well-pruned peach tree. Both rise to approximately equal heights, indicating correctly that in their way the insects are as specialized as the birds or mammals. Since both insects and mammals have developed closely knit groups, this is further evidence that there is a widely distributed potentiality of social life.

Of course, what is distributed is not merely a latent potentiality but the entelechy which seeks cohesion on ever higher levels. We are indebted to F. Frazer Darling for a brilliant interpretation which disposes of at least one notorious argument from the armoury of the 'solitary animals theory'. This interpretation is important for it may serve as a basis of analogy in other cases. It concerns the well-known contention that territorial monopoly by single animals is a clear example of solitariness and, therefore, evidence against the universality of social needs. Frazer Darling writes:

I would like to put forward the hypothesis that one of the important functions of territory breeding birds is the provision of *periphery* —periphery being defined as that kind of edge where there is another bird of the same species occupying a territory. One pair of warblers in a wood have, in effect, no territory at all; they are merely existing in space. But by pushing up against each other, rather than spreading themselves out, the birds are giving themselves peripheries, and there are doubtless optimum peripheries for each species. The breeding territory has little to do with a sufficiency of feeding grounds for raising the brood . . . *If this hypothesis is correct, then territorial behaviour as a whole is a social phenomenon, and it has survival value*[1] [F. D.'s italics].

Some years earlier he stated in another publication, 'The observance of territory tends to draw animals together in groups in which they know each other, and it brings advantages'.[2] The so-called topological psychologists are familiar with the phenomenon of parcelling out 'social space' and they were not driven to think that this proved asociality. Ferdinand Toennies anticipated the later hypothesis of universal sociality when he wrote:

One distinguishes between animals which live together and those

[1] 'Social Behaviour and Survival', *The Auk*, April 1952, pp. 183–91.
[2] 'The Social Life of Animals', by F. Frazer Darling, *Proc. Roy. Phil. Soc. Glasgow*, 139th Session, 1940–1, LXV, pp. 104–20.

which do not, i.e. between social and unsocial animals. This distinction is correct, but the fact is overlooked that it refers only to different stages of collective life ... it is also forgotten that staying together is a natural phenomenon, while in every instance special reason has to be given for separation.[1]

To insist, therefore, that cohesion is the product of a mutation and that the species are classifiable into 'collective' and 'non-collective' categories is theoretically unsound.

Ever since the Darwinian image of 'nature red in tooth and claw' captivated the minds of *laisser faire* business men, co-operation had to be reinstated as an instrument of evolution. Since Kropotkin's *Mutual Aid*, many have claimed that Darwin's picture was one-sided. In an excellently documented work by Ashley Montague the case against the monopoly of competition is conclusively stated and supported by a large number of authoritative sources. Montague is mainly concerned in combating the Darwinian fallacy that competition is the key to evolutionary advance. It is well and proper that this should be done but we must here point out that the rehabilitation of 'co-operation' does not terminate the dualism of competition-co-operation. Neither of these two reigns supreme. Darwin himself sensed this dualism for in *The Origin of Species* he wrote: 'I should premise that I use this term, (Struggle for Existence), in a large and metaphorical sense including dependence of one being on another, and including (which is more important) not only the life of the individual, but success in leaving progeny'. On the other hand, the opponents of the view that competition alone matters felt obliged to make concessions to this same dualism. Geddes and Thomson, for instance, who wrote that '... love and sociality, co-operation and sacrifice (are) the highest expressions of the central evolutionary process of the natural world'[2] also admitted that 'Competition and survival of the fittest are never wholly eliminated, but reappear on each new plane to work out the predominance of the higher, i.e. more integrated and associated type, the phalanx being victorious till in turn it meets the legion'.[3] The true meaning of competition is that in it individuation (growth) asserts itself at

[1] *Community and Association*, 1955, p. 59.
[2] *The Evolution of Sex*, 1901, p. 330.
[3] Op. cit., p. 329.

the expense of socialization (cohesion); thus my dualism can look back upon the competition-co-operation schema as its ancestor. The anthropomorphic element in 'competition-co-operation' cannot be detected in 'growth-cohesion': 'growth' and 'cohesion' are non-committal, empirical concepts whereas competition and co-operation project human experiences into the life of non-human nature.

The doctrineo f sociability by mutation pretends to have received empirical support whereas all it has to offer is a hypothesis which is more cumbersome than mine. The theory of 'sociability by mutation' does not even obey the law of parsimony, known as Occam's Razor.[1] Instead of devoting any further attention to this doctrine, it is much more important for me to show how closely the ultimate principle of cohesion, working on the fifth level, is connected with the social instinct. Animal ecologists widely confirm that the social organizations of animals spring from the more stable family bonds. Among species where gestation is not a hurried episode and where nursing follows birth the young remain with the parents for varying periods even after they have learnt to fend for themselves. N. Tinbergen, who is an opponent of the theory of a social instinct writes, 'By comparing solitary, intermediate, and higher social groups . . . it is found that the social organization has evolved from a family of mother with the brood, then a division of labour with increasing complexity of co-operation developed'.[2] And commenting on flocks he remarks, 'This type of community . . . begins as a relationship between an individual and one of its organs, and it changes gradually into one between individuals'. And later on he notes, 'Most insect states take their origin in a fertilized female. Many insects abandon their eggs as soon as they are laid and the 'community' never passes beyond the relationship between individual and organ' [italics mine]. This is a telling observation: Tinbergen confirms here that there is a continuity between the two kinds of bonds, that which links gestator and offspring and that which links members of the same community. Darwin himself concurred with this when he offered

[1] I.e. that we should not multiply our entities or principles unless it is necessary. 'Frustra fit per plura quod potest fieri per pauciora.' According to Professor Flew this is Occam's original formula. ('It is futile to do with more elements what can be done with fewer.')

[2] Social Behaviour in Animals, 1953, p. 121.

13

a similar account of the origin of the social instinct, 'The feeling
of pleasure from society is probably an extension of the parental
or filial affections, since the social instinct seems to be developed
by the young remaining for a long time with their parents . . .'[1]
W. M. Wheeler arrived at the same conclusion some thirty odd
years ago. He found clearly manifested tendencies towards
social life as far back as the Carboniferous period and shows
that at the beginning of the Oligocene between some 55 and 65
million years ago ants were as fully socialized as they are today.
He claimed that social behaviour developed twenty-four times
in more or less distantly related families of insects and asserted that in every case this came about through the prolonged
association of a mother or of both parents with eggs and the
young. In his view, ants are the dominant insects on the earth,
probably exceeding all other insects in numbers, and their
dominance is due in large measure to their social life.[2] Sir
Arthur Keith based his 'group theory of human evolution' on
the doctrine that human society issues from the kinship group.
He agreed with '. . . the opinion that the original grouping of
mankind was by kinship, and that it was only when such groups
settled on the land that the demarcation became territorial'.[3]

Robert M. Yerkes' *Chimpanzees* contains a delightful account
of the transition from maternal dependence to social dependence; Yerkes concludes 'The initial specific dependence upon the
mother gives place rapidly to a generalized dependence on the
extending social environment which may combine for years and
ordinarily weakens or disappears only in late maturity or old
age'. It is fascinating to compare the findings of a zoologist such
as Yerkes with those of a cautious empirical psychologist such
as Piaget; the latter remarks, '. . . as soon as the individual
escapes the domination of age, he tends towards co-operation
as the normal form of social equilibrium'.[4] That 'love is cloaked
in parenthood'[5] was perceived by Hume and there have been
several philosophers who regarded the state or the community
as the family 'writ large'.

Nevertheless some works on animal ecology question this con-

[1] *The Descent of Man*, 1932, p. 161.
[2] *Social Life Among the Insects*, by W. M. Wheeler, 1923, p. 7.
[3] *A New Theory of Human Evolution*, 1948, p. 5.
[4] *The Moral Development of the Child*, 1932, p. 99.
[5] *Essays and Treatises on Several Subjects*, Vol. I, p. 237.

tinuity between the biological and social bond, for example, 'Although insect societies are doubtless primarily developments of family systems, adaptive group life may emerge from aggregations of adults not necessarily associated with family and sex relations'.[1] In the first place this is difficult to substantiate; surely no one can assert that these aggregations do not absolutely depend on the extended family bonds which characterize the early life of each separate individual before aggregation comes into being. Migrating birds form enormous aggregations at times but the birds are not unfamiliar with the idea of co-operation and group life before they take part in it. Secondly, we may recall that the principle of cohesion functioned in a two-fold manner even on the fourth level of cohesion, i.e. protozoa grew into metazoa by mitosis without separation or they achieved this state through the formation of colonies. It is probable that the former was the dominant method of cohesion and that the latter was a delayed-action effect of the same principle. The process to which Allee *et al.* refer is analogous to colony formation on the protozoan level. Another criticism of the view that family life, and in particular protracted nursing, is the source of the later social needs is this: how is it that both gregarious and non-gregarious animals may receive extended maternal care? Tiger cubs and calves may experience an equally solicitous mothering, yet how different their social behaviour! These puzzling variations show no more than that the social behaviour of animals is widely different in form and not that some species are altogether unsocial. Anyone who observes the silent togetherness of domestic cats, their eyeing one another and their scuffles, cannot help feeling that feline social life consists in communications of an apparently non-co-operative kind which is yet unmistakably social.

2. *The Ontogenesis of Man's Social Need*

The ontogenetical evidence tallies well with the foregoing phylo-genetical account. Every time growth passes its saturation point and issues into a new individuality reaction sets in, as if cohesion claimed its rights. Evidence for this is supplied by modern

---

[1] *Principles of Animal Ecology*, W. C. Allee, A. E. Emerson, P. Park, T. Park, K. P. Schmidt, 1950, p. 687.

15

psychology. If the principle of cohesion is effective even in the moment of separation what would its effect be in the course of mammalian birth in general and human birth in particular? If the appearance of a new individual is the manifestation of the principle of growth, what is the manifestation of the principle of cohesion on this occasion? The Rankian Theory of the birth trauma, anticipated by Freud also, comes to my aid and supports my thesis. The Rankian 'birth trauma' has been received with incredulity by most people. Surely the experience of being born could not be construed as a shock or injury to life when it is, in fact, the supreme affirmation of life itself! The logic of nature came into conflict with the logic of temporal minds. Rarely does the temporal mind sense the realities of the universe to a degree where it is bold enough to question its own logic. There are, however, some inspiring precedents; Heraclitus taught that opposites not only are complementary and involve one another but that they are one and the same. One may also say that though the centripetal and centrifugal effects of revolutions are in opposition to each other they are both inseparably the content and meaning of the self-same revolutions. *'Das geeinte zu entzweien das Entzweite zu einigen ist das Leben der Natur'* (Nature lives by joining separate things and dividing those that are united), declared Goethe demonstrating how poetic insight could transcend the Principle of Contradiction.[1] 'What we call our "unconscious" (the deepest strata of our minds, made up of instinctual impulses)', wrote Freud, 'knows nothing whatever of negatives or of denials—contradictories coincide in it . . .'[2] But the temporal, and so often pedestrian, mind dare not risk as much as this. A naïve critic of *Solitude and Privacy* commented:

The author disposes briefly, but effectively with the Freudian idea of sex as the main basis of sociability, but the approved substitute is even less adequate, namely, the baby's craving for the security of the mother's womb. If one is to speculate on such a doubtful topic

[1] We have now reached a stage when the scientist too is obliged to follow the poet: '. . . in his recent Gifford lectures the Danish physicist Niels Bohr has propounded a doctrine of complementarity, which admits that human logic can interpret ultimate problems only by means of two antithetical hypotheses' (C. E. Raven, *Christianity and Science*, 1955, p. 37).

[2] 'Thoughts for the Times on War and Death', *Collected Papers*, 1946, Vol. IV, pp. 288–317.

surely it is reasonable to suppose that, as most babies finally struggle to get out, they have got a little bored with the close confinement.[1]

The Freudian and Rankian evidence of the trauma of birth is facetiously glossed over by this critic yet one must not get too impatient with his lack of comprehension; after all, the empirical proofs of the trauma are even scantier than those of some other psychiatric doctrines which have been received with no less incredulity. Even Freud himself did not attach much significance to the trauma of birth though he admitted that the individual's life does begin with it. In his famous essay, 'Analysis Terminable and Interminable',[2] he complained of the clinical uselessness of the Rankian hypothesis; he went on, 'Probably it has not accomplished more than would be done if the men of a fire-brigade, summoned to deal with a house set on fire by an upset oil-lamp, merely removed the lamp from the room in which the conflagration had broken out.' Indeed a significant metaphor! I do not think any more highly of the therapeutic achievements which Rankian insights have secured for us than Freud did, but the truth is no less a truth when it is not immediately useful: knowing that the oil-lamp was the cause of the fire is of little avail to the fire-brigade but it is the truth and Freud does not seem to deny it. From time to time, as a matter of fact, Freud stressed that we should be mistaken to consider birth—mammalian birth that is—as an abrupt beginning. The burden of individuality is hard to bear and 'the human being needs many years—namely his whole childhood—in which to overcome this first intensive trauma . . .'[3] The new life in the moment of its creation is a mere growth, a product of the principle of growth, a principle which imposes individuality on the product of growth. To illustrate this idea more vividly with reference to plant life: cut off any branch of a blackberry bush and replant it, it will become a new individual and a new bearer of the principle of growth. Here no dramatic birth is necessary and the continuity of growth is all but uninterrupted. Mammalian birth on the other hand seems to be an abrupt caesura in the interminable growth of life; here, instead of a smooth and continuous proliferation, as it happens with the blackberry bush,

[1] *J. Educ. Psychol.*, June 1952, Vol. XII, p. 151.
[2] *Collected Papers*, Vol. V, pp. 316–17.
[3] *The Trauma of Birth*, by Otto Rank, 1929, p. 11.

we have an apparent break. At the time of mammalian birth the will towards individuality is a transmutation of the principle of growth, for growth cannot continue to function without a periodic breaking-up (individuation) of what grows. At the same time the principle of cohesion radically resists individuation; the birth trauma is a reaction to the catastrophic imposition of individuality. A transmutation of the principle of cohesion ensues, the mother-child relationship and its profoundly intimate mutual dedication take the place of biological unity. Subsequently the mother-child relationship is superseded by the socialization of *both* (an important point this, the mother's resocialization being almost always ignored), and union on a 'higher' *social* level is sought in accordance with the principle of cohesion.[1] The growth of life in individuality would not be possible if the self-negating power of the principle of cohesion were allowed full scope. The will which, through the latter principle, strives to negate itself and craves for its own immolation is what the Freudians have labelled *Thanatos*, the Death Instinct. This is another example of the way in which my conceptions are related to the Freudians' hypotheses: I am describing the same phenomena but I am ordering them according to very different principles. That it is not death but an earlier form of life which is craved, Freud saw clearly; regrettably he chose the wrong label as he had done with the 'sexual' libido and caused many misconceptions among philosophically insensitive followers. Nevertheless let it be stated that the whole range of the widely accepted Freudian clinical interpretations would be only slightly affected by the adoption of my meta-

---

[1] In spite of the mother's obvious trauma in confinement and delivery successful parturition in optimal cases is compared to an orgasmic experience by Grantly Dick Read (*Revelation of Childbirth*, 1946). In a certain measure this is, of course, true and is made possible by the sudden triumph of the principle of growth. This is the ancestor of the sexual orgasm which itself is an *expulsion of life*. But the orgasm experienced in the successful diffusion of life must be countered by cohesion. The obvious and immediate form of cohesion is the mother's dedication to the child, yet soon this *mystica unio maternalis* must be supplemented by the resocialization of the mother for the mother-child bond is condemned to slacken as the child emancipates itself. Alice Balint is one of the few psycho-analysts who saw the mother's position clearly when she observed, '. . . one's own child is indeed not the external world'. She calls the early mother-child pair 'dual-unity' and describes its object relations as '. . . as old as their biological basis' ('Love For the Mother and Mother-Love', *Internat. J. Psychoanal.*, 1949, XXX, pp. 251–9).

18

psychological principles. The contemporary assessment of such matters as, for example, separation traumata of young children, as well as many of the traumata of the oral, anal, and phallic stages would be fundamentally unaltered. It is not my present task to work out the clinical implications of this metapsychology but I do not expect it to be an exacting undertaking.

Considered against the background of phylogenesis and ontogenesis the so-called social instinct of man is a materialization of a perennial and universal principle. The co-operation and individuation of man during the last half a million years has been determined in this way. On the human level the perennial principles work as a *Principium Sociale* and a *Principium Individuationis*: yet the terms I shall use in lieu of these in my subsequent reflections will continue to be the comprehensive principles of *cohesion and growth*.

There are still a number of issues which recently entered the framework of my hypothesis. A theory developed by Ernst Haeckel in 1874 and 1875 known as the 'theory of recapitulation' or 'biogenesis' stated that the embryonic development of more complex animals repeats, in order, the adult stages through which the race has passed during its evolution. The zygote can be compared with a protozoon, the blastula with a colonial protozoon, the gastrula with a coelenterate and so on. These comparisons, however, were later found to be oversimplifications and today the theory of recapitulation is, on the whole, discredited. Yet although the rule 'ontogeny repeats phylogeny' is no longer accepted some very useful accretions to our knowledge of evolution emerged from the prolonged debate over this rule. One of these gains is represented by the theory of 'neoteny' (foetalization', 'paedomorphosis') originally developed by Louis Bolk and Walter Garstang. This theory refers to certain evolutionary trends in widely differing species in which the reverse of what Haeckel taught seems to apply: the adult form of an animal resembles the young form of its presumed ancestors. That is a passage of foetal characteristics into adult life and hence the other names, quoted above, which are sometimes given to the process. G. R. De Beer explains Bolk's theory with the following illustrations:

Apes when new born have very much lighter skins than adults; additional pigment becomes deposited during later development,

19

and the same is true of the Negro. In this respect the white races are neotenous for they retain the embryonic condition of other forms. One of the most interesting cases of this is that of hair, for Bolk has shown that a progressive series in reduction can be made out in the monkeys, apes and man

1. The Monkey is born with a complete covering of hair;
2. The Gibbon is born with the head and back covered with hair and other regions covered later;
3. The Gorilla is born with the head covered with hair, and other regions are partially covered later;
4. Man is born with the head covered with hair and the other regions are scarcely covered at all later.

The more advanced the species, at any rate in this series, the more foetalized it is. The hairless embryonic condition becomes more and more prolonged and in man it goes scarcely beyond the embryonic achievement. At the same time, instances of neoteny are observed among other species, e.g. Miastor, one of the flies, axolotl, a Mexican newt, several groups of crustaceans, and others, where neoteny is not accompanied by an advancement in the direction of social life. But just as Allee sees a relationship between the level of specialization of the social ants and of man, so we too may observe here that in these widely differing species a point of saturation must have been reached in their evolution forcing them to slow down the rate of their ontogeny. Be that as it may, my deep concern with this process consists in this: *foetalization is a dramatic manifestation of the principle of cohesion.* The clinging to embryonic forms is combined with adequate individuation, yet this clinging very suggestively points to the stage in which the individual is tied down during its ontogeny: in case of the mammals this is the habitat of the embryo, the womb. Marston Bates in a pungently appropriate comment on neoteny reveals much, '. . . I find a particular pleasure in thinking of man as a kind of mammal that has lost the ability to grow up'.[1] In proportion to his neoteny man developed an intense degree of sociability and if similar achievements are lacking in the axolotl and the miastor it is probably because if there is no long period of gestation neoteny is not inevitably found with social behaviour. My point here is not to prove that neoteny and social behaviour are invariably linked

[1] *The Nature of Natural History*, 1951, p. 97.

but that the phenomenon of neoteny—as yet unaccounted for—is adequately explained with reference to the principle of cohesion. It is also possible that subtle and concealed forms of neoteny are universal;[1] we don't know whether they are and even if they are not there may be other evolutionary trends through which, in the absence of neoteny, the principle of cohesion would assert itself. The gradual extension of the mammalian gestation and nursing period is one such evolutionary trend. One may say, of course, that this was a consequence and not a cause of increasing socialization; one may claim that man was given the opportunity to gestate and nurse longer by social co-operation. But why should man use the opportunity to extend these periods? It seems to me that prolonged maternity and social co-operation developed side by side throughout man's evolution with the initial impetus on the side of prolonged maternity. This impetus is permanently sustained and is the chief manifestation of the principle of cohesion, for delayed parturition and prolonged nursing extend the period of biological contact between mother and child.

The earliest considered opposition to the theory of a social instinct came from Freudian metapsychology. The Freudians have been astonishingly physiological in their arguments: they demanded that we produced 'social organ' or 'social glands' similar to the sexual organs and glands. Indeed, from this point of view, the sexual libido was safe and sound, the genitalia and their internal apparatus were clearly inherited in the germ plasm.[2] Alas, there is no record of a physiological substratum

[1] Cf. A. C. Hardy, 'Escape From Specialization', in *Evolution as a Process* (ed. by J. Huxley, A. C. Hardy, and E. B. Ford, 1954). One of the characteristics of neoteny is that it involves an accelerated development of the reproductive organs so that they become functional before the structure of the other organs matures to its adult form. The phenomenon of infantile sexuality in man is, therefore, a neotenous development. The relevance of this to my argument consists in the following: *firstly*, it calls attention to the intimate relationship which obtains between neoteny and the psychoanalytical accounts of personality development; *secondly*, it suggests that the accelerated sexual development—itself a product of the principle of cohesion—bursts out in substitute solutions after the *caesura* of birth even when these solutions (e.g. infantile sexuality) are anomalous.

[2] Modern endocrinological research plainly disproves the all-embracing claims of pan-sexualism. The organization of the endocrinological system is controlled from the hypophysial (pituitary) centre and the feedback control of peripheral—among others sexual—secretions merely operates to ensure the homeostasis, the automatic balancing of the organism. The anterior lobe of the pituitary which is

having been discovered to serve Thanatos, the Death Instinct. There is no specific organ of self-destruction in the body of the human infant. But the postulation of a hereditary disposition, an instinct, cannot depend on our ability of finding a morphological agent in the human body to serve it. The ultimate principles of life pertain to the *Gestalt* of the organism in an as yet inscrutable way and not to any part-system of it. In fact, when a function is reserved for any part-system we can be sure that this function is phylogenetically derived from those ultimate principles. Sex is a case in point: reproduction, a manifestation of the principle of growth, preceded the sexual division of labour, the interpenetration of strains. Contemporary microbiology is a witness to this. Meanwhile every level of evolution has its own derivative laws; we saw this in the working of our two basic principles. These principles express themselves in *ad hoc* forms; for example, the principle of cohesion becomes a *Principium Sociale* among social animals. Similarly, the specialized organs of sex have become,—after asexual reproduction has been superseded,—extremely powerful controllers of the human Gestalt; yet, phylogenetically, the sexual instinct is an offshoot, however early, of the principle of growth.

The psycho-analytical scepticism about the social instinct received a certain support from the work of some zoologists. Tinbergen's conclusions on the social instinct are summed up in the following passage,

Contrary to current views there is, in my opinion, no 'social instinct' in our sense. There are no special activities to be called 'social' that are not part of some instinct. There is no such thing as the activation of a system of centres controlling social activities. An animal is called social when it strives to be in the neighbourhood of fellow members of its species when performing some, or all, of its

responsible for the normal function of several endocrine glands, including the gonads, is in turn, in an as yet unknown way, controlled by the hypothalamic region. Now it is ridiculous to claim that either the hypophysis or the hypothalamus are 'sexual' in their dynamic charge. Cf. *Textbook of Endocrinology*, by Hans Selye, Canada, 1948, p. 22. Even psychoanalysts are sometimes troubled by the arbitrariness of this pan-sexualism. Yet they still permit themselves extravagances of the following kind, 'By "sexual" Freud meant "sexual" in the ordinary sense, but he widened the popular conception of what things *are* sexual' (Ernest Jones in *Sigmund Freud, Life and Work*, 1955, Vol. II, p. 317). One may as well say that all men on earth are Englishmen if we only widen the popular conception of what people are English.

instinctive activities. In other words, when these instincts are active, the fellow member of the species is part of the adequate stimulus which the animal tries to find through its appetitive behaviour.[1]

According to this there is no specific 'social instinct' but the other specific instincts contain a kind of highest common factor, i.e. a need for 'adequate stimulus situation' which is a social situation. It is rather a futile reservation that this social need, i.e. the need for 'adequate stimulus situation', which is social, arises only when other instincts are active. Surely, some instinct or instincts are always active and a complete quiescence of instinctive activity amounts to death.[2] Thus if the social need is a component of some or all instincts then the social need is a permanent force of life. To say that the readiness to respond to social releasers is part of the organization of all instincts is the same as saying that *all instincts are social*!

It seems Tinbergen must have been aware of this possibility for later he remarks:

> There is, however, another classification which cuts across the neurophysiological classification. While many behaviour elements are directly advantageous to the individual, there are other elements that are of no direct benefit to the individual but are of advantage to a group of individuals. *In social species each instinct may contain such elements* [italics mine].

Tinbergen's position is briefly this: the so-called 'maintenance activities' of feeding, breeding, and defence against predators are more effective in social co-operation than in isolation. Hence social co-operation is an evolutionary discovery of some species which manage to prevail on account of the favourable social mutation. Now this is no less hypothetical than to claim that the 'social instinct' is universal but fails to manifest itself when it would be in disharmony with the forms of 'maintenance activities' established in the face of life's basic principles. The so-called solitary species breed, feed and fight or defend themselves in solo, for these maintenance activities are organized and ingrained in a way which would conflict with a co-operative solution.

---

[1] *The Study of Instinct*, by N. Tinbergen, 1951, p. 112.
[2] Tinbergen is very emphatic about the instinct of sleep!

With Tinbergen's observations we appear to be back again at the old game of arguing about the specificity of instinct-categories. When William James and William McDougall drew up their lists of instincts they were repeatedly attacked for their inclusions and omissions. And the controversy has continued to this day because no decision has ever been reached whether the postulation of an instinct should be based on physiology or ethology or some combination of the two. In my opinion neither of these solutions can compete with the accuracy of a phylogenetic classification of instinctual forces. This method inevitably reduces us to metaphysics and monism. And this is as it should be, for, let us face it, because instincts are metaphysical entelechies, they have no business to meddle with general metaphysical consistency. In my scheme the ultimate entelechy splits into two principles at the dawn of life or possibly before that. These two principles continue to govern life notwithstanding specialization on the various levels of evolution. The fountainhead of energies, the ultimate entelechy, is the same as that of the physicist.[1] Yet this common platform with the physicist no more commits us to materialism than it would involve the physicist in pan-psychism or mysticism. As a matter of fact one may take it for granted that the nature of the ultimate entelechy is such as to be beyond the scope of all our experience, past, present, and probably future.

Adhering to an empirical picture of the present I am obliged to concede that two forces in particular, namely sex and aggression, have differentiated themselves from growth and cohesion sufficiently to appear rightful claimants to the status of basic force. Sex has a strong claim to this status on many accounts which are, as a rule, stated in the following form though not necessarily in the following language: (a) sex has the power to prevail over the principle of growth: individuation is often subordinated to the sexual drive; (b) sex has the power to take precedence over the principle of cohesion: socialization is often defeated by sexual desire. Let us consider these objections to

---

[1] The physicist's position has not changed since Faraday confessed that, 'I have long held the opinion, almost amounting to a conviction ... that the various forms under which the forces of matter are made manifest have a common origin; or, in other words, are so directly related, and mutually dependent that they are convertible, as it were, into one another, and possess equivalents of power in their action.'

24

my dualism. *In the first place* the 'principle of growth' was selected to stand for a comprehensive force which may take many forms. It includes individuation with all its attendant functions such as the self-preservative drives of hunger, flight, and so on. But the true interpretation of self-preservation as well as of individuation is that through these it is the species which preserves itself. Self-preservation in the individual is a share of self-preservation in the species. The principle of growth is really a principle of self-preservation through continuous dynamic adjustment. This principle would come into severe conflict with itself if the self-preservation of the individual endangered the self-preservation of the species. The individual relegates his individuation into the background when the self-preservation of the species is at stake. The principle of growth draws away energy from individuation and passes it on to the so-called sexual and parental functions. Biologists often point out that the denial of parenthood deprives the individual of the immortality of his genes and psychologists have been equally vociferous in describing fruition in parenthood as a condition of mental health. *Secondly,* it is true that sex may appear to conflict with socialization and thereby with the principle of cohesion. These are, however, superficial and, at best, temporary conflicts. I have stressed that the phylic bond of mother and child is—from the point of view of the child—the universal beginning of socialization and that the principle of cohesion is a resistance to separation. Sex operating as an agent of the principle of growth is responsible for the creation of this phylic bond and often contributes to energize the social co-operation in this bond. The privacy and conflict which sex entails are amply repaid by the support which its sublimated remnants give to the principle of cohesion. Also, sex, far from being of necessity in conflict with socialization, provides one of the archetypes of mutually beneficent co-operation. One may say that sex is the frontier area between the principles of growth and cohesion or that it is the conciliating agent invented by the evolutionary process to ensure the continuation of life in spite of the basic opposition between its fundamental principles. Some psychoanalysts have seen this; one of the earliest among them was Ferenczi who equated the penetration of the vagina with a return to the womb, i.e. the sex act is the symbolical expression of the principle of cohesion.[1] Otto Rank quotes Strindberg whose portraiture of love-making and of its *post coitum triste* sequence curiously suggests the rhythmical, fluctuating battle between the two basic principles of life (Strindberg speaks from the point of view of the male), 'In love, he melts together with the loved woman, but then when he has lost himself and his form, the desire for self-preservation grows, and in the anxiety at "losing his ego through the equalizing power of love" he attempts to free himself from her in order to find himself again as self-existing.'[2] Sexual love derives its energies from the principle of growth but it seems that *on the level of culture* it harnesses the frustrated yearnings of cohesion as well. 'It seems to me that the complete passion of love integrates genital appetite with that "love" or tenderness which is the descendant or derivative of infantile need. It utilizes it, as it were, *as a means of restoring the lost sense of union with the mother. . . .*' [italics mine].[3] The doctrine which 'sexualizes' the basic forces of man is the product of a screen-memory[4] for the amnesias which go beyond infantile sexuality simply resist further analysis. Hence the error of pan-sexualism. No one saw this more clearly than W. R. D. Fairbairn whose 'object-relations theory of personality' is perfectly congenial to my metapsychology. He stated that 'Erotogenic Zones are not themselves primary determinants of libidinal aims, but channels mediating the primary object-seeking aims of the ego'.[5] This 'primary object-seeking' is, of course, the principle of cohesion. Remarkably enough Freud could not truly be regarded as out of sympathy with this thesis; he speaks of 'sexual instincts' in the plural and goes on to say that,

We do not . . . believe that there is a single sexual instinct which is from the first the vehicle of the impulse towards the aim of the sexual function, that is, the union of two cells. On the contrary, we

[1] *Versuch einer Genital Theorie*, (Congress Report), Zschr. VIII, 1922, p. 479.
[2] *The Trauma of Birth*, p. 72.
[3] *The Origins of Love and Hate*, by Ian D. Suttie, 1935, p. 72.
[4] 'Screen memory'—according to Freud—is the kind of childhood recollection which most people have and which bars the way to the recall of earlier repressed material usually of great significance to the individual's personality structure.
[5] *Psychoanalytic Studies of the Personality*, 1952, p. 162. Also cf. a forerunner of Fairbairn's, Michael Balint's 'The Final Goal of Psycho-analytic Treatment', *Internat. J. Psychoanal.*, April 1936, XVII, pp. 206–16.

see a large number of component instincts, arising from various regions of the body, which strive for satisfaction more or less independently from one another, and find satisfaction in something that may be called 'organ pleasure'.[1]

Now 'organ pleasure' presumably means a diffuse pleasurable excitation in various parts of the body funnelling severally rather than any one of these parts monopolizing the pleasure of the body *Gestalt*. It is of great importance to us to know whether there are 'a large number of component instincts' or a 'polymorphous perverse' diffusion of a homogeneous sexual libido. If it is the former we could, at least, claim that the sexual instinct has components which are not sexual. They could not all be sexual, for 'components' do not make a biological whole by arithmetical addition; they are rather like a parallelogram of forces. Can it be, therefore, that the sexual libido is the synthesis of the principle of growth and cohesion, and although inherited in the germ-plasm, from the point of view of evolution only apparently *sui generis*? There is a great deal in the study of early micro-evolution which tends to confirm this conjecture. Moreover when Freud writes about the 'conservative nature of instincts' and the expression of this in 'repetition compulsion' one cannot help associating these ideas with the working of the principle of cohesion. This stubborn, initially regressive principle which for ever tries to revert to the embryonic union and reveals its workings through phenomena like neoteny and birth trauma, is both conservative and compulsively repetitive. Both the most striking point of contact and the most fundamental metapsychological difference between the present reflections and Freudian conclusions are related to this. They concern the Freudian theory of aggression and the so-called Death Instinct. This brings me to the second of those two forces which have hitherto demanded an equality of status with my two basic principles.

The Freudian Death Instinct, Thanatos, is an infantile urge towards self-destruction, a craving for return to an earlier stage of existence. Or stated in Freud's own words, and indeed in a more radical form:

In the multicellular living organism the libido meets the death or destruction instinct which holds sway there, and which tries to

[1] *New Introductory Lectures in Psycho-Analysis*, p. 127.

27

disintegrate this cellular being and bring each elemental primary organism into a condition of inorganic stability (though this again may be but relative). To the libido falls the task of making this destructive instinct harmless, and it manages to dispose of it by directing it to a great extent and early in life—with the help of a special organic system the musculature—towards the objects of the outer world. It is then called the instinct of destruction, of mastery, the will to power.[1]

The points of agreement and of the differences between this doctrine as well as the body of doctrines to which it belongs on the one hand, and my present scheme on the other, must be clearly brought out: firstly, the dualism of Eros and Thanatos resembles my dualism of growth and cohesion only in as much as they are both dualisms. Secondly, the concept of infantile masochism is a mournful rendering of a life-affirming tendency: the protest against separate, individual existence is not equivalent to a protest against existence. It is not death that is craved but reunion. The late Professor Flugel admits almost as much as this:

Among the motives in which escapism predominates it has been shown that fantasies of death can be combined with those of love ('Dying together' *Liebestod*), that death is unconsciously equated with travelling or going away, and above all with the notion of life before birth (intra-uterine 'omnipotence') in which there is 'peace' and in which gratification is achieved without effort or frustration. But it is Nirvana, a *life* of peace, free from worry, pain, exertion or annoyance, that is wished for, rather than a cessation of life, which is indeed, as psycho-analysts themselves have often stressed, extremely difficult to envisage except in the most abstract way.[2]

In these circumstances Professor Flugel had to struggle valiantly to justify the conception of a 'Death Instinct'. The principle of cohesion describes the infantile protest in a form much more in keeping with our empirical findings, whereas no empirical proof is available or is even conceivable for the conception of Thanatos. Thirdly, the conversion of infantile masochism into aggression by a complicated process of projections and introjections is the Freudian and, in particular, Kleinian method

---

[1] 'The Economic Problem in Masochism', *Collected Papers*, Vol. II, p. 260.
[2] 'The Death Instinct, Homeostasis and Allied Concepts', *Internat. J. Psychoanal.* Supplement, 1953, pp. 43–73.

of accounting for aggression. 'At the beginning of post-natal life the infant experiences anxiety from internal and external sources. I have for many years held the view that the working of the death instinct within gives rise to the fear of annihilation and that this is the primary cause of persecutory anxiety.'[1] The infant having projected the internal danger into the external world, now introjects the external world's destructive designs and adopts them *against* the external world. Is this circuitous process really the true account? In my opinion the infant's craving for reunion is—in the infant's fantasy life—frustrated by the mother who expelled him and who now refuses to receive him back. The archetype of aggression is directed against the mother for she features as the one who frustrates the principle of cohesion. This aggression is analogously extended on to other persons and objects. The frustrating mother-image is so much the more inevitably plausible to the infant as she is the sole provider of all his needs, which, by virtue of being insatiable, are inevitably frustrated even in the most satisfactory circumstances. This construction harmoniously fits into the well-known 'frustration-aggression' theory of aggression which is both empirically and logically the sturdiest of the aggression theories.[2] Furthermore, it leads towards a profounder understanding of the nature of aggression, an understanding perhaps too simple for the sophisticated psycho-analyst. I formulated the foregoing theory of aggression in the following words, 'The true target of aggression is not the victim but the "difference", the gap, which is neither tangible nor destructible. It is the "otherness" of the "other" which is to be annihilated, if the gap is to be forgotten.'[3] This slightly 'guilt-allaying' interpretation of aggression aroused the suspicions of some people. Others thought it was an oversimplification and passed it with a shrug of shoulders. One critic remarked that this was indeed a kind description of the masters of Dachau and Buchenwald. Strangely enough only a year after the publication of this passage the following statements were made by Albert Camus, 'Terror and concentration camps are the drastic means used by man to escape solitude . . .', and, 'Terror is the homage that the malignant

[1] Melanie Klein in *Developments in Psycho-Analysis*, 1952, p. 198.
[2] Cf. Ian D. Suttie, op. cit., particularly p. 31.
[3] *Solitude and Privacy*, p. 7.

recluse finally pays to the brotherhood of man.' And finally, 'He who loves a friend loves him in the present and revolution only wants to love a man who has not yet appeared.'[1] It seems that the line of thought I followed is by no means isolated. There are passages in Erich Fromm's *The Fear of Freedom* which clearly concur with this view. The difference between 'congress' and 'aggress' is a difference in technique, both are trying to achieve the same end. At the same time it is very instructive to watch some Freudians engaged in putting carts before horses. We have seen the derivation of social bonds from aim—inhibited sexual libido; the criticism of this has already been given elsewhere.[2] But now we encounter another attempt at getting rid of man's social instincts.

The sublimated masochism of the normal individual reveals itself even more clearly in his relationship to the organized group in which he lives. Man's tendency to become a part of a larger unit, appears to be in part identical with the moral—masochistic impulse, as members of the organized group we cease to some extent to be independent individuals, we relinquish our personal existence, this in itself is a kind of self-destruction.[3]

So it seems that now, in addition to the aim-inhibited libido, we must also admit sublimated masochism as the core and substance of the social need. For me, cohesion comes first, and aggression follows only in the wake of the former's frustration: for the Freudians, Thanatos was there before man became social. One must remember that the longing for reunion obliges the individual to preserve itself for it and receive its fulfilment. The difficulty is this: how can he preserve himself and not preserve himself? How can he exist as an individual in reunion and yet not exist? This problem is vigorously alive in the writings of modern philosophers and theologians who advocate 'personality in communion'. In spite of all their criticism of modern psychology they have done little to resolve this antithesis. My controversy with the Freudians is not a mere matter of dispute over terminology or labels. I am not in the least averse from the metaphorical language of the school of psycho-analysis. All

[1] *The Rebel* (L'Homme Revolté), 1953, pp. 216, 217, 208 (in the above order).
[2] *Solitude and Privacy*, Chapter I.
[3] 'Masochism as a Pathological and as a Normal Phenomenon in the Human Mind', by René de Monchy, *Internat. J. Psychoanal.*, 1950, XXXI, pp. 95–7.

science uses metaphorical language; in fact, all language is metaphorical. But sometimes the connotation of a metaphor fits its referent as an outsize Homburg fits a toddler's head; one can't see the head at all. The repudiation of the Death Instinct has, no less than its acceptance, momentous philosophical repercussions and therapeutic consequences. Some of these I shall have the opportunity to examine later. For the time being I propose to deal briefly with the claim of aggression to the status of a basic principle of life. While there have so far been grounds for refusing this claim, there are none for questioning the universal frustration of the principle of cohesion; and of this frustration universal aggression is a consequence. This aggression though universal certainly varies most widely according to the treatment the child receives, and also according to his hereditary frustration tolerance. Yet the aggression which thus universally manifests itself is a derivation from and a reaction to the principle of cohesion and to a lesser degree to the principle of growth. Aggression is not a *sui generis* force equivalent in seniority and rank to the principle of growth and cohesion.

Whilst refusing sex and aggression a status equal to that of my basic principles I do not wish to deny that both of them are of the order of instincts. If by instinct we understand a hereditary disposition there is no doubt that even aggression forms part of the organization of other instincts, the part which begins to function when a specific instinct is frustrated. Nevertheless I retain my fundamental dualism for—as I hope to show in the following essays—its explanatory potentialities surpass systems so far recommended by others. The reason for this confidence is not far to seek: instincts vary according to species and they modify when passing one level of evolution to another but the fundamental principles of life do neither. Man's functioning in sexual life and in conflict invariably depends on the balance of these two principles. This is the cornerstone of most of my arguments in this volume. There is no radical departure here from well-trodden paths of reflection; the dualistic conception of life is as ancient as the myths of heaven and hell. The Empedoclian love and hate, the Chinese Yang and Yin, Kant's *Ungesellige Geselligkeit* (unsociable sociability), the Spencerian differentiation and integration, Nietzsche's Dionysian and Apollonian men, Pierre Curie's symmetry and asymmetry, the

Autonomy and Heteronomy of Angyal, Eros and Thanatos, to mention a few random examples, have all sought the solution in antinomies of which mine merely claims to be more accurate for it emerges from a synthesis of more up-to-date information. Neither is the relegation of sex to a second place the rationalization of resistance to psycho-analytical insight. There is nothing much I take exception to in the clinically established insight of psycho-analysis. It is its metapsychology which is incoherent and unsound. Otto Rank was the first who guessed right the relation of sex to the fundamental issues of living. Rank's psycho-analytical training is well-known and it may anticipate psycho-analytical reactions if I refer to the following passage in Rank's *Trauma of Birth*:

> The essential factor in the development of neuroses seems to be that man, in the biological as in the cultural overcoming of the birth trauma, which we call adjustment, comes to grief at the cross road of sexual gratification, which most naturally approaches the primal situation, yet does not completely re-establish it in the infantile meaning.

The whole gamut of those developments which are associated with infantile sexuality are secondary to the fate of the fundamental balance between my first principles. This is why most strictly empirical and behaviouristically conducted researches on psycho-analytical generalizations have failed.[1] Thus the variables which lie in the area of antenatal history, labour-confinement, and the first year of life assume decisive significance. It is largely during the latter that the pattern of socialization—individuation is fixed.

3. *The Disbalance of Basic Principles*

It remains for me to consider the interaction between my two basic principles; this I shall survey both in general terms and with specific reference to the human level of evolution.

Parts have to grow first before they can cohere into wholes. Yet on the lowest levels of life there could be no growth without the coherence of that which grows. In fact the initial impulse to

---

[1] Cf. Robert R. Sears, *Survey of Objective Studies of Psychoanalytic Concepts*, Social Science Research Council, Bulletin 51, New York, 1943.

grow is simultaneous with and equal to the impulse to cohere. It is only later, when a whole period of evolution is viewed in its entirety, that a dialectical, neck-and-neck precedence of the two principles can be observed. For instance, in the transition from protozoa to metazoa one notes that first there is a proliferation through division until, at one point, the principle of cohesion catches up and division ceases. Similarly it is the principle of growth which has driven man towards the proliferation in mass societies, into the creation of legions of bondless individuals, whilst the principle of cohesion has been lagging behind in search of community and fellowship. Judaism, the two millennia of Christianity, the modern humanistic versions of fellowship, and the socialistic, communistic collectivisms of our age are thus products of the principle of cohesion searching for expression in terms of culture. If the attempts at cohesion have failed they have done so on account of the striving to attain too much or the fear of aspiring for enough. The failure of the principle of cohesion to match the principle of growth cannot continue indefinitely without consequences to the human species. Human culture is an entirely novel mutation in the evolutionary process of life. As a negative factor culture has profoundly aggravated the otherwise subtly oscillating disbalance between the two basic principles of life; as a positive factor it created the self-knowing man who can intervene in his own evolution. The lesson of evolution is that either of my two principles can get out of hand and leaping ahead leave its partner recklessly behind. The division of the protozoa for countless millennia without a sign of cohesion asserting itself in a one-sided advance of the principle of growth. The emergence of undifferentiated colonies of cells without a metazoic individuality is a similarly one-sided advance of the principle of cohesion. On the cultural human level this is more dramatically illustrated by the excesses of individualism and communalism. The dialectic fluctuation becomes also more frequent, it is no longer merely evolutionary but also historical.

A number of observations have to be made on the nature of this fluctuation. In the *first* place we are not dealing with forces which change in intensity either one or the other getting stronger and thereby prevailing. I postulate the intensity of the basic principles to be equal. It is the changes in the biological vehicle

33

as well as the environmental medium which allow one or the other to predominate from time to time. *Secondly*, this fluctuation, far from being harmful to the species, is the very process of its evolutionary development; an absolute balance continuing indefinitely spells a static condition and as environmental circumstances are *never* stationary it is a sign of decline. And *thirdly*, the most frequent and most profound environmental changes occur in the culture of man thereby necessitating a perpetual state of *intensified* disbalance of the basic principles of life. The optimum condition of survival for man is, therefore, not balance but an optimum disbalance. I shall seek the measure of this optimum in the following essays; in the meantime I should like to pose the question whether the one or the other of the basic principles could furnish me with a point of departure for my inquiry?

Notwithstanding the equality of the basic principles a circumstance of metazoic life seems to endow one of them with greater significance. The metazoa cannot seek the fulfilment of cohesion on a biological plane. The realization of cohesion has become more problematical and a new platform must be found upon which it could come about. The social platform of cohesion may operate adequately on the animal level. But the self-awareness of man in culture has denied man spontaneous sociability and spontaneous cohesion. It is this sudden hiatus in the fluent style of evolution which has committed so many thinkers to the thesis that 'fellowship is life' and 'life is fellowship'. I am no exception to this bias which I regard as essential to us if we are to solve some of the problems of our survival. It is a necessary 'bias', a necessary metaphysical 'error' which we must heartily cultivate at a time when the principle of cohesion is at a low ebb. The stifling atmosphere of an overheated room in the winter can be made habitable only by opening the windows for a short while; our reason for opening them is not to reduce the temperature of the room below freezing point.

Hence, whereas one is inclined to regard this bias as salutary, for it is, relatively to our historical-cultural existence, not a bias at all, we should beware of hastily assuming that it reflects an ultimate priority of the principle of cohesion. The following passage from Toynbee's *Study of History* is an edifying example of a mistake from which I too have not been immune:

34

The withdrawal is an opportunity, perhaps a necessary condition, for the anchorite's transfiguration; but, by the same token, this transfiguration can have no purpose, and perhaps no meaning, except as a prelude to the return of the transfigured personality into the social milieu out of which he has originally come: a native environment from which the human social animal cannot permanently estrange himself without repudiating his humanity and becoming either a beast or a god. *The return is the essence of the whole movement, as well as its final cause* [italics mine].

It is true that individuation is a tool of the species, that it serves the totality of the species and not the myriad purposes of myriad individuals. Admittedly the purpose of life in general is inscrutable enough but these myriad purposes would merely raise our demand for explanation to the nth power. Furthermore, all our experience teaches us the indestructibility of life in general and the pathetic ephemeralness of individual life. Yet all these concessions to the whole at the expense of the parts can be reversed; the species exists in its individuals and in nothing else; the more resourceful in their various specializations are these individuals, i.e. the more they are individuals, the more sturdily and adaptably the species exists. The resolution of this conflict may be suggested through a modification of Toynbee's conclusion, 'Both withdrawal and return together are the essence of the whole movement, as well as its final cause.'

This dualism seems self-evident from our daily experience. Its detailed substantiation in physics and in the other sub-psychological sciences is yet to be carried out. The radical comprehensiveness of this dualism need be no impediment to its universal validity; in fact, it is more likely than not that only a principle so broad and general can possess the maximum explanatory power we need in all sciences.

'. . . While the eye that can perceive what are the wrong things increases in an uncanny and devouring clarity, the eye which sees what things are right is growing mistier and mistier every moment, till it goes almost blind with doubt.'

> G. K. Chesterton, in the essay
> 'On the Negative Spirit'.

'There is a story of a reincarnated King of Babylon visiting one of our modern cities. His host and guide undertook to show him the sights of the city. He took him the rounds of the brothels, the gambling joints, the opium dens, the saloons, the hideouts of gangsters, and the like. The king was polite and bored. He said, "We had all this in Babylon three thousand years ago and on the whole we did it rather better. Have you nothing new to show me?" His guide reversed his field and took his guest to the children's play grounds, the libraries, the high schools, the hospitals, the research laboratories, the centre for the visiting nurses. "Ah!" said the king, "All this is new, we didn't have these things in Babylon" . . . once a vicious man has exhausted the resources of evil there is nothing left but dull and monotonous repetition to the point of satiety and often suicide. Contrariwise, the resources of the good are inexhaustible.'

> Willard L. Sperry in *The Ethical Basis of Medical Practice*, 1951, p. 62.

'. . . Let me point out that all who have branded you as "mad" are quite as mad as you.'

> Horace: *Satires*, 'This Lunatic World', Book II, 3.

II

THE SEARCH FOR THE MEASURE

OF OPTIMUM DISBALANCE

WITHIN the context of the present chapter no ethical content should be attributed to the term 'optimum'. Animal ecologists often speak of 'optimum populations', meaning thereby some numerical median, some degree of density in which the species has the greatest chance of survival. It is in this sense that I apply the term, 'optimum disbalance' of the basic principles in human life. This is the measure of discrepancy which will provide the greatest expectation of survival for man even under rapidly changing conditions in his environment. Under culture man's environment changed more frequently and more profoundly than it had done throughout long periods of his whole prehistoric evolution. The adjustment of man to this unprecedented acceleration of man-made changes is our problem and the pursuit of its solution begins in an examination of the concept of 'adjustment'.

1. *The Concept of Adjustment*

The scientific use of the term 'adjustment' has a longer history than is generally recognized. 'Borrowed from juristics by mechanics, adapted to biology, and finally taken over by psychology, the history of the word "adjustment" is one of accretion of meanings.'[1] In all these disciplines the word 'adjustment' has two distinct applications: it has been used to indicate either a process or a condition.

Adjustment primarily suggests a *process* leading up to a goal,

[1] 'Adjustment in Psychology', T. R. Sarbin, *Character and Personality*, Sept. 1939–June 1940, VIII.

a condition of being adjusted. There is no finality in this condition, which is at best an intermediate state, for the life-process cannot reach a static position: both the individual and its environment are in a constant process of change. One could do no better than quote Samuel Butler on this:

All our lives long, every day and every hour, we are engaged in the process of accommodating our changed and unchanged selves to changed and unchanged surroundings; living in fact, is nothing else than this process of accommodation; when we fail in it a little we are stupid, when we fail flagrantly we are mad, when we suspend it temporarily we sleep, when we give up the attempt altogether we die. In quiet, uneventful lives the changes internal and external are so small that there is little or no strain in the process of fusion and accommodation; in other lives there is great strain, but there is also great fusing and accommodating power. A life will be successful or not, according as the power of accommodation is equal or unequal to the strain of fusing and adjusting internal and external changes.[1]

Modern psychologists and psychiatrists distinguish two major stages in the process of adjustment. The instinctual development of the infant on the one hand and the treatment he receives from his environment on the other combine in a *primary process of adjustment*. The outcome of this process is the basic personality structure of the individual. This structure possesses what Butler calls a 'power of accommodation' which is its principal characteristic; this power we call adaptability. *Primary adaptability* determines whether the individual will respond—in the course of his later life—in an aggressive or submissive manner, with sadistic or masochistic inclinations, with a heterosexual or homosexual tendency, with depressive, obsessional, hysterical, or anxiety symptoms, and so on. The actual forms these responses take—for example, the ideological content of political aggressiveness, or the manifestations of a latent homosexuality —will be decided mainly by a *secondary process* of adjustment which goes on from about the fifth year of life till its end. In the course of this secondary process primary adaptability, a mere frame, is filled up with content and becomes *secondary adaptability*.[2] The dominant features of secondary adaptability are

[1] *The Way of All Flesh.*
[2] Freud used the term 'primary and secondary process' in a different sense from what I give them here. Cf. *The Interpretation of Dreams*, 1948, p. 555.

fixed on a primary level for life though, admittedly, prolonged, deep psychotherapy may reach back to this level and effect fundamental changes in it. It is often claimed that longstanding conditioning, energetic education and drill, rigorous discipline or self-control may also have such results as these. There is, however, as yet no certain indication of the degree to which these methods may change primary adaptability. If apparently fundamental changes do take place, it is probable that changes in secondary adaptability are mistaken for those in primary adaptability. There has been some resistance to the determinism which this view inflicts on us. In the face of this resistance it may be interesting to recall Lorenz's theory on 'imprinting', a phenomenon which is the result of a young animal's early experience and which thereafter characterizes his behaviour for the rest of his life. Following Lorenz several ethologists have given further evidence that a certain specific early period of the individual's life permanently fixes the social adjustment of gregarious animals. This period, or 'critical period', is usually the initial period of life and corresponds to my primary process. We are told by one of these ethologists that the rearing of newborn lambs by human beings results in the animal's noticeable independence of the flock. When such animals as these grow old they not only show indifference to other sheep but are also little concerned for the welfare of their own lambs.[1] Elsewhere we read that puppies—though seemingly immune during the first four weeks (neonatal period)—during the 'critical period' following it are deeply susceptible to traumatic experiences which will affect them for the rest of their lives.[2]

Both primary and secondary adaptability are structural qualities of the personality and not processes; accordingly we should discriminate primary adjustment process from primary adjustment condition—the latter being a condition of adaptability at any time during the infantile and early childhood period—and

[1] 'Social Behavior, Organization, and Leadership in a Small Flock of Domestic Sheep', by J. P. Scott, *Comparative Psychology Monographs*, 1945, pp. 1–29.
[2] 'Critical Periods Affecting the Development of Normal and Maladjustive Social Behaviour of Puppies', by J. P. Scott and M.-V. Marston, *J. Genetic Psychol.*, 1950, LXXVII, pp. 25–60. Also cf. 'Experimental Exploration of the Critical Period Hypothesis', by J. P. Scott, E. Fredericson, and J. L. Fuller, *Personality*, April 1951, I, pp. 162–83.

secondary adjustment process from secondary adjustment condition—the latter being a condition at any time during the subsequent life of an individual. When referring to these structural results the term 'adjustment' stands for a condition arbitrarily 'abstracted' from the process at a certain point of time. There is, however, one abstraction which is not arbitrary, for strangely enough it is an abstraction from a condition all major features of which are permanent. This condition is the terminal adjustment condition of childhood which is customarily believed to consolidate towards the fifth year of life. A certain amount of arbitrariness still appears in this for finality could be claimed on behalf of several major features of personality acquired much earlier. The first twelve months of life, for instance, are often shown to be vitally decisive for the later adjustment process up to the end of the infantile period. We do not yet know, however, how later infantile experiences superimposed upon these very early imprints affect them, and thus we should be wiser to restrict the term 'primary adjustment condition' to the end-product of the infantile period. Naturally, a clinical worker attending to a child of two or three years of age would have to take the personality profile of the child at the time as reflecting a 'primary adjustment condition'; but he should not exclude subsequent major changes, quite apart from those caused by therapeutic intervention, for diagnosis here is far more of the nature of abstraction than it is later in life. Later, no matter what stage of the adult's life is selected for diagnosis the permanent core of his personality, the primary adjustment condition, is comparatively static. Abstraction in adult life consists in ignoring the constant changes which characterize an adult's way of handling his own primary adjustment condition.

Adjustment as process connotes interaction between one entity or tendency and another. It is often taken for granted that adjustment occurs between two factors, the individual and his environment, and that an adjustment condition is the permanent effect of the interactions, an effect which will subsequently determine later interactions. Let us see whether this conception of adjustment, namely that it is interaction between individual and environment, is a correct one.

Sarbin writes, 'Organisms, in their trial and error behaviour in nature, within certain limits adjust to their environment or they perish. Thus adjustment is a process of survival.' Then he adds the following apology to this statement. 'The author is aware that he is guilty of artificial fractionation when he dichotomizes behaviour into organism and environment. Existentially, behaviour is interaction of objects with a field. The dichotomy between environment and organism is made for practical, literary expediency.' This apology, in my view, is pointless. If 'behaviour is interaction of objects within a field' and if we conceive of the person as an object and of the relevant elements in the environment as other objects the dichotomy survives unimpaired. Even when adjustment is said to be effected between, say, instinctual needs and assimilated precepts (superego), the latter are residues (introjections), of the earlier impact of environment-objects. Lawrence K. Frank oversimplified this when he said, 'The ancient dichotomy of the individual and society will sooner or later be resolved as we understand that society is in each individual, and what we call "social adjustment" is essentially the individual's relation to himself."[1] Admittedly, in adjusting to environment the individual 'adjusts himself' but this 'self-adjustment' depends on two factors one of which is originally external to the individual in more than one sense. There is no call for 'self-adjustment' in an unchanging vacuum; there is no need for 'self-adjustment' in the absence of precepts which could be internalized but are always external. In the ultimate resort adjustment *is* between the individual and his environment. Of course, it would be a mistake to think of these two factors as if they were simple entities; they are two complexes of factors which *meet* internally. The complexity of the two factors is well expressed in Herbert Spencer's definition of life which is, 'the continuous adjustment of internal relations to external relations'; I would have to modify this definition only slightly to bring it into line with my own concepts and then it would run, 'life is the continuous balancing of the forces of growth and cohesion with the environment'. At the same time it is obvious that a psychological process is, by definition, an internal process; psychological adjustment, though a function of the relationship between ego and environment, takes place internally. Thus in a narrower sense adjustment consists in the balance of growth and cohesion.

[1] *Society as the Patient*, 1949, p. 165.

I have so far not mentioned *norms* which we invariably place side by side with adjustment conditions. Practitioners and writers are in the habit of implying some kind of norm in the very word 'adjustment' by their use of the antithesis 'adjustment-maladjustment'. By this they mean that a condition which approximates to their norm, whatever that may be, is an adjusted condition and one which departs from the norm is a maladjusted condition. This is, on the whole, a regrettable practice, for 'adjustment' is a positive term and not a normative one; its proper meaning in psychology amounts to no more than a 'psychodynamic compromise'. In this way—absurd though it may seem to many—even a psychotic condition is an adjustment for it is certainly a psychodynamic compromise. Moreover it would seem reasonable to insist that the universe and all that it contains is ever in a condition of adjustment and it would be inconceivable that this should not be so. Consider the perfect harmony of a living organism which, even in illness, rises to the occasion and battles with the illness in the most intelligent manner; what is this if not perfect adjustment? Whilst there is life there is adjustment. The antithesis of this is equally plausible: nothing is ever adjusted in life or in the universe, for adjustment means rest, finality, completeness, none of which are compatible with existence, whose essence is motion. Both of these are metaphysical meanings of the term which should be distinguished from a positive sociological meaning: this sees adjustment as a compromise solution which is neither good nor bad, neither healthy nor sick—what David Riesman calls a 'sociopsychological fit'.[1] A good example of this interpretation of 'adjustment' is the following passage from one of Erich Fromm's books, '. . . the vast majority of people in our culture are well adjusted because they have given up the battle for independence sooner and more radically than the neurotic person. They have accepted the judgment of the majority so completely that they have been spared the sharp pain of conflict which the neurotic person goes through. While they are healthy from the standpoint of "adjustment", they are more sick than the neurotic person from the standpoint of the realization of their aims as human beings.'[2]

[1] *The Lonely Crowd*, 1950, p. 288.
[2] *Psychoanalysis and Religion*, 1950, p. 83.

One may complain that the norm 'realization of their aims as human beings' is too vague, and also that 'healthy from the standpoint of adjustment' stretches the boundaries of health a little too far; nevertheless one thing is clearly admitted here, i.e. that a human being can be both adjusted and sick at the same time provided, of course, that nothing more is meant by the term adjustment than a so-called sociopsychological 'fit'. Since adjustment in this sense so often means that, as Kenneth Burke put it, 'people may be unfitted by being fit in an unfit fitness', nothing less than a universally valid bio-psychological norm, a measure of pan-human normality, would betray whether an adjustment impairs health or not. On the other hand it is obvious that if such a norm as this brands a culture as abnormal only those individuals who are not adjusted to this culture could achieve the pan-human standard of normality. Thus there are two normalities, the normality of the individual and the normality of a culture. Ultimately the former will determine the principles of the latter though certain social-cultural categories may appear hopelessly intractable to us at the present time. Here again I should like to point out that a 'sociopsychological fit' is strictly speaking an absurdity for it assumes no major changes in the environment. It is at best a concept of short-term validity and as such of limited use.

2. *The Relativistic Use of the Term 'Normal'*

This brings us up against the as yet unsolved problem of defining the human norm and human normality. Before I consider this problem at length I must emphasize that because sociology claims the status of a scientific discipline it may not rest content with the social-cultural definition of adjustment ('sociopsychological fit'). In my view it falls within the scope of the sociologist to use his resources to discover a bio-psychological definition of adjustment. This definition would be also a definition of normality enabling us for the first time to use the correct terminology, the correct antithesis: 'normal adjustment—abnormal adjustment'. The point of view which asks sociologists to extend their inquiries into the field of this study is by no means shared by many; Edwin M. Lemert declares that such activities as these properly belong to the realm of philosophy and not sociology.

45

Those who argue that sociologists in their research on human culture and societies must push beyond this function to evaluate the uniformities or sequences of socio-cultural events which they discover are saying in effect that sociology is not a science, that it is a philosophy . . . we cannot, in the light of recent history of sociology, give any serious consideration to this claim.[1]

In the last chapter of the present work I shall give careful consideration to the view that the search for a positive norm is in fact an attempt to 'evaluate'. Optimum disbalance, which is my norm, is of such a nature that it determines our existence irrespective of what we think we 'ought' to do or think and irrespective of any evaluation. That the confirmation of a positive norm inevitably *leads to* evaluation is beyond the control of the sociologist. But more of this later.

In my search for the norm I find, from the beginning, that it is hopelessly inaccessible. A spate of literature assures us that there are no catholic norms discoverable. 'Normality . . . within a very wide range is culturally defined.'[2] 'What is deviant or abnormal in thought, speech or act . . . depends largely on the cultural definitions of the same as this is qualified by interaction and by the individual's unique organization.'[3] 'The average individual is the fictitious individual who ranks at the midpoint in all distributions of test results. The normal individual is one who is integrated, healthy, and without any great variation from the average individual.'[4] The same note of scepticism recurs in the following, 'any judgment concerning the adjustment of an individual in any frame of reference is relative to a norm or standard with which it is compared'.[5] (This is, of course, true, but the implication is that it must be 'a' norm and it cannot be 'the' norm.) According to Karen Horney a condition is to be diagnosed as neurotic '. . . only if it deviates from the pattern common to the particular culture'.[6] And lastly, 'My final conclusion is that what are called normal and abnormal . . . are

[1] *Social Pathology*, 1951, p. 5.

[2] 'Anthropology and the Abnormal', by Ruth Benedict, *J. General Psychol.*, Jan. 1934, X, pp. 59–82.

[3] *Personality and Problems of Adjustment*, by Kimball Young, 1947, p. 622.

[4] 'A Theoretical and Clinical Study of So-called Normality', by A. S. Edwards, *J. Abnormal and Soc. Psychol.*, Jan.–March 1934, XXVIII, pp. 366–76.

[5] 'The Concept of Adjustment and the Problem of Norms', by R. P. Hinshaw, *Psychol. Rev.*, May 1942, Vol. II, pp. 287–92.

[6] *The Neurotic Personality of Our Time*, 1937, pp. 28–9.

in reality . . . similar . . . and that their only distinction inheres in differing sets of value judgment which are embedded in the mores.'[1]

Cultural relativism—the principal theme of these excerpts—lies at the root of our problem. Were we to try to derive the norm from actual behaviour, i.e. were we to attempt to find some kind of a highest common factor of the great variety of norms and of actual behaviour, we should be told that each and every society is unique and that there are no common factors.[2] On the other hand, when we inquire for the norm in one particular society we are referred to statistics: majority behaviour patterns are elevated to the status of cultural norm. These two are the main elements of cultural relativism: (a) the uniqueness of each society and (b) the statistical basis of the norm in every one of them. One may add to the latter that we never know whether we should derive the norm from majority behaviour or from majority aspirations; it is notorious that this discrimination is rarely made.

Most sociologists affirm, at least by implication, that the absolute norm is not accessible to them or that it is not their task to look for it. We read in anthropological accounts that there are societies in which cataleptic seizures are marks of nobility or in which paranoid behaviour is virtuous; we come across accounts like this, 'Within his everyday behaviour the Yurok cries to his gods "like a baby"; he hallucinates in his meditations "like a psychotic"; he acts "like a phobic" when confronted with contamination; and he tries to act avoidant, suspicious, and stingy "like a compulsive neurotic".'[3] Among the Balinese a schizoid or dissociated condition of adjustment is the lot of the majority. Writing of this Kimball Young states:

Among the Balinese this is the *norm*, and though we may find certain parallels among our own dementia praecox patients, we must not forget that the common acceptances and expectancies—which in Bali are put chiefly into group ceremonials—provide a standard of conformity and interaction that is, for the self and others, thoroughly normal and proper.[4]

[1] 'An Examination of Criteria for the Determination of Normal Society', by J. M. Gillette, *Amer. Sociol. Rev.*, Aug. 1937, II, pp. 501–7.
[2] Cf. *The Human Group*, by G. C. Homans, 1951, p. 46.
[3] *Childhood and Society*, by E. H. Erikson, p. 157.
[4] *Handbook of Social Psychology*, by Kimball Young, 1946, p. 56.

Now there are 'common acceptances and expectancies' in a prison too, in fact anywhere social life persists, yet the sociologist continues to ignore the possibility that these 'acceptances and expectancies' are also comparable on the basis of a pan-human norm. In despair at the range of cultural variations and exasperated by their differences, the sociologist withdraws, to allow revelation and tradition to dictate the norm. Partly responsible for this failure is his exclusive reliance on the analytic method and his relative neglect of the genetic method. He has not yet come to appreciate fully that actual behaviour is not the only kind of ontology from which the norm can be obtained. The bio-psychological potentialities, i.e. inherited potentialities, of human beings are not realized in the majority behaviour of any culture and it is my contention that these potentialities constitute the ontological basis of the pan-human norm.

Sociologists from Durkheim to, say, G. A. Lundberg have not shown much interest in going beyond the normalities of the several specific cultures with a view to discovering what pan-human normality consists of. According to Durkheim, 'In order that sociology may be a true science of things, the generality of phenomena must be taken as the criterion of their normality'.[1] In Lundberg's more recent version of this the same idea gains expression:

Most of the confusion regarding the 'normal' in the social sciences has arisen from the failure to recognize the purely statistical nature of the concept as it is used in science, and consequently the complete relativity of the 'normal' to a specified criterion, system, social segment, or culture. Most frequently, normal is defined (by implication) as that state of affairs which the writer in question considers desirable. That is, it is an 'evaluative' term. Now 'evaluating' is from our point of view a kind of behaviour as much as any other.[2]

No one would doubt that in the social sciences 'normal' has a purely statistical nature. But everything depends on what is being counted: so long as actual behaviour and actual personalities are the basis of our statistics we shall always have a wide selection of normalities; there will be as many of them as there are groups to which we relate them. By all means take the generality of phenomena as the criterion of normality, but if by

[1] *The Rules of Sociological Method*, 1938, p. 75.
[2] *Foundations of Sociology*, 1939, p. 213,

'generality' we mean all humanity then the phenomena must be culturally uncontaminated bio-psychological tendencies. The 'uncontaminated' state is, of course, a kind of *tabula rasa* which we cannot observe, only infer. The inference is made via genetic psychology, going backwards in the life of the individual first empirically and later by the increasing use of hypothesis we establish these virgin bio-psychological tendencies. This genetic approach to the definition of the norm is well expressed by Walter Hollitscher, '. . . when we answer the question whether an illness is to be called psychological, we pay attention not only to which functions are disturbed, but also to how these disturbances arose. . . .'[1] Already some forty years ago, Wilfred Trotter voiced objections against the superficiality of any method which ignores the genetic study of man's culturally unadulterated potentialities:

If once the statistically normal mind is accepted as being synonymous with the psychologically healthy mind . . . a standard is set up which has a most fallacious appearance of objectivity. The statistically normal mind can be regarded as a mind which has responded in the usual way to the moulding and deforming influence of its environment . . .[2]

So long as the basis of this 'statistical normality' remains the culturally differentiated, and, therefore contaminated, behaviour and personality I shall have the following objections against it:

(*a*) Lundberg complains[3] that 'Most frequently, normal is defined (by implication) . . . as desirable.' Yet he insists that the concept of 'normal' has a 'purely statistical nature'. What does this amount to? That majority behaviour is normal because it is majority behaviour? But his own phrase 'most frequently' indicates that the majority regards 'normal' as 'desirable'! According to Lundberg we are obliged to conclude that the *normal* meaning of the term 'normal' is 'desirable'. It is true that the majority may be in error as to the correct usage of a word or a phrase. But even if this is the case at least the usage shows the majority's need for an absolute norm which is part of the

---

[1] 'On the Concept of Psychological Health and Illness', by W. Hollitscher, *Internat. J. Psychoanal.*, 1943, XXIV, pp. 125–40.

[2] *Instincts of the Herd in Peace and War*, 1947, p. 81.

[3] In his later writings Lundberg seems to have departed from the relativism implicit in the quoted passages. Cf. *Amer. Sociol. Rev.*, Feb. 1944 and Dec. 1948.

majority's evaluative behaviour. This can be ignored only at the risk of a breakdown in communication.

(b) We come across the following comment on the statistical conception of normality in the Kinsey report, '. . . many items in human sexual behaviour which are labelled abnormal, or perversions, in textbooks, prove, upon statistical examination, to occur in as many as 30 or 60 or 75 per cent of certain populations. It is difficult to maintain that such types of behaviour are abnormal because they are rare.'[1] They are abnormal because the norm is *not* given by majority behaviour; so far as the textbooks are concerned the norm is either a bio-psychological constant of which their authors are unaware or which they don't care to define, or it is a cultural precept of some sort.

(c) If Durkheim and Lundberg are right what should be the meaning of the statement, 'This man is healthier than the average'?[2] Is the man in question abnormal? G. E. Moore had every right to ask:

Was the excellence of Socrates or of Shakespeare normal? Was it not rather abnormal, extraordinary? It is, I think, obvious in the first place that not all that is good, is normal, that on the contrary, the abnormal is often better than the normal: peculiar excellence as well as peculiar viciousness, must obviously be not normal but abnormal.[3]

Surely, the deeply ingrained connotation of the word 'abnormal' forbids us such a usage as this.

(d) Werner Wolff writes, 'Just as we have a model of normality for the physical build and bodily function, so we may also have a model of normality for psychological functions, especially since body and mind seem to be interdependent.'[4] No one can question psychosomatic unity any longer and it is perfectly right that we should learn from physical medicine and from its approach to the conceptions of 'health' and 'ill-health'. I agree with Trigant Burrow who, rejecting the statistical conception of normality, exclaims,

[1] *Sexual Behaviour in the Human Male*, by A. C. Kinsey, W. B. Pomeroy, and C. E. Martin, 1948, pp. 199–201.

[2] W. Hollitscher, op. cit. Cf. 'Psycho-analysis and the Concept of Health', by Heinz Hartmann, *Internat. J. Psychoanal.*, July–Oct. 1939, XX, pp. 308–21.

[3] *Principia Ethica*, 1929, p. 43.

[4] *The Threshold of the Abnormal*, 1952, p. 7.

THE RELATIVISTIC USE OF THE TERM 'NORMAL'

It is, of course, quite unthinkable that there should not exist for
the phylosoma as a whole a definite functional norm, a determinable
central constant that is as basic and dependable as the universal
structural norm recognized as protoplasm. It is unthinkable that
there should not exist a primary principle of functional constancy or
interrelational balance within the phyloorganism that discloses deviations in function correlative to those existing in the structural
sphere.[1]

Trigant Burrow suggests that this principle consists in 'the
solidarity of individual and phylum . . . a biologically consistent
norm of behaviour'. Though this principle mistakenly elevates
my principle of cohesion to the rank of exclusive authority in
these matters, the assumption that a principle of some kind is
in fact operative could not be denied by the sociologist. But if
there is a bio-psychological norm, there must be a bio-psychological normality! C. Daly King offered the following solution
of this problem. 'The normal . . . is objectively, and properly,
to be defined as that which functions in accordance with its
design.'[2] This is indeed the only sensible interpretation of a
term which has so much been misused; except, of course, this
formula imposes on us the task of defining the *normal design*,
for that which functions in accordance with an abnormal
design is abnormal.

(*e*) Arguing for the statistical conception of normality Lundberg presents the following example, 'If, for example, the group
considered consists of advanced cases of typhoid fever, a temperature of 102 may be normal (i.e. most common for such
patients) although this is regarded as "abnormal" for an un-
selected group.' Now I should have thought that what is 'most
common' is 'true to type'—it is 'typical'—a phrase much more
appropriate for the menial task of statistical description than
'normal'. As it happens the varieties of typhoid fever are of a
great number; a different kind of temperature may be 'normal'
for some of these varieties. What is 'normal' for the *septicaemic*
form may be 'abnormal' for the ambulatory variety. In fact,
almost every kind of temperature could be described as 'normal'
so long as it appeared in the appropriate kind of typhoid fever.

[1] *The Neurosis of Man*, 1949, p. 189.
[2] 'The Meaning of Normal', *Yale Journal of Biology and Medicine*, Jan. 1945,
XVIII, pp. 493–501.

Applying this to human behaviour, every kind of human behaviour becomes normal if we can relate it to a category within
which it is *typical*. For example, it is normal for paranoid dic-
tators to persecute and to wage war, it is normal for homicidal
maniacs to murder, it is normal to be a leper in a leper colony,
and so on.

*I contend that the use of the term 'normal' for the description
of average-majority-conditions carries with it a sometimes unin-
tended and implicit denial that an absolute norm exists.* After
all, if normality may signify cultural (relative) standards only,
what term if any, would be left available for the description of a
bio-psychological (absolute) standard?[1] We must remember that
Lundberg wishes to *reserve* the term for relativistic application,
ignoring the possibility of arriving at an ultimate "statistical'
norm to which all cultural norms would be relative. Whether
we can formulate plausible hypotheses about the ultimate norm
or succeed in actually defining it, one thing is certain, that the
ultimate norm has an indisputable priority for the adjective
'normal'. If a sociologist uses terms—which the majority regards as normative—in a merely statistical sense he is implicitly
affirming ethical relativism or scepticism. This he has no right
to do. The sociologist's scrupulous abstention from value-
judgments would be even more complete if he showed no less
concern for the choice of his terms and concepts.

3. *The Concept of 'Abnorm'*

Assuming that we have succeeded in recapturing the term 'normal' from the relativists it shall henceforth signify conformity
with a universal and absolute bio-psychological principle. The
'normal' shall hereafter shed its inverted commas for it is no
longer just the 'so-called' normal but 'the' normal. But what is

[1] 'It is a semantic misfortune that the word "norm" used in statistics, and the
word "normal" used in speaking of health, have a common pool', from Lawrence
S. Kubie, 'The Fundamental Nature of the Distinction between Normality and
Neurosis', *The Psychoanalytical Quarterly*, 1954, XXIII, pp. 167–204.

'At present the idea of abnormality seems to be hopelessly confused with the
entirely different idea of a departure from the average; what is average is supposed to be normal and what is not average is supposed to be abnormal, although
objectively it is quite possible that the average may be the most abnormal of all,
and any departure therefrom is *ipso facto* in the direction of the normal', from
Integrative Psychology, by Marston, King, and Marston, 1931, p. 434.

this norm, this basic principle? If I had the audacity to attempt a definition of the absolute norm I should be conspicuously lacking in wisdom, for there are some very good reasons why the absolute norm cannot be defined.

The first of these is that at one particular juncture of history no one is in a position to circumscribe the area of normal behaviour for all times to come. The range of normal behaviour is always widening and the differentiation of normal personality types continues all the time; new forms of normality are always possible in the civilizations yet to come. This is what Ruth Benedict had in mind when she wrote, 'No one civilization can possibly utilize in its mores the whole potential range of human behaviour.' She would be misunderstood by those who might regard this statement as entirely pessimistic: it is not only that civilizations fail to exploit the whole range of the bio-psychological potential of man but that in every civilization the range widens *while* it is being exploited. This process may well be the essence of what is usually described as 'progress'. According to this, human progress is the ever greater realization of the bio-psychological principles of life through the growth of the range of normal forms of behaviour.

Secondly, even when there seemed to be some consensus on normality it never went beyond vague generalities. On the other hand, people's agreement on abnormalities, i.e. on what to call as such, is very often specific. It appears that abnormalities are more concrete and distinctive than normalities. 'When we come to psychological ill-health we are, it seems to me, on firmer ground; there is much more likely to be agreement about what is bad for us than what is good for us.'[1] Indeed a similar situation prevails in the realm of medicine regarding physical health and ill-health. Though there may be many theses and arguments about the definition of physical health there is no doubt that, say, *poliomyelitis* is a disease. More success may attend our efforts if we turned our attention towards the 'abnormal' first to see whether in this manner 'an indirect approximation' of the norm would not be feasible? After all, it is reasonable to hold that the freer a condition is from abnormalities the more of the absolute norm is being realized.

[1] 'The Problems of Discipline', by W. J. H. Sprott, *The Listener*, 28 June 1951, also *Social Psychology*, by W. J. H. Sprott, 1952, pp. 226–30.

The inability or unwillingness of some to approach the problem of normality from the side of a seemingly negative concept —'ab'—normal or 'non'—normal—is understandable enough.[1] Elementary logic will tell us that we cannot define 'not-English' before first giving a definition of 'English'. I propose the following solution of our problem: The definition of normality is not possible if we expect this definition to guide us clearly in concrete instances. Nevertheless a theoretical definition was suggested in the previous chapter which I may now put to work with some chance of success. I said there that there is a specific range of disbalance between the basic principles of growth and cohesion which furnishes an optimum chance of survival for the human species. This is, of course, vague and, in its present form, a well-nigh useless guide. But it is rash to claim that, ignorant though we are about what this 'specific range' should be, we know when it is grossly overstepped? We may not know what to call an 'optimum disbalance' but we are, as we shall see, in no doubt about what is a gross deviation from this optimum disbalance. '. . . Although we do not possess any general definition of normality, either from a statistical or from a normative viewpoint, we, experts and public, are in reasonable agreement about extreme abnormality. But even extremely abnormal behaviour has not been described in a fashion which will lend itself to an unequivocal definition.'[2] We must, therefore, abandon the search for a *sufficiently specific* definition and instead find out whether other kinds of definitions would not be equally effectual and 'unequivocal' even in the not so 'extremely' abnormal cases. We will have occasion to see whether this is in fact possible.

[1] Cf. 'Before we can speak of the abnormal we must already have a conception of the normal', *Psychology and Morals*, by J. A. Hadfield, 1949, pp. 4–5. F. T. Hacker speaks of the 'methodological impossibility of defining something by the absence of its disturbance', 'The Concept of Normality and its Practical Significance', *Amer. J. Orthopsychiatry*, Jan. 1945, XV, pp. 47–64. Carl Binger utters the same *caveat*, 'Maturity is not simply the opposite of immaturity—at least we probably shall not arrive at a sound understanding of it if we proceed by describing an immature individual and then by saying, "a mature man is everything that this one is not",' ('What is Maturity?' *Harper's Magazine*, May 1951, pp. 70–8). It is important to remember that I do not aim at the *definition* of normality through the definition of abnormality; I claim, however, that the time has come to agree what is definitely *not* normality.

[2] 'The Concept of Normality', by F. C. Redlich, *Amer. J. Psychotherapy*, July 1952, VI, pp. 551–76.

If normality can come into being only when the pan-human forms of abnormalities are absent, a definition of the abnormal is, in fact, a definition of one of the most important frontiers of the normal. We must, however, admit that the definition of the abnormal is a progressive act of psychiatry and that the concept of the abnormal grows with every psychiatric discovery. At the same time, strangely enough, the area of normality does not correspondingly narrow, for discoveries of abnormalities more or less keep abreast with discoveries of novel forms of normality. There are, therefore, two progressive series: the growth of the abnormal, i.e. the more and more subtle discernment of the abnormal, and the refinement, enrichment, and consequent growth of the normal. Yet the core, the essence of both, remains the same throughout the career of the human species. The evidence is plentiful to show that this is true of the abnormal, though to prove it true of the normal is more difficult. Thus tuberculosis or hyperthyroidism have always been abnormal conditions and will never become normal conditions, and Aretaeus about 2000 years ago identified διαβήτης as a disease: it is a disease today no matter to what degree our conception of diabetes has been changed by Banting, Best and Macleod.[1] So in view of psychosomatic unity, by analogy, what is abnormal adjustment today will be abnormal adjustment in the future. There is no such persistence of agreement as this in the realm of the normal. There may be certain general principles of normality which manage to survive social change—for example, our approval of charity, justice, courage, and so on—but there is nothing in these which corresponds to the specificity and concreteness of a psychological disease-syndrome as defined in modern psychiatry. Also, whereas a Nietzscheian dissident of charity and justice is possible in moral philosophy no school of psychiatry is ever likely to declare that, say, paranoid behaviour is normal.

In rejecting cultural relativism I have insisted that abnormality is not a thing that varies according to culture, but that cultures vary according to the degree of abnormality they encourage and legitimize. Ruth Benedict, in spite of her repeated affirmation of cultural relativism, must have felt this when she said, 'Western civilization allows and culturally honors

[1] Cf. *A History of Medicine*, by Douglas Guthrie, pp. 71–2, 365.

gratifications of the ego which according to any *absolute category* would be regarded as abnormal,' or when she wrote, '. . . it is quite possible that a modicum of what is considered right and what wrong could be disentangled . . .'[1] She was aware of the presence of absolute categories, though she, as many others, seemed to expect a definition of the normal and not that of the abnormal to emerge with the help of these 'absolute categories'. In her treatment of this subject she repeatedly suggests this. For example, 'No society has yet achieved a self-conscious and critical analysis of its own normalities and attempted rationally to deal with its own social process of creating new normalities within its next generation. But the fact that it is unachieved is not therefore proof of its impossibility.' Others have gone further than this by demanding an arbitrary postulation of the elements of normality; for example, '. . . All the symptoms associated with the psychoneuroses seem best defined by a normative approach which arbitrarily postulates, on the basis of the best psychiatric opinion, a theoretical integrated, balanced personality, wide deviations from which would be looked upon as "abnormal".'[2] Here I am asking for something much more modest than this. I am seeking a minimum definition of what is *certainly abnormal* under all circumstances and in all cultures. Such a definition as this would not necessarily point to an ideal or indicate what is meritorious; yet the quest for this definition follows the most promising line of inquiry into the ways in which one can successfully combat the unrecognized relativistic bias of contemporary sociology, as well as lighten the miseries of contemporary moral philosophy.

It would be idle to pretend that a 'definition' in the strict logical sense is possible even here. A sharp dividing line between the normal and abnormal adjustment of personality or between normal and abnormal forms of behaviour is likely to remain elusive for ever. Let us suppose that we were to define the meaning of the phrases 'long life' and 'short life' as they are customarily applied to human beings. There would be no gainsaying that a child dying at the age of three had a short life and that an octogenarian has a long life behind him. Of course,

[1] Op. cit.
[2] 'A Critique of Cultural and Statistical Concepts of Abnormality', by H. J. Wegrocki, *J. Abnormal and Soc. Psychol.*, 1939, XXXIV, pp. 166–78.

we are aware of the considerable changes which have taken place in the human life span and which are anticipated to take place in the future. One thing is certain, that if premature death at the age of three is taken as a parallel to our 'abnormal' no matter what advances we may make in longevity, death at the age of three will always be premature, and, as a matter of fact, the more advance is made the more premature it will become. At the same time any sharp dividing line between 'short' and 'long' would be arbitrary in this case. Now, just as we can say with certainty that death at the age of three is premature—without allowing that a four year old is 'longlived'—we can also say that, by certain criteria to be considered later, adjustment is abnormal—once again, without allowing that in the absence of those criteria the adjustment is normal. Thus what we can legitimately aim at is not a definition of abnormality, but the definition of the *minimum area* of abnormality, i.e. the definition of what is certainly abnormal. What are the criteria of this condition?

Before we examine whether a plausible answer to this question is available we should remind ourselves that it is not abnormality in general but 'abnormal adjustment' in particular that we seek to define. We should, therefore, disregard those abnormal conditions of the personality which are generally believed to be hereditary as well as those mental conditions which are concomitants or consequences of a physical injury or disease. This proviso will eliminate most of the psychoses, though not all of them. I shall retain within my concept of abnormal adjustment only those conditions which are predominantly the outcome of the adjustment processes (see above).

Yet the exclusion of the organic and, even more important, of the hereditary variable from my discussion may be criticized as a method guilty of a serious omission. It may be, after all, that the range of hereditary variability is so wide and its influence so decisive as to invalidate a purely environmentalist definition of abnormal adjustment. *Firstly*, it will be said that there are many viable and serviceable deviations from any norm. To illustrate, André Gide argued strenuously that homosexuality was a legitimate variant, nay, a necessary complement of the species.[1] Although there are only a comparatively few cases in

[1] *Corydon*, 1952.

which homosexuality is genetically determined one must examine this argument for it may be possible to extend it by analogy to other cases as well. Gide quoted Magnus Hirschfeld, according to whom there were all kinds of intermediate degrees of sexuality each of which must be allowed to run its course unless one wishes to violate the freedom of a perfectly natural variation. These *Sexuelle Zwischenstufen* are legitimate variations in sexuality, insists Gide, and there are no grounds upon which they could be condemned. The fallacy of this argument is not difficult to reveal. Why not regard the various degrees of hereditary visual or other sensory defects, e.g. shortsightedness or partial deafness as *Zwischenstufen*? Also if inversion is in some cases part of the range of hereditary variability it will not make acquired inversion a legitimate variant. From the point of view of the evolutionary process both are unserviceable. *Secondly*, far more important are the implications of a recent research[1] which examining the correlations between the neurotic traits of identical twins and fraternal twins found that the former amounted to 0·851 whilst the latter was only 0·217. A careful perusal of this research report, however, could suggest no more than what we have always suspected, i.e. that 'predisposition', 'susceptibility' or 'vulnerability', play some part in deciding whether or not the individual is going to succumb to noxious psychological influences of a certain intensity and frequency. It is still not ruled out that there is a minimum area of these influences to which all would succumb. And this is sufficient for the purposes of the minimum definition I seek. *Thirdly*, the problem whether the psychoses and the neuroses fall into a single order, a single continuum, need not concern us here. If there is only one continuum (which we may call adjustment continuum) its minimum abnormality is covered by an environmentalist definition; if there is more than one, the others are necessarily outside my field of interest.

There is yet one more specification I must introduce into my task. Earlier I pointed out that primary adjustment conditions —though hidden in the overlay of the secondary adjustment process—persist and remain with the individual for life, unless he is subjected to some form of anamnesic psychotherapy.

---

[1] 'The Inheritance of Neuroticism: An Experimental Study', by H. J. Eysenck and D. B. Prell, *J. Mental Science*, July 1951, XCVII, pp. 441–6.

Furthermore I put it forward that the secondary adjustment process cannot undo the primary adjustment condition or introduce into it fundamental changes. From this it follows that when I define 'abnormal adjustment' I am, in fact, defining *abnormal primary adjustment condition*.

4. *The Casuistic Criteria of the 'Abnorm'*

My task is now definitely circumscribed: I am to examine whether it is in our power to define the minimum area of abnormal primary adjustment conditions. There are two paths which converge towards this objective.

(A) The first is the development of a general principle, a universally applicable criterion, of abnormality. This general principle will tell us whether cohesion and growth are so grossly out of balance during the primary adjustment process as to prejudice a *serviceable* disbalance during the course of the individual's subsequent life. The construction of an inventory of experiences during the primary adjustment process should follow from the definition of the general principle.

(B) The second is the construction of an inventory of those syndromes, i.e. manifestations of primary and secondary adjustment conditions which certainly signify that unserviceable disbalance characterized the preceding primary adjustment process.

That medicine is casuistic is obvious; that the absence of absolute and general theoretical standards in medicine is no impediment to the application of that science is palpable. On the contrary, absolute standards are too far removed from the concrete instances of living and are thereby to some extent almost irrelevant.[1] If casuistry is the accepted and effective rule in medicine it seems unreasonable to object to this rule in psychology. It is probable that psychology's closer historical association with moral philosophy has been responsible for the philosophical distrust of casuistry making itself felt in psychology as well. Casuistry acquired a notoriety in moral philosophy largely on account of its Jesuitic exploitation. Yet today, in spite of its unsavoury reputation, casuistry is being rediscovered as a logical necessity. Hastings Rashdall, Moore, Laird, and others came

---

[1] Cf. 'Optima of Mental Health', by Brewster Smith, *Psychiatry*, XIII, Nov. 1950, pp. 503-10.

to the conclusion that 'casuistry is the goal of ethics'[1] and Moore reminded us that 'so far as ethics allows itself to give lists of virtues or even to name constituents of the Ideal, it is indistinguishable from casuistry . . .'[2] Now a 'casuistic definition' is no novelty to logicians. It is no other than the so-called 'extensive definition', a definition by examples. It is true that there are some grounds upon which a protest could be made that a definition by examples is not a definition at all. Yet it would be fastidious to repudiate an extensive definition when it is both useful and the only one available.[3] Such is the case in medicine, and psychology may follow suit without compunction.

5. *The First Inventory*

(A) The infant's and the young child's relationship to his mother is a psycho-biological relationship and the archetype of all subsequent social relationships. It is this relationship during which the final pattern of balance between growth and cohesion is formed. Certain objective essentials of what I call unserviceable disbalance at this time can be worked out. These essentials are the following:

(*a*) The continued or repeated interruption of physical proximity between mother and child, or even in the absence of this, the child's emotional rejection by the mother.

(*b*) The practice of child-rearing up to the age of five containing disciplinary measures based on the sanction of pain infliction or on the systematic and radical frustration of instinctual needs.

---

[1] *The Theory of Good and Evil*, by Hastings Rashdall, 1924, II, p. 418.

[2] *Principia Ethica*, 1929, pp. 4–5.

[3] Susan Stebbing, who was sceptical as to the propriety of calling a set of examples an 'extensive definition', observed that an extensive definition could be achieved only by someone able to select the 'typical' instances. She quotes J. N. Keynes (*Formal Logic*, 1906, §22), whose illustration of this sort of definition is particularly useful to me as a model of what I have in mind: '. . . A chemist might be able "from the full denotation of metal to make a selection of a limited number of metals which would be precisely typical of the whole class; that is to say, his selected list would possess in common only such properties as are common to the whole class" . . . the chemist would take metals "as different from one another as possible, such as aluminium, antimony, copper, gold, iron, mercury, sodium, zinc". These selected metals define the class *metal* by example' (*A Modern Introduction to Logic*, by L. S. Stebbing, 1942, p. 422).

(c) The exposing of the child to experiences which he will construe as threats to himself or to his love-objects.

(d) The creation of an atmosphere of insecurity either through deliberate teasing or through parental instability and fickleness.

In all these experiences the transmutation of the principle of cohesion in terms of reciprocated love suffers a rupture and henceforth I shall bring terminology into line with my theory and refer to these experiences as 'rupture experiences' to distinguish them from the so-called traumatic experiences. *This is my general principle: rupture in the smooth transmutation of cohesion into love is unserviceable.* Once again, at this point, a reminder is needed to stress why I am preoccupied here with the principle of cohesion and make no mention of the principle of growth. Once man has reached the level of culture, co-operation, reciprocation of love, and an experience of communion are far more problematical than growth and individuation. For *all* metazoa the realization of the principle of cohesion is immeasurably more difficult than that of the principle of growth. The evolutionary process has not as yet reached a stage when it is apparent how cohesion on the fifth level[1] should be realized. Most of what is abnormal in the human adjustment process is so on account of the failure of the principle of cohesion. The consequence of rupture experiences is that the child's cohesion urges intensify and the disbalance between the two basic forces becomes unserviceable. This is, of course, a deliberately simplified schema and it is understood that a very early sexualization, as well as an early reactive aggression, introduces great variety into the forms of disbalance. Nothing would be gained here by rewriting the psycho-analytic clinical record against the background of my first principles.

An inventory of rupture experiences should be drawn up in the spirit of my general principle which would introduce the maximum specificity into the four points listed above. There are three major objections I anticipate here.

(1) Let us suppose that we draw up an inventory of those experiences of the primary adjustment process which try the child's frustration-tolerance. The hereditary variables of this tolerance do not cause us much trouble for a minimum defintion would make use of a highest common factor. But what

[1] Cf. pp. 5–10.

specific experiences should we include? Whether a certain experience should be included and another not would be as a rule decided by the empirical evidence of its syndrome-producing power. But then the question why a certain manifestation-pattern should be regarded as a syndrome, is usually decided by finding out whether it is rooted in social-sexual frustration during the primary adjustment process. *The obvious circularity of this argument is cut through by saying that 'syndrome-producing power' may have led us to the discovery of rupture experiences but these latter are not derived from the syndromes; the experiences are postulated as criteria of abnormality for they constitute an infringement of the basic principles of life.*

I derived the principle of cohesion and growth (see Chapter I) *inductively* from a large number of disparate observations. These principles now serve as a point of departure for *deductive* reasoning; I infer that an abrupt severance of the phylic bond between mother and child or any interference with the gradual weaning of the child from this bond is unserviceable to the individual as well as to the species. The syndromes are regarded as syndromes of abnormal adjustment because they are rooted in rupture experiences and not the other way round, i.e. that rupture experiences are to be declared abnormal because they have been shown to result in certain syndromes.

(2) But what are we to do with the problem of measurement? These experiences which we may list in an agreed inventory can be of all conceivable degrees of intensity and frequency; when are we to pass the verdict that they should be listed? After all, we know of no cultures in which at least some of the experiences we would readily list are not tolerated or indeed institutionalized. No doubt the limit of the minimum will have to be arbitrarily drawn but it will be a safe arbitrariness well within the area of the palpably abnormal. One should also consider that even if we could not agree on absolute and universal limits we could still regard our list as one containing *directional criteria, ideal types,* or negative signposts which we must leave as far behind as possible. A disagreement on operational limits does not preclude an agreement on directional criteria. A disagreement on 'how much' is not crippling to an agreement on 'what'. Sociologists and moral philosophers should remember, when complaining of the vagueness or tentativeness of my speci-

fications, that they have produced no agreement even on directional criteria. To show how a casuistic listing of rupture experiences may acquire an immediate practical value irrespective of the serious difficulties in measurement I offer the following illustration. In a recently published paper on 'Research Strategy in the Study of Mother-Child Separation'[1] the writers of this paper give an exhaustive list of all the principal classes and subclasses of this rupture experience:

1. Separation from the mother *before* a stable and secure dependency relationship has been established with either

(*a*) lack of subsequent opportunity to form a stable relationship with any one mother-figure, as in institutionalization—the case of *complete privation*; or

(*b*) a temporary lack of opportunity to form a stable relationship with any one mother-figure but with later opportunity to establish one, either with the natural mother or with the mother-substitute—the case of *temporary privation* of greater or lesser duration; or

(*c*) immediate substitution for the mother of a substitute mother with whom the child can establish a stable and secure relationship, as in early adoption; this probably results *in no appreciable privation*. [This, of course, is *not* a rupture experience.]

2. Separation from the mother (or substitute-mother) *after* a stable and secure dependency relationship has been established and before the child is old enough to be independent of the mother, with either;

(*a*) severance of the relationship and no subsequent opportunity to form a stable and secure relationship with the original or a substitute figure—the most severe case of *deprivation*; or

(*b*) severance of the relationship but with opportunity to form a stable and secure relationship with a substitute-mother; despite the provision of the substitute figure this may involve *temporary deprivation* through the very breach of relationship; or

(*c*) a temporary interruption of the relationship followed by reunion with the mother. This case is also one of *temporary deprivation*. It may occasion more deprivation than (*b*) if it lasts a long time and there is no substitute figure. Even with a temporary mother-substitute there would not only be a breach of the original relationship but a breach of the second relationship with the substitute (if such was formed) upon reunion with the mother.

The writers further list a large number of variables which

[1] By Mary D. Ainsworth and John Bowlby, *Courrier*, International Children's Centre, March 1954, Vol. IV, No. 3.

would appreciably or even profoundly affect the severity of the rupture experienced by the child. Indeed it is not possible to think of more than a list, an inventory, of the standard cases which in their totality would constitute a minimum definition of rupture. Even so the absence of identifiable quantitative limits would still defeat me were it not that I will make full use of a second inventory when specific diagnoses are needed, and that I can put the definition of rupture to immediate use even without a second inventory: the significance of the definition of rupture experiences does not lie in its use as a diagnostic tool for the assessment of individuals but as a yardstick of preventive action both in individual life and in institutional planning. *Thus if we agree on this definition we would not commit ourselves to arbitrary judgments on the adjustment conditions of single individuals but we would commit ourselves both to social policies and to precepts of individual behaviour.* With the aid of this inventory we can not only decide that certain kinds of individual behaviour are unserviceable but also that certain kinds of cultures or certain specific cultural traits are unserviceable. Herein lies the *immediate* and *practical* significance of such an inventory as this.

(3) To locate the cause of abnormal adjustment in rupture experiences without reference to the social, physiological, and physical ramifications of these experiences will be branded as a 'single cause explanation'. An objection on this score may take the following form.

In psychiatry ancient thinking still is strongly represented. For example, there exists the belief that if one could find that one 'Factor X' which is responsible for a given nosological entity such as schizophrenia, one could cure such a condition. The fallacy of such argument is obvious. Raising the question of the cause of schizophrenia presupposes that certain behaviour features can be classified, isolated, and localized and that the hypothetical cause can be likewise isolated and related to the disease entity. In such reasoning, the organism is not considered as a whole but is split up in part functions. Likewise, in psychotherapy, there exists still the tendency to make single events such as traumatic childhood experiences responsible for later behaviour. Causal and lineal thinking are also revealed in fashion trends of psychoanalysis, varying from the 'primal scene' over the 'castration complex' to 'repressed aggression'. This strong nineteenth century orientation of psychiatric theory is likely to be replaced in time by other views. These hold that whenever one factor changes, all the other factors likewise must undergo change . . .[1]

Jurgen Ruesch, the writer of this prediction, goes on to say that, '. . . the psychiatrist has to realize that he himself, and also the individual he is studying, are but minimal parts of larger super-personal systems and that theories of causality which the psychiatrist establishes are usually valid only within the framework of very narrow considerations, special situations, and limited delineations of the scientific universe'. It was desirable that this veto should be cited at length for its warnings deserve most careful attention. To begin with, the protest that the organism is not considered as a whole is a *non sequitur*. Should single factors suffice to explain etiology and to suggest adequate therapy they do not oblige us to split up the organism into part functions. *Single factors can be total organismic factors, all-enveloping, decisive principles; growth and cohesion are of this kind.* Furthermore, I have never suggested that a single rupture experience should ever be made sufficient to account for syndrome formation. In the first place rupture experiences take place in time and constitute a series. Secondly, they almost always appear in clusters, in Gestalts, the character of which does not altogether defy description or even definition. And finally, the omission of treating the sociological, physiological, and physical ramifications of these rupture experiences *as causes* is made here partly for reasons of economy and space, and partly on principle. The former needs no separate justification, whilst to give the reasons for the latter will suffice: the bio-psychological abnorm is realized during the primary process of adjustment and *all* sociological, physiological, and physical factors are funnelled into the psycho-dynamic experiences of the child. Many extraneous events may cause rupture experiences, but unless they exert an influence on the framework of life within which the primary process takes place, unless they are converted into psycho-dynamically relevant experiences, they are *not* causes from the standpoint of the abnorm. Yet as a certain quantity of these extraneous factors are invariably so converted, their obvious status in the causal series is not for a moment questioned. What I am doing here is to insist that the appeal to

[1] *Communication*, by Jurgen Ruesch and Gregory Bateson, 1951, pp. 74–5.

'larger superpersonal systems', however sound, sabotage the unique opportunity to understand and appraise those very superpersonal systems themselves. Moreover, the virtuous and vicious circle formed by individual and environment is legitimately cut at the point where interaction is most simplified. Hankering for total explanations simultaneously rendered may be salutary in the service of truth but it will inevitably postpone the intervention of social science in social affairs for ever. Meanwhile I repeat, it is not this expediency that makes me advocate the definition of the abnorm but the bio-psychological absoluteness of the latter.

6. *The Second Inventory*

The definition of abnormal primary adjustment stands or falls with the arguments of the foregoing section. The second approach which leads to this definition is merely supplementary to what has already been said. This consists in the construction of an inventory of syndromes which the concurrence of world-wide psychiatric research correlates with the experiences linked in the first inventory.

The sceptic, not unexpectedly, may look upon this second inventory most unfavourably. He may regard it as intolerably arbitrary; he may say that a syndrome is what the psychiatrists agree to call as such, an agreement by no means guaranteed. Lamentable as the uncertainty is from which disagreements issue, they are also observed in general medicine although, admittedly, to a lesser extent. No one would doubt that, say, a hundred years ago an inventory of the identified disease-syndromes would have been agreed upon by the medical world at that time. There *was* a consensus on what was a disease-syndrome and a near-enough consensus on what were to be regarded as the constituent symptoms in these syndromes. Even if this agreement did not result in a formally agreed, subscribed and ratified inventory it was there implicitly. Now this inventory has grown considerably during the last hundred years by the more subtle specificity introduced through the discovery of new symptoms and also by the addition of newly discovered syndromes. Yet what was agreed upon a hundred years ago, concerning the description of certain conditions *as abnormal*, has changed only very marginally. Disagreements between the past and the present surround problems of etiology, specificity of diagnosis, prophylaxis and therapy, but not the decision whether or not a condition is abnormal. Gregory Zilboorg is right in stressing that '. . . the clinical manifestations of a mental disease undergo changes in the course of time and that clinical pictures were different at various periods of history. . . .'[1] Yet is it not possible to identify the highest common factors in these 'changing manifestations' if mental disease itself is not alleged to have changed? Zilboorg admits that *plus ça change plus c'est la même chose* and that '. . . Hippocrates, as well as the Roman compiler Celsus described mental conditions highly similar to those found today . . .' To argue that there is no *grande hysterie* today whereas it was very frequent in the 15th and 16th century would not impress us either for it is not my thesis that a syndrome will never cease to plague us.

Excerpts from a correspondence between Professor Aubrey Lewis and myself may reveal what in my view is meant by 'marginal' changes in the conception of the abnormal. Professor Lewis wrote (12 Jan. 1953):

A condition once regarded as abnormal may now be regarded as normal, but the name it formerly bore may have been gradually shifted to something else which is undoubtedly abnormal. *Albuminaria* supplies an instance of an abnormal condition now regarded as harmless. In the 19th century the presence of albumin in the urine, which so frequently betokens acute nephritis or Bright's disease, was assumed always to indicate a morbid abnormality; consequently the form which we now call orthostatic albuminaria (viz. albuminaria occurring in healthy adolescents, especially when they change from the recumbent to the erect posture) was considered to indicate disease, and appropriate precautions were taken by insurance companies, military services and so forth. Now, however, we regard this condition as compatible with perfect health (although, of course, it falls outside the statistical norm). There are other such symptoms which have been mistakenly assumed to indicate disease and even built up into a disease per se.[2] Constipation (or more properly,

[1] Cf. *Amer. J. Orthopsychiatry*, Oct. 1938, VIII, pp. 597–600.
[2] Further instances are mentioned by John A. Ryle ('The Meaning of Normal', *The Lancet*, 4 Jan. 1947, Vol. 252), such as myotatic irritability of the pectoral muscles, palpable epitrochlear glands at times as large as a cherry stone, stethoscopic misinterpretations of innocent cardiac murmurs, and so on.

infrequent defaecation) is another example of something previously regarded as abnormal, with consequent mistaken efforts to improve it by drugs, alteration of the diet, etc., whereas we now recognize how wide the range of the normal and healthy is in this respect. While I would, therefore, agree that it is most difficult for positive science to define the normal (whereas definition of the abnormal in the form of minimum definition—is usually practicable and lasting), it is hardly possible to accept the unrestricted assertion that 'what is identified as abnormal in one age is never rehabilitated as normal in another'.[1] I think that the difficulty in agreeing with this statement is much greater when the phenomenon is mental than when it is physical.

This is, of course, a wise and restrained comment with which I am in agreement. In my reply I explained that I wished to emend my former statement thus, 'What is identified as an abnormal syndrome in one age is never rehabilitated as normal in another.' I went on to explain that as albumin in the urine or constipation are not syndromes but symptoms, I hoped that the new formula would be acceptable. Professor Lewis replied (27 Feb. 1953): 'I think the modified sentence disposes of most of the difficulties I mentioned. It raises, of course, a potential crux, in the criteria for distinguishing between a symptom, a syndrome, and a disease. . . .' In connection with this Professor Lewis referred to Scott Buchanan's *The Doctrine of Signature*. Buchanan's analysis did much to save me from overlooking important conceptual difficulties. But, as we shall see, these difficulties will not affect my minimum definition even in the realm of the 'mental'. Buchanan turns our attention to the realities which lie behind terms such as 'symptom' or 'syndrome'. He calls an item of nature, as observed in experience, a signature. Signatures (*sensa*) are never wholly discrete and merge with others into syndromes. On the other hand, these signatures or symptoms may feature in the *Gestalt* of many different syndromes. It appears to me that symptom-status is a very ephemeral thing:[2] everything depends on the precision of our instruments in analysing the *sensa* reported by the subject or identified by the physician. One may even say that symptoms are hardly ever indivisible into further constituent symptoms.

---

[1] Quoted from my first letter to Professor Lewis.
[2] So is 'part-function' which Professor Lewis seems to favour.

Should this be the case the difference between symptom and syndrome would disappear and both would occupy their positions along a continuum of various complexes of *sensa*. Indeed, in these circumstances, it will not be possible to discriminate between the two for the difference will be one of scope, and not between multiplicity and singularity. The fact that a disease picture consists of incommensurabilia (Buchanan, p. 83) comes to our rescue. So long as the disease picture contains *disparate manifestations* which together make up the *Gestalt* of the disease picture we have no reason to doubt that we are dealing with a syndrome. For our minimum definition we need look for no more than this. That symptoms have a habit—in the course of the progress of medical knowledge—of breaking up into component symptoms and thus to become syndromes is quite true but does not affect my argument.

The future discoveries of psychiatry may lengthen an inventory of the definitely abnormal as well as further differentiate its items, but the discarding of items from the area of a minimum agreement is improbable if not impossible. To the question, 'What evidence can you offer of such a contemporary consensus as this?' we may reply that the evidence is of the same nature as that to which we would refer were we asked to prove that there was an agreement in physical medicine on what constitutes a disease syndrome. The evidence is in the broad unanimity of the literature and of clinical diagnosis. No matter whether he is a Behaviourist, a Freudian, Kleinian, Reichian, Rankian, Adlerian, Rogerian, Jungian, or anything else, the practitioner's description of what constitutes the paranoid syndrome will be substantially the same. His language, his conceptual scheme, his metatheoretical assumptions and therapeutic recommendations may widely differ but not his discernment of an abnormal condition. It is significant that this agreement embraces those who belong to different cultures and whose field of work is in different cultures. This is already obvious in the work of psychiatrists throughout the western world, the culture of which is by no means homogeneous. Recent literature on psychiatric disagreements, though salutary, is also misleading. Whereas it is true that disagreements exist on taxonomy and classification this is no more than a dispute over labels. Disagreements on quantitative expression, on limits, represent a very real issue complicated by cultural variations in values; a minimum definition will have to be provided with an operational ceiling for 'No amount of classification will get rid of the borderline cases', as Dr. Helen Witmer observed twenty years ago.[1] The point is that basic theoretical agreement exists even though its diagnostic application is faulty for want of definite quantitative criteria. It is only a question of time until the objective testing and assessing methods reach the moderate degree of precision necessary to implement a minimum definition of abnormal adjustment.[2] The writers on psychiatric disagreements bent on demonstrating the wisdom of scepticism invariably come across a core of agreement which, with a little cultivation, would amply suffice for my purposes. F. Elkin finds, for instance, that, 'among the great majority of analysts . . . there was rather general agreement on . . . personality traits'[3] and Philip Ash admits almost regretfully, 'It perhaps should also be pointed out, as a limitation of the findings presented here (i.e. concerning the unreliability of psychiatric diagnoses), that agreement between two psychiatrists with respect to specific diagnoses in, say, even 30 per cent of a series of 50 cases would be far beyond 'chance' agreement if the criterion were blindfold selection. . . .'[4] Admissions on agreement in papers designed to demonstrate disagreements are more significant than is generally felt. At any rate, here I do not insist that today an all-round precision in clinical diagnoses obtains. Nothing is further from me than to claim something as obviously untenable as this. Yet far more attention ought to be paid to the fundamental and precise agreements in genetic theory and to the basic agreements on concrete assessments actually observed. If personality assessment methods aimed at accuracy in a minimum area of abnormal adjustment instead of striving to furnish us with a picture of its total ramifications we might be less reluctant to realize that a basic agreement already exists.

[1] A comment on 'Reliability of Observation in Psychiatric and Related Characteristics', by C. R. Doering and A. F. Raymond, *Amer. J. Orthopsychiatry*, April 1934, IV, pp. 249–57.

[2] On 'objective behaviour tests' cf. *The Scientific Study of Personality*, by H. J. Eysenck, 1952.

[3] 'Specialists Interpret the Case of Harold Holzer', *J. Abnormal and Soc. Psychol.*, Jan. 1947, XLII, pp. 99–111.

[4] 'The Reliability of Psychiatric Diagnoses', *J. Abnormal and Soc. Psychol.*, April 1949, XLIV, pp. 272–6.

With these reflections as my background I find a large measure of agreement in assessment methods between oriental and occidental psychiatrists who practise in widely different cultures. The variations in the cultural contexts may result in differences as to what should be considered the norm but not as to what is the minimum area of the 'abnorm'. Moral philosophers are incredulous and somewhat impatient when confronted with such 'immoderate' hypotheses as the foregoing; for instance:

> While Christians and Muslims, Marxist and Liberal, American and Chinese doctors would rarely disagree about whether or not some (physical) condition in which the clinical facts were known was to be counted as an illness or not, the same could scarcely be true of a similarly mixed bag of psychiatrists consulting about mental disease.[1]

Christians and Muslims would certainly disagree whether a visionary experience is to be counted as a hallucination or a revelation. Yet they did not agree in the past whether a certain physical or astronomical discovery was to be 'allowed', and the story of Galileo Galilei makes it irrelevant that Christians will 'disagree'. Disagreements in the face of empirical evidence are inspired by dogma and are of no significance to my present hypothesis. They are just as irrelevant as the certainty that African witch-doctors too would disagree with our conception of mental disease. The Marxist and Liberal interpretations of the universe are at variance for similar reasons. A theory according to which the primary adjustment process is a decisive phase of the individual's development is unacceptable to the Marxist on *a priori* grounds, *irrespective* of clinical-empirical evidence. So long as there is to be a 'Marxist-Leninist truth' and an 'objectivist distortion' of it the disagreement in this area is equally irrelevant. Then there is the 'American and Chinese' antithesis. So far as today 'Chinese' spells 'Marxist' I have nothing new to say. But let us replace the Chinese with another, non-Marxist and oriental nation, the Japanese. J. C. Moloney's recent paper in *The International Journal of Psycho-Analysis*[2] provides us with some excellent material for thought. He explains

---

[1] 'Crime and Disease', A. G. N. Flew, *Brit. J. Sociol.*, March 1954, V.
[2] 'Understanding the Paradox of Japanese Psychoanalysis', 1953, XXXIV, pp. 291–303.

that Japanese culture under the Meiji (authoritarian) type of oligarchy demands fixed status for everyone, gives little value to individual life, attributes extraordinary importance to the prestige of the family and supreme value to the 'national entity of Japan'. In these circumstances a psycho-analytic therapy cannot aim at the liberation and emancipation of the individual from oppressive family bonds. One would expect the Japanese psychiatrist to veil any insight he may have acquired from western teaching and to continue to tell a childish and incoherent tale to his patients who would respect much that has the trademark of western science; and this is precisely what Japanese psychiatrists do. Now to a large extent Japanese psychiatrists are ignorant of psycho-analytical discoveries and those few who have read and studied the accounts of psycho-analytical work have not been analytically trained.

The psychiatric staff members of the Kiushu University Medical School are quite firm in their 'non-Freudian' approach to mental disease. They explain their position by saying that Japanese psychiatry like Japanese medicine has developed under the strong influence of the Germans who have not, in their opinion, given support to Freudian theory.[1]

The opposition of those who are familiar with the cardinal principles of western psychologies, be they psycho-analytic or not, is clearly determined for them by the all-powerful cultural leadership in Japan which is no less tradition-bound today than it was before the war. Yet in spite of all their scepticism regarding the 'vague, presumptuous and unscientific' Freudian theory they follow Dr. Morita who teaches them that 'in considering the life histories of (his) patients he found that many of them were brought up in homes that were "too rigid or permissive" '. We understand that

the most widely used system of psychotherapy in Japan to-day was developed about 30 years ago by Doctor Morita, Professor of clinical psychiatry at Zikei University in Tokio. He developed his method specifically to treat a group of neuroses which he called 'Shinkeishitsu'. Literally translated, 'Shinkeishitsu' means nervousness.

[1] 'Japanese Psychiatry and Psychotherapy', A. Jacobson and A. N. Berenberg, *The Amer. J. Psychiatry*, Nov. 1952, CIX, pp. 321–9.

Jacobson and Berenberg explain that this concept embraces three sub-groups which correspond to some of the recognized neurotic syndromes in the West although they overlap in many ways. Notwithstanding all the scepticism it seems that vaguely conceived and incoherent reductive principles are at work which cannot become explicit on account of cultural censorship. There were signs of this in Moloney's report where we find the following interesting aside, 'Dr. Muramatsu, who is . . . a psychiatrist, says of psycho-analyst Kosawa: "Dr. Kosawa seems bravely to lead patients 'individualistically' and seems sometimes to cause trouble among their families (by this psycho-analytic approach) . . .." ' In other words the Japanese psychiatrist who acquired the clinical-empirical training necessary for valid insight to develop finds that his culture is even more abnormal than the one from which he borrowed his knowledge. He also finds that although he is in agreement with our abnorm he cannot deliver a frontal attack against his culture. He has to modify his analytic therapy to avoid clashing with an abnormal culture. The few undercover psycho-analysts in Hitler's Germany were in a similar predicament. It isn't that these practitioners did not agree as to what was a mental disease but they had to accommodate patients with the existing order of society or not at all. Further interesting evidence emerges from the handling of the Hess case at the Nuremberg trials. The International Military Tribunal appointed a psychiatric panel which consisted of three American, three British, one French and three Russian psychiatrists. Commenting on the work of this panel the Journal of the American Medical Association writes:

The appointment of psychiatrists from four geographically widely separated countries, speaking three different languages and coming from other cultures, assured a diversity of point of view and breadth of approach. . . . The hearing of the tribunal on Nov. 30th, 1945, concerning the mental state of the defendant was noteworthy on several counts. First among these is the remarkable degree of accord revealed in the report of the groups of psychiatric experts representing the four countries responsible for the trial. This essential agreement between the groups, whose examinations, with the exception of that of the French, who participated in all three, were carried out separately, strengthens the conclusions of the psychiatric panel.[1]

[1] 23 March 1946, p. 790, quoted in The Case of Rudolf Hess, ed. J. R. Rees, 1947, p. 166.

It was recognized that Hess's syndrome was of neurotic origin and thus the agreement is of so much the greater in significance. It is, after all, obvious that the ten psychiatrists separately arrived at unanimity in spite of their widely differing theoretical premises.

Professor Flew is, therefore, somewhat overconfident in his denial. There *is* a sufficiently large measure of agreement to support a minimum definition of universal abnormality in adjustment.[1] It is, of course, possible that the agreement to which we refer will be described as the result of the spreading of a psychiatric culture from one source and of its uncritical acceptance elsewhere. But then who is to say that the diffusion of physical medicine is not just the successful propagation of an ideology?

The psychiatric textbook embodying this agreement on diagnosis and on my two inventories has not yet been written, largely because it would be difficult to find a language which did not favour one school, or offend another. Indeed a work of this kind, properly conceived, would not be a psychiatric textbook at all but a sociological and possibly an ethical primer.

These arguments are in defence of the secondary inventory, the inventory of syndromes. The first inventory, the inventory of rupture experiences, requires no such defence as this. I derive the items of the first inventory from the empirical study of child behaviour as well as from the compared and sifted introspective reports of individuals, both therapists and patients.

A definition of abnormal adjustment supported by an inventory of syndromes (symptoms) will not be heeded unless I make an effort to anticipate some criticisms of this definition. Yet before I proceed I should like to stress that my principal criteria

[1] Here I am concerned with an agreement on abnormal primary adjustment conditions, in other words with the neuroses. It is far easier to demonstrate an agreement regarding the psychoses. 'We believe that the "relativity" concept of psychosis is based on criteria which do not include all of the essential symptoms. Our experience with psychotic patients in our own culture has led us to the conviction that mental illness manifests itself not only in ideas and emotional attitudes which differ from the accepted norms, but also in personality disturbances which affect the whole sphere of behaviour and result in an indifference to the most fundamental and universal realities, such as self-care, working ability and relation to other individuals. We believe that such a syndrome would stand out as abnormal in any culture, though its particular form and content may differ in different settings' (*Chamorros and Carolinians of Saipan*, A. Joseph and V. Murray, 1951).

74

of abnormal adjustment are listed in the inventory of rupture experiences; the criteria listed in the inventory of syndromes are not relied on exclusively.

(1) The most probable line of attack would be the view voiced by Karen Horney:

> . . . it is difficult to find characteristics common to all neuroses. *We certainly cannot use the symptoms*—such as phobias, depressions, functional physical disorders—as a criterion, because they may not be present. Inhibitions of some sort are always present . . . but they may be so subtle or so well disguised as to escape surface observation. The same difficulties would arise if we should judge from the manifest picture alone the disturbances in relations with other people, including the disturbances in sexual relations. These are never missing but they may be very difficult to discern. There are two characteristics, however, which one may discern in all neuroses without having an intimate knowledge of the personality structure: certain rigidity in reaction and a discrepancy between potentialities and accomplishments.[1] [Italics mine.]

I am in agreement with Horney's remark that symptoms are elusive, but I cannot see my way to regarding 'rigidity in reaction' or 'discrepancy between potentialities and accomplishments' as other than symptoms. Though Horney appears to reject a symptomatological definition of neurosis, (i.e. abnormal primary adjustment condition), she has, in fact, formulated such a definition as this. Later, when she gives a so-called 'description' of neurosis she says, '. . . a neurosis is a psychic disturbance brought about by fears and defences against these fears, and by attempts to find compromise solutions for conflicting tendencies'. But fears, defences, and compromise solutions are themselves symptoms or express themselves symbolically in symptoms. Another example of this sort of thing is the position occupied by Lawrence S. Kubie; he writes, 'Orthodox psychiatry distinguished neurosis from health by the presence of symptoms, the "phenomenology" of neurosis. The limitation of this differential criterion was that it overlooked the most widespread neurosis of all, namely the neurosis expressed not in overt symptoms but in subtle distortions of character.' Once again, how else can we speak of 'subtle distortions of character' unless these are *manifested*? If they are, the manifestations are nothing but

---

[1] *The Neurotic Personality of our Time*, 1937, pp. 21–2.

75

symptoms. The whole issue turns on what manifestations are to be regarded as symptoms and not whether or not to accept symptoms as criteria of neurosis. Professor Aubrey Lewis, who in an address to the British Sociological Society[1] offered 'inadequacy of part-function' as a criterion of abnormality, clearly recognized this, for even 'inadequacy of part-function' is a manifestation. Replacing 'symptom' by 'inadequacy of part-function' also implies that a quantitative appraisal of the manifestation will be possible eventually. If one wishes to affirm this expectation, then Professor Lewis's term may prove more appropriate. Nevertheless this accretion of meaning will not change the symptomatological character of his definition.

There are legions of definitions of normality which give us 'ideal types' of puppets instead of models of normality. A standard example of this is Karl Menninger's 'all this and heaven too':

Let us define mental health as the adjustment of human beings to the world and to each other with a maximum of effectiveness and happiness. Not just efficiency, or just contentment, or the grace of obeying the rules of the game cheerfully. It is all of these together. It is the ability to maintain an even temper, an alert intelligence, socially considerate behaviour, and a happy disposition. This, I think, is a healthy mind.

This, I think, is a *fata morgana*, not a norm. Also, once again, this 'definition' is just as symptomatological as any of the others so far considered. Each of the many splendid virtues therein can be diagnosed only in the absence of disqualifying symptoms. Thus a definition of abnormal adjustment cannot be other than symptomatological (syndromic). No other definition is logically possible for a definition requires a *definiens* and the *definiens* always turns out to be a symptom.

(2) We may be told of instances in which the presence of a clinically identifiable symptom does not permit the diagnosis of abnormal primary adjustment. An *enuretic* child who *seems* otherwise symptom-free and whose behaviour comes up to the expectations of his environment may be described as having an isolated functional disorder only. If the *enuresis* has no demonstrable somatic cause it must be assumed psychogenic. This in-

[1] Cf. 'Health as Social Concept', by Aubrey Lewis, *The Brit. J. Sociol.*, June 1953, IV, pp. 109–24.

volves the whole personality. And as a tiny drop of ink is sufficient to change the total hue of a tumbler of water so the whole adjustment character of the child is influenced by the apparently isolated disorder. At any rate, should we find it justified, we could always decide to leave such conditions as these outside the minimum area of abnormal adjustment.

(3) Another dispute may arise from attaching the label 'symptom' to a manifestation which is not a symptom at all. The delinquent acts of A and B may be similar in every respect yet A's act is a symptom rooted in his primary adjustment condition whilst B's act is the outcome either of an *ad hoc* provocation or of non-conformity of some kind in B's family and upbringing, e.g. B may steal because he is starving or because stealing is a family virtue. I claimed above that a manifestation which is a true symptom of abnormal primary adjustment condition is never an isolated phenomenon; it is always part of a network of symptoms. (*a*) Sometimes the intensity or frequency with which an isolated manifestation appears clearly shows that it is a symptom; (*b*) at other times one has to examine the individual to discover whether the isolated manifestation is part of a system of manifestations or not. When a network of this kind is discovered to possess one of the clinically identifiable patterns of abnormal primary adjustment condition the queried manifestation can be safely labelled 'a symptom'. To illustrate these two extremes: (*a*) if someone tells us that he has had violent nightmares over a number of years the communication of this single manifestation enables us to say that it is a symptom of abnormal primary adjustment condition; (unless subsequent discovery of other symptoms relegates it into the area of the psychoses), (*b*) if someone displays hatred of an object, person or persons of certain category the observation of this single manifestation must be supplemented by some evidence of a system of symptoms, i.e. we require proof of the presence of other complementary symptoms, e.g. irrationality, self-contempt, possible social-sexual inadequacies, somatic complaints, and so on.

In other words, for a manifestation to be regarded as a symptom it must be part of a syndrome. The syndrome may be legitimately inferred (*a*) or subsequently proved (*b*).

(4) Of course, adjustment may be abnormal even when the

occasional symptom or syndrome is not recognized as such by anyone. This should not disconcert us unduly for we are in search of a minimum definition. To the degree unreserve, communicativeness, as well as familiarity with psychiatric casuistry spreads, the recognition of symptoms and, consequently, the applicability of a minimum definition increases. On the other hand it is not warranted to judge a *single* manifestation as a symptom or syndrome. Lawrence S. Kubie recommends that '. . . we should limit ourselves to an effort to characterize the state of health of a single act or moment of life, and not the normality or neurosis of an entire personality'. Such a limitation as this is impossible; without the knowledge and assessment of past acts or moments in the individual's life, very few assessments of single acts or moments are likely to be correct. By agreeing to this Kubie contradicts himself:

Thus the essence of normality is flexibility, in contrast to the freezing of behaviour into patterns of unalterability that characterizes every manifestation of the neurotic process, whether in impulses, purposes, acts, thoughts or feelings. *Whether or not a behavioural event is free to change depends not upon the quality of the act itself, but upon the nature of the constellation of forces that has produced it. No moment of behaviour can be looked upon as neurotic unless the processes that have set it in motion predetermine its automatic repetition irrespective of the situation, the intensity or the consequences of the act* [Kubie's italics].

In other words one must go beyond the single act or moment (i.e. a symptom or syndrome) if one is to judge.

(5) What justifications have I in regarding an inventory collated in the manifestly abnormal cultures of the present and the past, as universally applicable? My justification rests with my premises which are not cultural but biological: the aprioristic foundations are not built on culture but on the psycho-biological relationships of parents and children. My readiness to call our culture abnormal may have a flavour of familiarity: certainly there have been reformers and revolutionaries who were always vociferous about the abnormalities of the society which they were determined to change. But these set out with the affirmation of an ideal, a norm, a utopia. The social psychiatrist of today on the other hand is like a mathematician going over the calculations of others; his job is to mark the mistakes. '. . . In

the present state of western civilization we have no grounds for assuming that normality and complete reality adaptation are identical,'[1] writes Edward Glover and indeed he is moderate with his disclaimer. There is no clue for normality in any of the reality situations of historical humanity. In fact one should bluntly admit that there has been no such thing as a 'perfectly normal mind' in cultural man.[2] On the other hand the psycho-biological nature of man is a constant; it is to this that I turn for guidance. I have not been able to derive from these premises a precise measure of the range of 'serviceable disbalance'. I agree with Professor Harding that '. . . human normality, far from being uniform, includes immense variety'.[3] But I claim that there is already a residue of agreement as to what is defi-nitely *not* serviceable. We know that the survival of the species demands from us two things: first, resilient, resourceful and readily adaptive individuals, and second, intimately co-opera-tive highly integrated groups. We know when either of these requirements is grossly lacking in the individual or in the social system of his group. The task of specifying these instances should not be left to those whose sole field of work is the clinic or the consulting room. 'The psychiatrist is too close to the problems of his patients (which are disclosed within the same culture, usually, as that which the doctor lives in) that he forgets that some of these problems might cease to be problems if the culture changed.'[4] The specialist, whose training must comprise both sociology and psychiatry, the social psychiatrist, must be conversant with the sociology of bias including his own. Now I contend that the universal applicability of an inventory of rup-ture experiences as well as of syndromes would be generally confirmed by such specialists if and when the inventories were available.

[1] 'Medico-Psychological Aspects of Normality', *Brit. J. Psychol.*, Gen. Sec., Oct. 1932, XXIII, pp. 152–66.
[2] Cf. 'The Concept of the Normal Mind', by Ernest Jones, *Internat. J. Psycho-anal.*, 1942, XXIII, pp. 1–8.
[3] *Social Psychology and Individual Values*, by D. W. Harding, 1953, p. 123.
[4] Professor Aubrey Lewis in T. M. Tanner, *Prospects in Psychiatric Research*, 1953, p. 51.

7. *The Casuistic Definition of the 'Abnorm'*

The examination of the two approaches towards a definition of the minimum area of abnormal primary adjustment condition is summed up in the following:

(*a*) The infant's relation to his mother and to the other members of his family is a psycho-biological relationship in which the child's supreme need is individuation in the security of an unfailing bond of love between him and, primarily, his mother. This need is the human replica of the evolutionary principles of growth and cohesion. As culture has created much fewer novel impediments to individuation than to socialization it is the latter from which the malaise of cultural man develops. A rupture or disturbance in the mother-child relationship defeats or hinders the principle of cohesion and thereby arrests the socialization of the child. This is aprioristically affirmed as the general principle of abnormal adjustment. It is recommended that an inventory of experiences constituting rupture, disturbance, and so on, should be made explicit and agreed upon.

(*b*) An inventory of manifestations (symptoms), as well as of the rules according to which these manifestations fall into recurrent patterns (syndromes), is also recommended provided empirical evidence is available to show correlation between items of Inventory I and those of Inventory II.

(*c*) The general principle 'Unserviceable Disbalance' is measured with the help of both of these inventories and applied to whole cultures. In assessing the abnormality of individuals, who live in abnormal cultures, my rule is that the conforming individuals, i.e. those who are statistically normal, are likely to be absolutely abnormal and a reference to Inventory I is to decide whether they are.

(*d*) On the level of culture I equate the term 'social-sexual inadequacy' with the broader evolutionary term, 'unserviceable disbalance'.

In the light of the foregoing I propose to formulate the following definition of the minimum area of abnormal adjustment:

Abnormal primary adjustment condition (neurosis) obtains when the individual suffers social-sexual frustrations in any of a number of specified experiences listed in an inventory universally agreed upon, provided these experiences are followed by any of a number of specified manifestations listed in a similarly accepted inventory; the first of these two need not be ascertained under all circumstances as some typical patterns of manifestation conclusively prove the occurrence of specific rupture experiences.

Truly a laboriously construed, lengthy and complex definition! Yet anything less qualified would be an arbitrary simplification at the present time, and a premature offering to sociology and ethics. Such offerings as these have so far been politely and sometimes contemptuously rejected by sociologists and moral philosophers. It is my contention that at the present juncture all attempts at simplifying a casuistic definition would jeopardize its reliability.

(*a*) No sociologist or psychologist can safely deny that individuation and socialization are two major trends of personality development along which *all* human experiences can be logically arrayed. The description of these trends may appear elsewhere in the garb of a terminology uncongenial to my present theory yet it is always convertible into my description without injury to my conceptions.

(*b*) No philosopher can safely deny that the antithesis of one-many is central to all philosophical speculations which aim at exploring man's place in the universe. To regard, therefore, the success or failure of man in this universe as a function of the one-many antithesis cannot be repudiated by him.

(*c*) *My definition faithfully reproduces the criteria which psycho-analytically oriented clinical practice, biographies, sociological work, literary characterization, and so on, in fact, accept.*

8. *Some Further Comments*

Some further observations may increase the plausibility of my conclusions:

Whatever may constitute social-sexual adequacy it is not a condition of balance; it is, in fact, a serviceable condition of disbalance. Psycho-analytic literature bears this out down the line as far as the founder.

I do not think much of the objection that neurotics are a special class of people marked by a degenerative disposition, whose child-life must not be regarded as evidence of the childhood of others.

Neurotics are human beings like everyone else and cannot be sharply differentiated from normal people . . . they fall ill of the same complexes with which we who are healthy also have to contend. The difference is only that the healthy know how to overcome these complexes without great and practically demonstrable harm; while the suppression of these complexes in nervous people only succeeds at the price of costly substitute-formations, thus in practice proving unsuccessful.[1]

No further documentation is really necessary for this is a widely known thesis of the psycho-analytic theory. It is not unrelated to conceptions of life which regard pain, or in ethical parlance, evil, as essential to the maintenance and development of life. Yet there is a great gulf between pessimistic interpretations of this kind and the present reflections; I do not feel obliged to equate pain with disbalance. Consequently I do not submit to Conte Vecchi's '*Il solo principio motore del'uomo e il dolore; il piacere non e un essere positivo*' (The sole moving principle of human life is pain; pleasure is not a positive factor). Vecchi's proposition is unacceptable, for 'escape from pain' and 'seeking of pleasure' are synonymous and both optimistic and pessimistic emphases are unwarranted.

That 'normality' and disbalance are compatible has not escaped the attention of psychological literature. In fact, from time to time, one comes across definitions of normality which clearly make this disbalance its essential characteristic. For instance,

When an individual identifies himself to an extreme degree with a group, the effect is that he loses his value. On the other hand, a complete inability to identify has the effect that the environment loses its value for the individual. In both extreme cases the dynamic relationship between individual and environment is distorted. An individual behaving in such a way is called 'neurotic'. In a normal group each member preserves his individuality but accepts his role as participator also.[2]

It is significantly brought out here that excesses in both socialization and individuation characterize the victim of distortion.

[1] 'On the Sexual Theories of Children' (1908) by S. Freud, *Collected Papers*, 1946, II, p. 60.
[2] Werner Wolff, op. cit., pp. 131–2.

Another writer further simplifies this dualism by saying that 'anyone who has achieved a satisfactory dynamic balance between the need for self-expression and the need for self-repression has a normal personality'.[1] But by admitting that no one has succeeded in attaining to such a condition this writer too confirms the universality of disbalance. A third instance in which disbalance is universally postulated fails to attribute it to a fundamental dualism, 'Normality in both function and in structure, consists not in rigid, invariable activities and organs but in a ceaseless play of *constitutionally antagonistic forces* and structures'[2] [italics mine].

Whereas their insistence on the ubiquity of disbalance is sound, these writers erroneously strive towards a definition of the normal with its help. The truth is that certain forms of disbalance are normal and others are abnormal. The latter reveal themselves through their attendant syndromes provided that these syndromes are rooted in rupture experiences. The 'optimum disbalance' does not reveal its criteria to us; its measure is hidden. As with the process of life in general, so the process of social life and of culture in particular consists in the perennial transubstantiation of disbalance. Whether this transubstantiation goes on in a specific direction we do not know. That it is dialectical seems probable; the conversion of biological cohesion into social cohesion on the one hand as well as the fluctuation of individualistic and communalistic phases in the history of man's culture on the other appear to bear this out. This, my precious hoard of certainty, is a modest yet not insignificant capital for the present speculative venture. Abnormal primary adjustment condition consolidates a form of disbalance in the individual which prejudices the simultaneous unfolding of the growth-cohesion needs. This abnormality spells either over-socialization or overindividualization. The supremacy of either is a sham supremacy for a man who is hypersocial without the complementary individuality of a corresponding power of uniqueness and autarchy is not socializing a genuine person but merely goes through the motions of 'communion'. Whereas the man who strives for an alien uniqueness of individuality

---

[1] 'What is a Normal Mind?' by Nathaniel Cantor, *Amer. J. Orthopsychiatry*, Oct. 1941, XI, pp. 676–83.
[2] *The Unity of the Organism*, by W. E. Ritter, 1919.

without sustaining it by the life-blood of fellowship individuates not a person but a thing.

People always speak of 'stability' as an ideal state, little suspecting that should it be realized it would bring evolution to a standstill. The origin of this misconception is in some notions of physics such as those of Fechner according to whom every system moves from unstable to stable states. But 'stability' is possible only in the physical realm and only in isolated systems: for the living, 'stability' is found only in death. The fundamental anomaly of existence is not rectifiable; it is the very essence of life that it is nourished by discord, by disbalance. Yet the maintenance of a flourishing discord depends not only on the continued virulence of discordant forces but also on some measure of disbalance between these forces. This disbalance is serviceable when the opposing forces are poised almost equally and are challenged to exert themselves to their maximum capacity. The game is not worth playing when one of the two is plainly no match for the other; the game is over when one of the two contestants is defeated. In serviceable disbalance there is an alternation of supremacy, and even a fluctuation, between growth and cohesion. Some may say that this *is* balance; but balance is static and final whilst life is neither.

'I say unto you: a man must have chaos yet within him to be able to give birth to a dancing star. I say unto you: ye have chaos yet within you.'

Friedrich Nietzsche:
Thus Spake Zarathustra.

' "If there are no more people with a taste for disease," Ubu said softly, "then will disease have any, uh, what you call ethetic (esthetic) value?"

"Fortunately," Martin said, "that situation will never come about. The meekest, most self-effacing people will always, from time to time, spew up wild eyed self-assertive individuals with riot in their souls. And these deviants will always make up an amuck fringe-world ringing you subdued ones in. Which is probably a good thing for the normal ones, Ubu. The sleepwalkers should occasionally hear a spine-chilling bellow from the blowtops on the outskirts, just to keep them from falling asleep entirely. If disease isn't an esthetic good of and by itself, neither is stupor." '

Bernard Wolfe: *Limbo 90,*
1953, p. 16.

'The zealot gets things done. He cuts through established routine. A certain amount of zealotry is necessary to get habituated mortals out of their accustomed ruts.'

Dialogues of Alfred North Whitehead
by Lucien Price, 1954, p. 299.

'C'est la dissymétrie qui crée le phenomène!'

Pierre Curie.

'The completely integrated person is the complete bore.'

Arthur Koestler: *The Invisible Writing,*
1954, p. 430.

'Nothing could be more horrible than a world of completely happy people who didn't know suffering.'

Sibylle Escalona in *Symposium on the Healthy
Personality,* ed. by M. J. E. Senn, 1950, p. 241.

III

THE NECESSARY AND

MERITORIOUS DISBALANCE

1. *Evolutionary Relativism*

At This point I had better turn my attention to an objection which, if it is not parried, would render my minimum definition of doubtful value. This objection consists of what may be described as 'evolutionary relativism'. Whereas cultural relativism issues from the comparison of known cultures, evolutionary relativism is deduced from the comparison of phylogenetic and historical data. According to this objection the species, in the course of its interminable differentiation, throws up variants and deviants which may multiply and lead to a more efficient adaptation to changing circumstances. Such variants and deviants are, therefore, anything but abnormal. Though we may not lightly brush aside the possibility that major evolutionary changes may take place in the realm of the social and sexual needs of man we may safely ignore this process on account of its exceeding slowness. At any rate, my principal assumption is that growth and cohesion are the unchanging functions of life—no matter what form future individuation and socialization take—and so my conception of 'serviceable disbalance' will not be affected. The significance of evolutionary relativism is thus very limited and it is cited here merely because it serves as a basis for a perilous analogy. Frequently enough one comes across pleas for the neurotic deviant who is described as the leaven of social change and social adaptability. It is argued that the social process needs irritants to be prompted into advance by leaps when a merely ambulatory progress would be overtaken by disaster. Supererogatory deeds, brilliant

87

exertions and inventions, spectacular selflessness and daring rebellions are planned and executed by those, it is claimed, who would be only too often branded by psychiatric opinion as abnormally adjusted. That the oyster requires a speck of grit constantly rankling the poor creature's body for it to sweat out a pearl, is a metaphor sometimes quoted. And a disconcerting metaphor it is; for if culture, a secretion of society against deviants, benefits man only as much as the pearl improves the amenities of an oysterly existence the sooner we cleanse ourselves from chafing matter in our cultural epidermis the better it will be. We know that culture, the bearer of our distinctive humanity, is biologically impure and inconsistent, and that a biologically sound culture is probably both utopian and chimeric. We know that in culture the serviceable disbalance of evolution functions with far more friction and pain than it has ever done before. We also know that this cannot be otherwise and that the most we can aim at is the progressive transmutation of friction and pain away from what we regard as the definitely abnormal. It is now being suggested that even for this very purpose society needs neurotic spurs to ride culture through the quagmires of stagnation. If this latter metaphor truthfully interprets our utter dependence on the abnormal a society without its quota of abnormally adjusted individuals would be an abnormal society. There is nothing novel and surprising in this conclusion. What is strange about this sceptical point of view is that there are signs of its spreading to psychoanalytical theory and therapy in a manner the logic of which continues to elude most of us. Our confusion is worse confounded by statements such as this. '. . . I believe that for most people it is more normal to have slight peculiarities, anxieties, minor neurotic symptoms or bad habits than to be absolutely free from them, provided they are in a position to tolerate them without difficulty.'[1] What precisely does 'more normal' mean in this context? Is it implied that these people are more *valuable* with their minor neurotic symptoms than they would be without them? Isn't it possible that the therapist's failure to bring 'absolute freedom' from these symptoms to the patient induces him to indulge in this 'sour grapes' self-justification?

[1] 'After the Analysis . . .' by Melitta Schmiedeberg, *The Psychoanalytic Quarterly*, 1938, VII, pp. 122–44.

2. *Dr. Lindner's Rebellion*

Some years ago Dr. Robert Lindner, an American prison-psychiatrist at the time, wrote a book about the treatment and eventual redemption of one of his patients. The patient was 'doing time' in a penitentiary for a serious offence and Lindner treated him with a method which combined psycho-analysis and hypnosis. Neither the method, nor the revelations to which it led, were entirely new to well-informed readers yet the dramatic presentation of the life-history of this convict earned a wide circulation for the book, entitled *Rebel Without a Cause*. The non-professional readers were fascinated by the penetrating efficiency of this method of treatment; they were also impressed by Lindner's deft analytic skill in tracing back the cause of criminal behaviour to emotional shocks suffered in infancy. It is difficult to say what captivated the lay reader most—was it the graphic presentation of cause and effect, that is rupture experiences in infancy and crime in adulthood, or the hypno-analytic trance in which memories, however long forgotten, could be recalled, or the miraculous-sounding healing effect of recalling those memories? For all these things were most convincingly portrayed in Lindner's book. No one ready to accept the claims of this book would have been reluctant to say that indeed modern psychology has given us powerful insights and a great instrument of healing.

Now, Dr. Lindner has written another book which he calls *Prescription for Rebellion*. In this book Lindner declares that psychology has little to offer to the sufferer or the world at large. 'A few generalizations, a handful of suggestions, a small bundle of tricks, a bag of catch-as-catch-can techniques' comprise the healing arsenal of modern psychology. He complains that psychology has been overadvertised and oversold and that it cannot live up to the prestige which it recently acquired.

What led this sincere, though somewhat too emotional, writer to this bitterly sceptical conclusion? Does he now regard the brilliant hypno-analytic treatment of that convict as a sham performance? Were the great skills displayed in the course of that treatment a mere 'bundle of tricks'? What happened to Dr. Lindner since he wrote *Rebel Without a Cause?*

THE NECESSARY AND MERITORIOUS DISBALANCE

Like so many psychologists today Lindner had begun to ask philosophical questions and was disturbed by the answers he had contrived to find. What is the purpose of psycho-analytic treatment? he asks with laudable perseverance. He insists that according to the majority of psycho-analysts the purpose of psycho-therapy is adjustment. Lindner is very properly apprehensive of this vague concept and proceeds to examine it. He comes to the conclusion that adjustment means resignation to one's circumstances, that it means giving up distinctive efforts, and that it amounts to surrendering individuality. Consequently it means dullness, selfish complacency and a lowering of general vitality.

> . . . I intend to reveal the truth about adjustment, to show it for what it is—a mendacious idea, biologically false, philosophically untenable, and psychologically harmful. Together with a gradually increasing group of psychologists and scientists from other fields, I regard it as perhaps the single great myth of our time, and one to be exposed to its roots lest it continue to sap human vitality and exhaust the energies which men require to build the better society they seek.

Lindner charges contemporary psychiatry with transforming every dissatisfied Socrates who turns to it for succour into a satisfied ass. One is reminded of the physician who suggested in a medical journal some years ago that if Charles Darwin had been taken to a child guidance clinic, there might never have been *The Origin of Species*.[1] Lindner accuses psychiatrists with all the crimes in the Soviet calendar, that they are servants of the *status quo*, lieutenants of the vested interests and subverters of the evolutionary process itself. The future of humanity depends on a generous supply of rebels whose dissatisfaction with life as they find it is the leaven of the evolutionary process. Alas, the present day vogue of this so-called adjustment threatens us with the extinction of these rebels. Lindner regards the adjustment-cult of modern psychiatry as a grave danger and he vigorously enjoins us to show this thing up for what it is.

Dr. Lindner's line of attack is guided by a first principle which one finds difficult to accept. He believes that human beings are endowed with an instinct of rebellion and it is in the interest of both patient and society to express this properly.

[1] *The Times*, 23 Aug. 1954.

He prescribes the following formula to all psycho-therapists: do not aim at adjustment but at rebellion which is creative, productive and regenerative.

It is regrettable that Dr. Lindner should have allowed himself to be so much deceived, for there is no doubt that human rebellion is in fact a secondary reaction to continued frustration. A primary urge to rebellion would be meaningless; one could just as well say that all life is rebellion against internal and external environment. Eating our lunch is a rebellion against hunger and reading a book is a rebellion against ignorance. Could it be that Lindner's 'instinct of rebellion' is only a new and polite name for the Freudian Thanatos, the instinct of aggression? It is hardly probable that Lindner would willingly equate his instinct of rebellion with the better known instinct of aggression. For one thing it would make his first principle unoriginal, for another it would make his prescription impracticable: incitement to aggression would not have appreciable benefits in many cases unless the disposal of a few psycho-therapists by homicidal patients be so regarded.

What should we make of this 'instinct of rebellion'? To increase our difficulties Dr. Lindner introduces the distinction, positive and negative rebellion. This is an ethical distinction, but he cannot tell us how to agree on moral philosophy. He tells us that positive rebellion is the creative adventure of the individual beyond the boundaries of the conventional, the routine and the stagnating; negative rebellion is destructive, anti-social and arrests development. These and similar statements are laden with values yet we are not told how we should measure and discern them. Surely there are situations in which rebellion would be evil and accommodation or compromise would be virtue?

Whatever the weaknesses in Lindner's reflections one thing is certain: the necessity for them springs from his disillusionment with adjustment as a therapeutic goal. This disillusionment provokes sceptical thoughts in the minds of those who read Dr. Lindner's success-story, *Rebel Without a Cause*. They will ask now whether the convict's rehabilitation had not been a good deal less complete than the writer made us believe? There Lindner claimed success without having administered his prescription for rebellion. The goal of that therapy was

91

adjustment and we were told that that goal was all but achieved. Surely, successes of this kind do not make sceptical psychiatrists!

His misunderstanding of the adjustment-concept is somewhat of a mystery. Psycho-analysts who use this term do not understand by it a mechanical compromise between environment and individual or between impulse and conscience. Their sole aim is to light up the hidden springs of motivation in the patient's mind and to enable him to judge these consciously. They give no injunction to adjust, to compromise or to accept. It may be, of course, that Lindner had in mind some shortened methods of treatment which are, no doubt, fairly widely practised. These methods have been designed to meet the stupendous demands on psychological therapy in our age. A so-called classical analysis is costly and prolonged, the number of trained analysts is infinitesimal, whereas the incidence of neurosis in contemporary society is alarmingly great. To deal with this situation many psycho-therapists resort to suggestion, inspiration and persuasion which they may or may not combine with the more time-consuming analytic methods. Needless to say, this kind of treatment is often hasty and superficial, and the injunctions addressed to the patient arbitrary. It is in connection with this kind of therapy that Lindner's charges assume full substance. He is to be commended for the force of his arguments and the sincerity of his indignation. These so-called brief-psycho-therapists do indeed throw out the baby with the bath-water and when suppressing 'negative' rebellion in their patients they stifle 'positive' rebellion as well. Nevertheless, let us retain our sense of proportion: no psycho-therapist would deliberately work for such a 'negative' result as this; no psycho-therapist has as yet publicly affirmed that conformity with the mass is a supreme value and that conflict with the herd is an unmitigated evil. Even the brief-psycho-therapists make an attempt to explore the modes of self-expression most congenial to a patient and would discourage his rebellion only when this is almost certainly self-defeating. We may also remember that these shortened methods of treatment are rarely inflicted on people who would have made a distinctive contribution to society had they not been emasculated by a reactionary psychiatry. Dr. Lindner's case-histories are somewhat unconvincing when he exerts himself to prove that this is in fact what is happening. One's incredulity is fostered by seeing that these case-histories concern prolonged, analytic treatment and not some abbreviated form of therapy.

Psycho-analysts do give one suggestion quite openly; they instruct their patients not to make fundamental changes in their lives while under analysis. They ask their patients to postpone major decisions, if possible, until after the analysis is terminated. No doubt there is a moral principle lurking behind this policy. The moral principle is not that the present unanalysed motives are *a priori* inferior to the forgotten, infantile motives but that the unanalysed person is rarely conscious of the significance of *all* his motives. The moral principle is Know Thyself, an ancient yet ever youthful precept. The 'I' will still have to choose what course to follow but the adult 'I' may dismiss the infantile motives and refuse to act upon them. If the patient's 'successful' analysis ends in a lukewarm peace or in a contented sluggishness then that was all there was in him in the first place and analysis put his strivings in the right perspective, that is to say, in the perspective of his true potentialities and abilities. Hence when analysis issues in the abatement of rebelliousness there cannot be room for complaint.

The true meaning of adjustment, that is other than abnormal in our sense, is not a vacuous resignation to one's fate and circumstances. It is not automatic acceptance of an ill-chosen career, human relationship, or habit. It is insight into the intricacies of one's motives which prompted the mistaken choice. If the infantile motives leading to the original choice now glaringly show that a serious error was made the patient may decide on a radical change in career, human relationship, or habit. But why call this radical action 'rebellion'? Lindner's choice of the term rebellion and his apparent liking for it—it appears in the titles of two of his published works—is itself suspect. After all, insight or self-knowledge in the modern as well as in the classical sense entails composure, serenity and a considered circumspection, all of which are alien to the rebel. A radical revision of one's life-plan need not take place with the fury, violence and shock of a rebellion. Lindner's language betrays Nietzscheian yearnings and an exasperation with an undramatic, piecemeal betterment of man's condition. This reaction is all too familiar in political extremism but unprecedented in psychiatric clinical literature.

It is important for us to realize that rebellion has a number of meanings however much these meanings are fused together. We may think of rebellion as an attack by the individual against his own conscience. This may happen when upon achieving a new and fundamental insight a man discards some of his rigid, obsessive scruples and frees himself from what the Freudians would call a tyrannical superego. It may well be that this kind of rebellion actually introduces more conformity into the individual's life than was there previously. Instead of being a rebellion against the larger society this may be the rejection of a narrower code. The code was narrow because the parents of the patient may have belonged to a dissident minority. By rebelling against this minority code the individual declares that he does not wish to be different from the majority. This is hardly the sort of rebellion Lindner would like to encourage. Then rebellion may constitute an open attack on our environment or an open affirmation of our dissidence from its rules. Sometimes, only too often, the true motives of one's dissatisfaction with the environment are strongly coloured by motives of an infantile nature. It is true that successful psycho-analytic therapy divests our otherwise rational criticism of the environment of the rebelliousness of infancy, of the elemental revengefulness of early childhood. A good many fanatic as well as revolutionary ideologies are deeply apprehensive of psycho-analytic therapy for they fear that many a red-hot sentiment would fade in the dry-cleaning process of this therapy. Of course, their suspicion will not be couched in such an opportunistic language as this. They will assuredly speak of psycho-therapists as debunkers of idealism. The truth of the matter is that so long as criticism of and opposition to this and other kinds of psycho-therapy continues, the psycho-therapist is one of the rebels. His rebellion brings us to yet another meaning of this term, the meaning accepted by those who regard their opposition to society or some institution of it as perfectly rational and fair. Rebellion against an institution which countenances the abnormal forms of primary adjustment condition is of this quality. To rise against these circumstances may be dictated by the fundamental instincts of man as well as by some obscure and secret revengefulness of a

94

long-since injured personality. Psycho-analytic therapy aims at freeing those fundamental instincts, giving them their maximum share of spontaneity, and neutralizing the distortions of revengefulness.

Naturally, all these qualities of rebellion are present in most instances of it. The neurotic rebel, the rebel with an intimate personal grievance, often links this with rational appraisal of a just cause. On the other hand the rebels of the past, whose actions and achievements are today regarded as profoundly beneficial contributions to the weal of humanity, were often not a little fired by personal and infantile grievances. We may as well say that in matters like these there is always a modicum of the wrong reason for doing the right thing. The psycho-analytic view is that a just cause is best served when the motives of the protagonists are as uncoloured by their personal dis-balance as possible. So long as adjustment means a condition in which the influence of the emotional vicissitudes of childhood is reduced to a minimum I cannot share Dr. Lindner's condemnation of it.

3. *The Problem Stated*

Lindner's apprehensions are not isolated, they are representative of an ancient dualistic view of the universe characteristic of Zoroastrian as well as Christian cosmology and ethics. According to Christian theology the devil is engaged in essential and indispensable work; whoever should convert him to virtue would end by bedevilling virtue. Odd as it may seem the modern sociologist reiterates the ancient formula, Durkheim, for instance, 'What is morbid for individuals may be normal for society. Neurasthenia is a sickness from the point of view of individual psychology; but what would a society be without neurasthenics? They really have a social role to play.'[1] Durkheim was convinced that the pathological individual was but an 'imperfect individual' and that there were 'necessary imperfections' without which society could not function.

It is useless to maintain [he wrote], that evil does not cease to be evil even though it cannot be prevented; this is the preacher's language, not the scholar's. A necessary imperfection is not a disease;

[1] *Suicide*, p. 365, footnote.

THE NECESSARY AND MERITORIOUS DISBALANCE

otherwise disease would have to be postulated everywhere, since imperfection is everywhere. No organic function, no anatomical form exists, some further perfection of which may not be conceived. *Whatever is an indispensable condition of life cannot fail to be useful unless life itself is not useful.*

But the point is that the 'indispensable conditions of life' change as life changes: to Malthus, for instance, epidemics, wars, and a high infant mortality rate were remediless necessities. The unanimous consensus among those today, who would be called social psychiatrists, is that the present rate of incidence of abnormal adjustment conditions in man imperils the survival of the whole species; it is indispensable to disaster and not to life.

Let us survey the true scope of my predicament.

(*a*) I insist that the minimum area of abnormal adjustment is not serviceable to the human race.

(*b*) I am now confronted with the claim that no abnormal adjustment can be judged unserviceable because the species requires the hypersensitiveness, the explosive power, and even the convulsions of the abnormally adjusted. If we accepted that there was an intimate association between abnormal adjustment conditions and creative performances we should be obliged to answer the question—are the latter caused by the former? Should the answer be in the affirmative we could not escape the conclusion that creative performances are not instrumental to the survival of man, an absurd conclusion, for creative performances are the very adjustment acts of the evolutionary process. In ethical parlance, evil is necessary, because, without it, not only would the good fade and eventually lose all meaning, it could not even come into being.

The examination of this whole problem will be carried out in the following three sections: the first (4) will deal with the abnormality of the artist; the second (5) will treat the abnormality of the political leader; and the third (6), a rather brief study, will observe the position of scientists in general and of social scientists in particular.

4. *Artistic Creativeness and the 'Abnorm'*

We must sound the thinkers of many ages on this matter to ensure that no conclusion is reached without giving them a hearing. Their testimony makes fascinating reading, and, although some of their utterances have by now become tags, many of them are rarely mentioned and are little known. One of the earliest commentators on abnormality in creative artists was Democritus. We learn from the *Ars Poetica* by Horace that Democritus '. . . thinks that none but brain-sick bards can taste of Helicon'—Horace continues,

> So far his doctrine o'er the tribe prevails,
> They neither shave their heads, nor pare their nails;
> To dark retreats and solitude they run,
> The baths avoid and public converse shun;
> A poet's fame and fortune sure to gain,
> If long their beards, incurable their brain.[1]

Horace does not seem to agree with the view of Democritus that abnormality in the poet is an essential requirement of his art and deplores the first precedent to the fashions of Montmartre, Chelsea, and Greenwich village. This early testimony to the effect that it is easier to imitate the abnormality of the genius than his talent I shall discuss later at some length.

Plato, in the *Phaedrus*, takes up the same theme. He is as unequivocal about the conditions of admittance to Helicon as Democritus. He tells us about the ordinary madness which is a disgrace and dishonour as well as of inspired madness which is of divine origin.

I told a lie when I said that the beloved ought to accept the non-lover when he might have the lover, because the one is sane, and the other mad. It might be so if madness were simply an evil; but there is also a madness which is a divine gift, and the source of the chiefest blessings granted to men. For prophecy is a madness, and the prophetess at Delphi and the priestess at Dodona when out of their senses have conferred great benefits on Hellas, both in public and private life, but when in their senses few or none . . . (244).

And

The third kind is the madness of those who are possessed by the Muses; which taking hold of a delicate and virgin soul, and there inspiring frenzy, awakens lyrical and all other numbers; with these adorning the myriad actions of ancient heroes from the instruction of posterity. But he who, having no touch of the Muses' madness in his soul, come to the door and thinks he will get into the temple by the help of art—he, I say, and his poetry are not admitted; the sane man disappears and is nowhere when he enters into rivalry with the madman (245).

Before I consider what we might learn from these ancient verdicts on the necessity and even meritoriousness of madness I add two further pronouncements of Plato's. The first is from the *Ion*:

For all good poets, epic as well as Lyric, compose their beautiful poems not by art, but because they are inspired and possessed. And as the Corybantian revellers when they dance are not in their right minds so the lyric poets are not in their right mind when they are composing their beautiful strains, but when falling under the power of music and metre they are inspired and possessed; like Bacchic maidens who draw milk and honey from rivers when they are under the influence of Dionysus but not when they are in their right mind . . . and therefore God takes away the minds of poets, and uses them as his ministers, as he also uses diviners and holy prophets, in order that we who hear them may know them to be speaking not of themselves who utter these priceless words in a state of unconsciousness, but that God himself is the speaker, and that through him he is conversing with us (533).

And the second from the tenth book of the *Republic*:

. . . the peevish temper furnishes an infinite variety of materials for imitation; whereas the temper, which is wise and calm is so constantly uniform and unchanging, that it is not easily imitated; and when imitated, it is not easily understood . . . Hence it is clear that the imitative poet has, in the nature of things, nothing to do with this calm temper of the soul . . . (604/605).

In the Greek culture of Plato's time there seemed to be no question about the great moral asset which the ravings of Delphi and Dodona, the *Theia Mania*, represented to Plato's contemporaries. The Platonic views on these matters must have been quite widespread; according to Seneca Aristotle held that *nullum magnum ingenium sine mixtura dementiae fuit* (There has been no great brilliance without an admixture of madness). It is significant that over two thousand years ago the world's most incisive thinkers agreed on what was 'mad' in the poets, who were by no means obvious psychotics, and that we would, on the

98

whole, agree with their diagnoses. Yet whilst we still agree
with their diagnoses we no longer agree with, say, Plato's
reverence for prophecies and oracles. Whereas the fruits of madness are constantly changing, our idea of what madness itself
is changes little. Looking into the future we may well wonder
whether the fruits we savour with pleasure today will not have
gone bad a long time before the abnorm of human adjustment
is accepted? What aesthetic values will continue to live as long
as the abnorm of human adjustment? Surely, six or eight thousand years of culture and even its surprisingly stable aesthetic
valuations are not adequate grounds for certainty. The Platonic
reflections on prophetesses are particularly suggestive of a moral:
let us meditate on them in all humility. No less instructive are
the Corybantian and Bacchic analogies. But their analysis will
have to wait.

There are several oft-repeated passages in the world's literature which ply the same ideas as the ones already quoted. I
may as well throw them in for good measure, so much more
weight may I feel entitled to place in the other scale eventually.
There is, of course, Shakespeare's

> The lunatic, the lover and the poet,
> Are of imagination all compact . . .
>> *Midsummer-Night's Dream*, Act V, Scene I

Dryden's

> Great wits are sure to madness near alli'd,
> And thin partitions do their bounds divide.
>> *Absalom and Achitophel*

Shelley's

> . . . Most wretched men
> Are cradled into poetry by wrong:
> They learn in suffering what they teach in song.
>> *Julian and Maddalo* 544/6

Macaulay's

Perhaps no person can be a poet or can even enjoy poetry, without
a certain unsoundness of mind . . .
>> *Milton*

We learn from Charles Lamb that there were some who
thought '. . . that great wit (or genius, in our modern way of
99

speaking), has a necessary alliance with insanity . . .' (*Sanity of True Genius*). Lamb does not think so, and we shall have occasion to see whether we may feel entitled to agree with him. An impassioned protest of indignation can no longer allay our curiosity. 'You worthy critics', writes Schiller with ire, 'are ashamed or afraid of the momentary and passing madness that is found in all creators.'[1] And Goethe muses in his composed wisdom:

When I strictly scrutinized my own and other man's development in life and art I often found that what can properly be called an aberration turned out to be an indispensable digression for the individual on the way to his goal. Every return from error exerts a mighty formative effect on man, specifically or generally, so that it is easy to understand how the prober of hearts can take greater pleasure in one repentant sinner than ninety-nine righteous. As a matter of fact we often unconsciously strive in the direction of an apparently mistaken goal, just as the ferryman heads diagonally against the current when his only concern is to land exactly across from his starting point.[2]

The milder terms 'aberration' and 'error' need not mislead us: Goethe treats the same subject here as I am discussing. He also reminds us of the many points of contact which this subject has with the moral philosophy and theology of all ages.

In these historical examples truth and fallacy mingle in an almost impenetrable tangle. By citing them at some length I aimed at counteracting any complacency to which I may incline while defending my definition of abnormal adjustment. But this is not all. The modern formulations of the same point of view are even more insistent and, by being related to some fairly sound general doctrines of modern psychology, are also more plausible. In a trenchant analysis of the writers' and poets' personality Edmund Bergler finds that he can be a witness to the historical observations.

The real writer [he declares], produces not because there is a demand for his product, but because he solves a conflict within himself. If he does not do it for this reason, he is just a writer-racketeer. Ironically enough the real writer thus gets paid for his cure, while

[1] Quoted by F. L. Lucas, *Psychology and Literature*, 1951, p. 167.
[2] From a letter to Eichstadt, 15 Sept. 1804. Translated in *Goethe: Wisdom and Experience*, ed. Ludwig Curtius, 1949.

other neurotics have to pay the physician for theirs. This is one of the peculiarities of the business of writing.[1]

Bergler reflects the general psycho-analytical viewpoint in these matters; according to him the writer '. . . is a neurotic, unconsciously operating his defence mechanism without knowing it. Sometimes the defence mechanism will coincide with the general trend; then he will be successful.' The most instructive testimony of this paper is the one in which Bergler deals with the fiction of a 'normal writer'. He says there is no such thing as a normal writer, this is a contradiction in terms. (One of those instances when a prominent psycho-analytical publication openly admits its commitment to an absolute conception of normality!) In a recent paper Bergler further clarified his position, '. . . there is nothing neurotic *per se* in the *sublimation* of writing. The neurotic substructure, however, is visible in the fact that the writer's sublimation is different from any other sublimation. The artist's sublimation is *temporary*, and *"on probation"* . . .' He gives three reasons for this, that creative artists have a constant fear of barrenness, that their sublimation is complete only in the rare elated moments or periods of creation, and that the sublimation in creation is accompanied by an all round failure in private life. The artist is both more neurotic than others and neurotic in a special way—Bergler still maintains this view.[2] In the III/IV volume of *The Psycho-analytic Study of the Child* there is a paper on the relationship of 'normality' and sensitivity to stimuli in the young child. The authors of this paper are undecided whether sensitivity, or a 'thin protective barrier against stimuli' is inherited or acquired; they conclude that '. . . only research can tell eventually what the facts are and what the surviving hypotheses are going to be'.[3] Yet earlier on in the same paper they throw out the challenge, 'Can we find apparently normal persons, that is to say, persons who can stand a fair amount of frustration, and who show average or better "ego-strength" in relation to id, superego, and the outer world (the three forces with which, according to Freud, the

[1] 'Psycho-analysis of Writers and of Literary Productivity', *Psycho-analysis and the Social Sciences*, 1947, pp. 247–96.

[2] 'Can the Writer "Resign" from his Calling?' *Internat. J. Psychoanal.*, 1953, XXXIV, pp. 40–2.

[3] P. Bergman and S. K. Escalona, 'Unusual Sensitivities in Very Young Children', 1949, pp. 333–52.

ego has to contend), but who show in some ways that stimuli reach them with unusual intensity?' For the time being it is sufficient for me to answer that we do not know why sensitivity matures into creativeness at times and fails to do so at others.

Freud's own private admissions are of great value to us for they show in what way the present concern would be countenanced by Freud, the writer. 'I have come back with a lordly feeling of independence and feel too well'—Freud wrote to Fliess on 16 April 1896—'since returning I have been very lazy because the *moderate misery necessary for intensive work* refuses to appear.'[1] And on 6 September 1899, he wrote to Fliess on the same theme again, 'My style in it (*The Interpretation of Dreams*) was bad, because I was feeling too well physically; I have to be somewhat miserable in order to write well.' C. G. Jung, in spite of all his remonstrances, admits this much, '. . . it would never occur to a thinking lay mind to confound art with a morbid phenomenon, *in spite of the undeniable fact that the origin of a work of art must confess to similar psychological preconditions as a neurosis*'[2] [italics mine].

Among artists who venture to be articulate about matters of this kind today there is a variety only in the expression, not in the substance, of what they say, and this is in harmony with the principal ideas in the foregoing pages. 'The surrealists believe that the world is led by those whom the world calls insane: Hölderlin, Baudelaire, Lautréamont, Dostoievski, Kafka, by all those who have deep memory of time before history.'[3] Not only writers but painters testify too. 'The hidden means which Dali finds in the phenomena he studies, come to him, he claims, from temporary states of insanity.' And another example picked at random, 'Picasso believes that art emanates from sadness—and pain'.[4] An interesting commentary on Picasso's belief comes from E. Cunningham Dax, who reporting his observations on art-therapy in mental hospitals, states:

Composite figures are not infrequently found in schizophrenic art . . . If a person is 'two faced' he does not have to be painted in

[1] Ernest Jones, *Sigmund Freud, Life and Work*, 1953, I, p. 335 (Jones' italics).
[2] *Contributions to Analytical Psychology*, 1945, p. 228.
[3] Wallace Fowlie, *Age of Surrealism*, 1953, p. 62. Presumably this is a deep evolutionary memory which is just another way of saying that some men are more aware of their cohesion-growth conflict than others.
[4] Jaime Sabartes, *Picasso*, 1949, p. 65.

two situations, but he is conveniently shown so that both sides of his face or personality are displayed at once; this economic device was used by Picasso for some of his earliest heads . . .[1]

When one is unimpressed by frightful sounding psychiatric diagnoses one's artistic appreciation may lead to the following characteristic conclusion:

Many cases have been reported of patients whose artistic production showed an improvement after the onset of psychosis. This was particularly true among patients who had had previous training in technique and in whom mental deterioration had not yet progressed very far. *The products of such patients are often described as being more imaginative, original, novel, and interesting than those produced by the same individuals before the onset of psychosis, and they have sometimes been judged to be 'better art' !* [italics mine].[2]

And finally the most telling confession of all from the beholder, the critic, 'I speak of enjoying the work of art. To avoid misunderstanding let me say that I use the verb to "enjoy" in no hedonistic sense, but as people speak of "enjoying bad health".'[3]

If the artistic genius is in the habit of appearing among the socially and sexually inadequate, and if—as it has now so often been alleged[4]—his superior achievement is somehow the consequence of those very inadequacies then the definition of a pan-human abnormality—and the condemnation of what is defined—is not only mistaken but also dangerous,—*unless*, of course, we declare art itself a symptom of abnormality, or rather a syndrome, a disease, and in ethical language, an evil. Is it then true that creative work, initiative, persistence, and some other qualities of the artistic genius owe their existence to certain neurotic traits, i.e. to an abnormal adjustment condition? This question bears *two* entirely distinct meanings: *one* is that the artist is more neurotic than any other control sample of non-artists or at least that the artist's neurotic syndrome is of a

---

[1] *Experimental Studies in Psychiatric Art*, 1953, p. 38.

[2] Anastasi and J. P. Foley, 'A Survey of the Literature on Artistic Behaviour in the abnormal', *Psychological Monographs*, 1940, LII, No. 6 (237).

[3] Bernard Berenson, *Aesthetics and History*, 1950, p. 21.

[4] Cf. the following: 'The psychopath notoriously suffers from his lack of stability and from the sense of inferiority this engenders. But it is this very handicap which is a spur to intellectual creative endeavour and also gives a man increased insight into the infirmities of others' (W. R. Bett, *The Infirmities of Genius*, 1952, p. 20).

specific type; the *other* meaning of the question is based on the Freudian doctrine of the universality of the neuroses in childhood. The artist converts his neurotic disbalance (of which he has no more than the non-artist) into artistic expression while the non-artist manifests it in other ways or through symptoms. Nevertheless artistic sensitivity, imagination, and dedication are functions of the disbalance, tension, and pain which the artist has experienced or is experiencing, and these are essential to his creativeness. In other words Baudelaire's *l'indispensable douleur* and *la fertilisante douleur*, and Rimbaud's *le dérèglement de tous les sens* are not the privilege of the artist but it is the artist alone who can make art of it and without it he could make none.

Let us now restate our original question as two distinct questions and couch them in terms as unambiguous as possible:

(1) Is the creative artist more abnormally adjusted than other people or abnormally adjusted in a special way?

(2) Is the creative artist dependent on disbalance for creativeness although he is no more abnormally adjusted than other people?

In the following observations I shall dispose of the first imputation with comparative facility. But when I turn to the consideration of the second meaning my position will be much more difficult and the task I set myself will have offered me its severest test.

I

(1) When the incidence of neurotic disorders in contemporary western society is frequently put between thirty and sixty per cent, it would not be surprising to find thirty to sixty per cent of our artists similarly affected.[1] The findings of cultural anthropology allow us to claim that the incidence of abnormal adjustment is even greater in contemporary primitive societies where the abnormality of culture—in terms of its primary institutions —is frequently more obvious. Furthermore, throughout the history of human culture the deviations from an optimum disbalance in the primary adjustment process have often been wilder and more extravagant from time to time. Yet this does

[1] For some notes on the incidence of neurosis cf. *Solitude and Privacy*, pp. 90–1.

not commit us to the view that abnormal adjustment in the past was more frequent than it is today, but merely that it has always had a marked incidence, and that nostalgic suppositions about a saner humanity in the past are difficult to make plausible. Nevertheless one must consider the relationship between the problem of modern art and the hypothesis of 'greater incidence of neurosis in modern mass society'. Guyau, for instance, asserted that 'neuropaths and delinquents' increasingly swamp our literature.[1] This woeful plaint is caused by a misunderstanding. Modern art is no more neurotic in its dynamic inspiration than were its predecessors. The point is that modern art communicates more about the artist's disbalance without the censorship of a comparatively inflexible artistic convention. The modern artist obeys a convention which dictates unlimited flexibility, and grants a well-nigh unlimited licence of communication. It is as if the usual human struggle against depth perception had been given up entirely and the shield of formal orderliness, *Gestalt*,[2] had been thrown away. The artist is not more neurotic today, he has only changed his subject matter unashamedly to neurosis.

(2) The publicity given to the aberrations, foibles, that is to say symptoms, of the great is encouraged by the insignificant, the sterile, the lazy, and the nondescript who avidly receive morsels of gossip and chunks of scandal. The portraiture of the shady aspects of the artistic élite is gratefully beheld by those less generously endowed. Almost masochistically the creative élite readily obliges by supplying the biographer, the reviewer, the social psychologist, and the literary psycho-analyst with intimate details; of this Lionel Trilling wrote:

One reason why writers are considered to be more available than other people to psycho-analytical explanation is that they tell us what is going on inside them. Even when they do not make an actual diagnosis of their malaises or describe 'symptoms', we must bear it in mind that it is their profession to deal with fantasy in some form or other. It is the nature of the writer's job that he exhibits his unconscious . . . the writer is more aware of what happens to him or

---

[1] 'Névropathes et déliquants sont entrés dans notre littérature et s'y font une place tous les jours plus grande', (J. M. Guyau, *L'Art Au Point De Vue Sociologique*, 1930, p. 342).
[2] Cf. *The Psycho-analysis of Artistic Vision and Hearing*, by Anton Ehrenzweig, 1953, p. 50.

goes on in him and often finds it necessary or useful to be articulate about his inner states, and prides himself on telling the truth.[1]

(3) Psycho-analytic psychology and most of its derivatives have repeatedly claimed that successful treatment securing social and sexual readjustment invariably expands the creative powers and enriches the work of the patient. In other words, neurosis is far from being instrumental to creativeness, it in fact impoverishes creativeness. The gist of this claim is valid but we should hasten to point out certain inaccuracies lest we prejudice the consistency with which we wish to handle these problems. No psycho-analytic therapy is 'successful' in the sense that the rupture experiences and their residues are wiped clean off the slate of the unconscious. No psycho-analyst would dare claim as much. What may happen in 'successful' psycho-analysis is that the syndrome-formations which are crippling to the functions of the individual, be he an artist or anything else, are weakened or their precipitating causes are channelled in more serviceable directions. Success in these matters does not amount to more than that the patient is helped to live with his abnormal primary adjustment. Therefore, I accept the psycho-analytic claim, for on the basis of my own definitions the patient is removed from the area of the 'definitely abnormal': his syndrome may cease to be apparent and prevalent through his review of his primary adjustment. It seems unlikely that this review will have a neutralizing effect on creative skills and discernment. In this respect one would agree with Ernst Kris who spurns the idea of such 'sterilizing effects'. In his opinion, 'The gifted artist "spoiled by analysis" seems to be a rare occurrence.'[2]

(4) In almost all communities—and certainly in our own—the distribution of opportunities has not depended on abilities. This is still one of our more important social problems. Many exceptionally able individuals have to go through a very exacting secondary process of adjustment before they can realize their potentialities. Though the causes of neurosis do not lie in this secondary process the greater exertions during this process may elicit, in the exceptional individual, a more profuse symptom formation, whilst his primary adjustment condition would

[1] *The Liberal Imagination*, 1951, p. 169.
[2] *Psycho-analytic Exploration in Art*, 1952, p. 29.

not otherwise have bared its abnormality. I am aware that this is a factor which I deliberately ignored in the previous chapter: my justification for doing so was that I was engaged in a quest for a minimum definition. One should emphasize that research into this problem has been neglected and that the role of the secondary adjustment process as a variable of syndrome-formation should be systematized.[1] Here I must restrict myself to a limited statement which concerns the 'genius'. All through history religious, political, scientific, and aesthetic conservatism and authoritarianism have increased the volume of frustrations for the exceptional innovators, while the conforming masses have had the advantage of a comparatively smooth secondary adjustment process. In addition to this, 'to excel' in anything is to detach oneself from the homogeneous group. As there is already a good deal of sociological information available about the attitudes towards aliens, minority groups, and such like, it may be of some interest to see how much popular hostility is directed against the artist and how much of this hostility aggravates the artist's reality situation beyond the point which the economic hazards of his own occupation would not otherwise explain.

(5) We have no knowledge whatsoever of the nature and functioning of creative gifts. The use of the very word 'gift' is a commitment which we have no right to make without evidence. Our ignorance of the biogenetics of artistic talent is complete.[2] The psychogenetics of this talent ultimately boil down to sheer environmentalism. Now it is true that the first five years or so of an individual's life decisively set his basic personality structure, but it does not fix the materials, meanings, and techniques

---

[1] That Freud was not forgetful of the pathogenic power of this secondary process is shown by his essay, 'Analysis Terminable and Interminable'; he writes there, '. . . we have a justification of the claim to aetiological importance of such unspecific factors as overwork, shock, etc. These have always been certain of general recognition and psychoanalysis has had to force them into the background' (*Collected Papers*, Vol. V, p. 327).

[2] Bergler (op. cit.) expresses his personal belief that the 'mysterious ingredient "talent" ' can now be traced to biological factors. But instead of biology he speaks of orality and voyeurism as biologically conditioned. What can he mean? At any rate, if increased orality and voyeurism have genetic components, i.e. if there is such a thing as an inherited predisposition to them, it is not this which psycho-analysis is equipped to prove. Psycho-analysts have always concentrated their attention on environmental determinants, in particular on the mother-child relationship. They know nothing about inherited predispositions.

of its later manifestations. Surely if we take our stand with environmentalism we must also remember that predisposing experiences, such as, for example, artistic parents or sustained artistic influence of other kinds may have a critical importance in the development of the artist's genius. These experiences are often far more in evidence during the secondary process than before. The ability to assimilate 'craft', skill, and even discernment does not entirely depend on dynamic factors. Thus this contribution to creativeness is unrelated to disbalance.

(6) My last argument is bound up with allegations that the artist's neurosis is a specific kind of neurosis. According to Otto Rank, the artist's neurosis is characterized by extreme narcissism and exhibitionism; according to Hans Sachs it is a feeling of guilt which seeks relief in confession to all and thus in sharing the load of guilt with others; according to A. A. Brill and Edmund Bergler it is a heightened orality which is the hallmark of the artistic personality. Bergler also substitutes voyeurism for exhibitionism regarding the latter as a defence for the former. There is no doubt that some or all of these specific traits and tendencies may be recognized in the personalities of artists but they are equally traceable in a very large number of non-artists as well, and thus—by suggesting these things— no light has been thrown on the mechanism of artistic creativeness. On the contrary, were the artist's misery specifically his own, he could not communicate to others, he could not share his experience with others. The artist's misery, or in my parlance the artist's disbalance, is of the same stuff as the disbalance of the rest of us.

These six points are lined up against the romantic exaggerations of those whom the tragic role of the creative artist seemed to please and who derived no small measure of pride from the artist's elegant and even exquisite 'madness'. The arguments contained in the foregoing paragraphs are ranged also against those whose sensitivity to the creativeness of artists has been reduced on account of an exclusive interest in the monotonous and stereotyped uniformities of the artist's unconscious, or rather of man's unconscious. Interest in these matters is legitimate and fruitful but it becomes barren when it boycotts parallel and equally legitimate interests in the artist's cognitive performance.

These brief observations on the first meaning of my introductory question whether the artist is more abnormally adjusted than other people or abnormally adjusted in a special way—will amply suffice.[1] When I turn to the examination of the second question—i.e. whether the artist is dependent for creativeness on his share of the universal disbalance of man,— I am obliged to reflect at greater length.

II

The theory of art which satisfies me can be summarized in the terminology I have adopted. Artistic expression and communication is a tool of the principle of growth and a product of the principle of cohesion. In other words it is an instrument of inviduation and socialization. But as all other forms of creative activity, nay, of all activity, share these characteristics I must search further for what is distinctive of art. In art, individuation reaches its peak because the product of expression is uniquely novel. By this I do not mean that 'novelty' is an artistic ingredient in and by itself. It is, however, an essential requirement, for the fatigue engendered by the *vieux jeu*, by the stale idea, is a barrier to communication, to communion, to cohesion. What is not novel fails to serve this principle. How does this stricture allow communion with the artists of the past whose 'novelties' have ceased to be such? Notwithstanding the distance, communion is achieved because the criterion of novelty remains effective beyond the time in which it operated. The novelty of the past retains its 'surprise' because we are in rapport with the age or cultural climate in which it appeared.

Though the area has now narrowed, my conception of art still includes some other forms of creativeness especially in science, philosophy, and religion. To be called art the uniquely novel product must not deal with universals as do the products of science, philosophy, and religion. Art consists in the creation of uniquely novel representations of particular experiences no matter how pregnant of universals these particular experiences are. Yet unless these representations are put forward by the artist to be shared with others, in however limited and even symbolical

[1] Also cf. 'The Unhappiness of Genius', by Henry Harper Hart, *The Journal of Nervous and Mental Diseases*, July–Dec. 1934, LXXX, pp. 410–29 and 557–73.

a sense, no art would be produced. The artist who objectifies himself in his art invariably establishes a bond between himself and an imaginary other or others to whom he originally desired to address himself. That no immediate and actual communication may take place is not decisive but that the intention of communication is ever present is not questionable. No artistic creation is possible if it is not meant to be beheld by anyone. Even certain forms of 'doodling' practised by virtuosos in a semiconscious haze is a communication to some internalized audience-image, to say the least. There is a fairly widespread agreement on this nowadays; e.g. Ernst Kris states emphatically that, 'Wherever artistic creation takes place, the idea of a public exists, though the artist may attribute this role only to one real or imaginary person'. And, for instance, '. . . the writer writes for *somebody*, and would cease to write if nobody was there. In our day that somebody is almost infallibly another writer'.[1] Wyndham Lewis, whose view this is, says the same about painters. On the other hand, when communication does in fact take place the artistic experience of the recipient is even more clearly an instance in the workings of the principle of cohesion. The beholder enters into the unique expression of the artist which he now vicariously feels to be his own expression; he is also exhilarated to realize that his own latent and inarticulate perceptions have been shared by the artist. All artistic experience of the beholder is *shared* experience. But whereas the artist has the considerable extra reward of 'expressing', which to him means enhancement of his individuality, the beholder can experience this only vicariously, in fantasy as it were. To compensate for this, beholders usually have recourse to substitute solutions and hence we witness the phenomena of the 'aesthete', of literary salons, of social intercourse among connoisseurs, of recitals by dilettantes, and so on. But even without these I should question the imputation that the beholder is passive. The introjected person-images have a way of keeping the individual company even whilst he seems alone. The individual in his solitary meditations is often described as being engaged in a dialogue. Even when he does not put this dialogue into words, he experiences, within himself and in fantasy, the communion between the I and the Thou.

[1] *The Writer and the Absolute*, 1952, pp. 34–52.

A theory of the orectic (dynamic) origins and functions of art is incomplete without an account of its cognitive life. Yet, if what I have said of the dynamics of art is true it stands, even if it does not constitute a comprehensive theory of art. Without further indulging in this digression I now extract those elements of it which are essential to the development of my argument. (*a*) A continued *individuation* in the form of artistic uniqueness, novelty, and sensitivity is at the core of art but, (*b*) its essential experience is one of *socialization*, of sharing, of communing, without which it cannot be art at all. This revised and telescoped version of Tolstoy's[1] and Croce's[2] aesthetics is my point of departure.

Against the background of this brief outline I propose to give my answer to the second question in three progressive instalments: the first two will constitute a thesis and an antithesis, the third will attempt a resolution of our dilemma in a final answer.

(A) The question we are called upon to answer is this: 'Is the creative artist dependent on disbalance for creativeness although he is no more abnormally adjusted than other people?' We may with some justification observe that the artist, instead of succumbing to disbalance, displays a remarkable command over it. The artist's representation of his abnormal adjustment in creative acts would not be possible if his primary adjustment process had left him with a paralysing abnormality. One may even be so rash as to declare that the very fact of a creative accomplishment is a suitable operational criterion of a comparative freedom from abnormality. I do not for one moment deceive myself and think that this is anything else but excessive complacency.[3] The biographical records of the greatest artists would make such an operational criterion of abnormality farcical. Nevertheless, *in the area of the artist's creativeness*, we find a remarkable degree of resilience, of adaptability, of articulate expressiveness, a will as well as an ability to communicate, and a patience, sometimes loving and dedicated—some or all of

---

[1] Cf. Aylmer Maude, *Tolstoy on Art*, 1924.

[2] Benedetto Croce, *The Essence of Aesthetic*, 1921.

[3] In popular treatises on mental hygiene matters one not infrequently comes across complacency of this kind. A good example of this tendency is apparent in the book, *The Mature Mind*, by H. A. Overstreet, 1950.

111

which are conspicuous by their absence in the non-artist neuro-tics. When an individual possesses these qualities he also pos-sesses vitality, health, and the realism of sanity too in at least some sectors of his experience.

Nowadays our theory of poetic creation holds [Lionel Trilling notes in his essay on Keats] that the poet derives his power from some mutilation he has suffered. We take it for granted that he writes out of a darkness of the spirit or not at all. But this was not the belief of the great poets of Keats's own time, and it was not Keats's belief. Wordsworth and Coleridge thought that poetry depended upon a condition of positive health in the poet, a more than usual well-being.[1]

I am not sure that Keats who wrote, 'Ye love-sick Bards, madmen that ye are!' (in one of the sonnets *On Fame*), would have confidently agreed with this. Yet it is equally possible that Keats's 'madmen that ye are' was not a considered psychiatric diagnosis but a temporary self-deprecation. Moreover one must admit that even when a poet's or an artist's brilliance consists largely in a narrowly focused clear-sightedness it surpasses the perspicuity of ordinary sanity. One should also remember that even when the artist's profundity is that of a deep well and not of the ocean he is so much the better equipped to quench our thirst, to cool and refresh us. At times one is vividly impressed that the artist's vision is *the* sane vision and that all that is in-sensitive and artless is nearer to the 'darkness of the spirit' than art could ever be. Then again it seems that this matter of sensi-tivity is not really a reliable guide. There are great artistic talents with their deep and painful sensitivity who are ever paralysed by their hesitation and the 'grossness' of any commitment. Sen-sitive people often lack the creative audacity so necessary to stop revising, correcting, retouching, and rethinking. Some-times too, sensitivity is 'seismographic' and fails to discern the rumblings of a six-ton lorry from those of a remote earthquake. Also, 'An artist is not necessarily more sensitive than an art-lover, and often less so than a young girl; but his sensitivity is of a different order . . . an artist supremely gifted for quickening emotion is not necessarily sensitive, and the most sensitive man in the world is not necessarily an artist.'[2] On the other hand,

[1] *The Opposing Self*, 1955, p. 7.
[2] *The Voices of Silence*, by Andre Malraux, 1954, p. 278.
112

that lasting creation can be, and at its best sometimes is, sheer hard work of the fortunately endowed and of the not-too-roughly-treated, that art could be the felicitous record of serene concentration or of emmet-like industry—these accounts are not dramatic enough to inspire reverence. 'To say that *only* persons exhibiting a special psychological dynamic are capable of creative writing is a form of crude reductionism; it leads to the nothing-but fallacy in which complicated patterns of talent and effort are dismissed with a nod towards Oedipus.'[1] One may not agree with this protest yet its indignation is not altogether undeserving of sympathy. After all, is it really true that only merciless self-searching inspired by tireless discontent, conflict, and unceasing disbalance can dispel the haze of common vision? Is it really true that without madly obsessed preoccupation there is no creation? And above all, is this preoccupation invariably the offspring of abnormal adjustment conditions working themselves out painfully, yielding only occasional drug-like reliefs? In this brief passage no more is suggested than a moderate measure of doubt concerning an affirmative answer.

(B) This half-hearted plea is closely followed by a discourse of reckless scepticism. With all its attendant risks this device is adopted to reconnoitre all the routes even those which cannot but lead to a morass. I believe that useful lessons may be learnt from this method of exploration. *Whereas the following reflects some of my anxieties, my rounded views should not be sought in this passage.*

There is and has been all through history a masochistic and tragic element in art which at times becomes its predominant feature. Indeed we must distinguish between art's inspiration to transvalue our disbalance and its invitation to wallow in our miseries, between therapy and epinosic indulgence.[2] This is neither an aesthetic nor a moral difference at first but a positive one. In this sense one could fairly say that not even Sophocles and Shakespeare are exempt from the charge that they ennobled misery by lending to unserviceable disbalance an air of tragic respectability. It is no excuse that this sort of reaction is prompted by the sick motives of sick beholders and that there is no warrant for this response in the essence of the poet's

[1] 'Poetic Creativity', by R. N. Wilson, *Psychiatry*, May 1954, XVII, pp. 163–76.
[2] 'Epinosic' = pertaining to the secondary gain or advantage through illness.

communication. The plea that *pro captu lectoris habent sua fata libelli* is too naïve. Though some are healed, my suspicion is that some are corrupted, or at least confirmed in their corruption. Canon Ainger's view that 'there is an unmistakable ethical flavour purifying and elevating the general atmosphere in almost every one of Shakespeare's dramas', is no longer held unreservedly. Ainger is quoted in the Introduction to the Chiswick edition of *Coriolanus* and one is tempted to ask whether Caius Marcius and Volumnia in the grandeur of their cruel pride really purify us of evil passions or inspire us to cultivate similar dignity. Think as we may, the possibility of corruption is worth at least some attention. Let me once again stress this: six or eight thousand years of culture are but a ripple on the ocean of time whilst the principles of life from which my discourse took its beginning span the whole course of life; even a few thousand years of recognition and respect for an artistic reputation are not inviolable evidence of perennial worth. Of course, neither is this impassioned protest a decisive testimony—from the world of the present. Yet the whole array of witnesses from Democritus to Freud tell us of the fetid soil from which the flower of art takes its nourishment, and so long as there is the smallest chance that the flower—in spite of its deceptive attractions—may pollute the air and contaminate the soil in which the rest of the flora thrives, the flower of art will not be safe from being eventually condemned as a weed. This is indeed a sacrilegious idea but I am curious to see where the present argument will take me.

Even the plea, that exceptional persistence need not be spurred on by conflict, is suspect. Creation could not come about through cursory asides and be assembled from desultory fragments. Perseverance is essential yet this perserverance is by no means the hall-mark of serenity. The taut, shackled energy of perseverance is kept up by the tug of war between individuation and socialization. The perseverance of the ambitious, the tireless industry of the aspiring, are maintained by a craving for triumphant recognition, acclaim, and love; meanwhile the rejection of the common, the vulgar, the hackneyed, and the insensitive, is prompted by the radical demand for growth, and unique independence. This is the paradox of all exquisite human achievement not only of art; in art, however, we are more aware of it.

Christopher Caudwell described this paradox of art as '. . . man withdrawing from his fellows into a world of art, only to enter more closely into communion with humanity'.[1] This so-called 'paradox' is only a special instance of disbalance, of the universal need for having it both ways, the need for communion as well as uniqueness, love as well as independence, socialization and individualization—cohesion as well as growth. In this sense the 'paradox' itself is universal and I shall have to find some other criterion to aid one in recognizing what is and is not art. Professor D. W. Harding, having given us three stimulating sketches of the 'innovators' Manet, Cézanne and George Fox, came to the conclusion that this criterion consisted in the *intensity* of the disbalance. 'The rareness of innovators is probably due in part to the need for (the) unusual combination of determined and even combative independence of mind with a strong, active need for approval and esteem.'[2] Or as he put it later, 'The combination, superficially paradoxical, of craving for affection and appreciation of one's group together with a life's work that centres round combative antagonism to its standards . . .', is a definition of disbalance as it most familiarly appears in the average adult in our time. It is interesting to observe the remarkable spreading of this dualistic interpretation in psychological literature on aesthetics. R. N. Wilson, for instance, acknowledges that there is a duality of forces bearing down on the artist; one of these is the individualism of the artist springing from 'idiosyncratic reactions to certain stimuli' and the other is the artist's inevitable need to be 'minimally' communicating to others.

The whole profession of art is profoundly involved in the moral of this analysis. Creation, this plaything of two irreconcilable forces, is precariously set in the course of cultural development. No one can say when it goes off the rails and no one can be certain whether equanimity in respect of this erratic course is logical and consistent with our fundamental and universal aspirations. The voices of doubt are more frequently heard these days though to extend Freud's sceptical thesis on religion (cf. *Future of an Illusion*) to the realm of art has not yet been

[1] *Illusion and Reality*, 1937, p. 20.
[2] *Social Psychology and Individual Values*, 1953, p. 138. The whole of his Chapter XII is most relevant to my conception of disbalance.

115

attempted.[1] There are cautious, self-conscious, and even apologetic criticisms, for the opponent is even more powerful than Freud's opponent, i.e. religion, was. Whenever the ephemeral fashions in certain neurotic syndromes become too vociferous one comes across pained wonder and even irritation; for instance:

We have acquired a tendency nowadays, when all standards have toppled into chaos, to murmur bashfully in front of the latest artistic abortion—'Well, I suppose there must be something in it, or people would not like it.' No doubt there *is* 'something in it'; but it may be something deadly sick. Tolerance is excellent; one should respect, if possible, the tastes of others; but a goitre is not a thing to be respected. It is a thing to be cured. The world is perhaps more

---

[1] Here again I deliberately carry the argument to its logical extreme. It is not at all certain that this extremist view would lead to an all-round nihilism such as for instance the nihilism of Bazarov in Turgenev's *Fathers and Sons*. Some sixty years ago Max Nordau, an irate and erratic aesthete, misled by Lombroso's psychiatry, hopelessly muddled the issues which I am here considering. Yet Nordau's broad erudition and independent mind arrived at some conclusions which are, even now, of interest. For instance, he foretells the disappearance of art, without the obligatory brave-new-world-despair, in a passage which suitably illustrates the present stage of my argument, a passage disconcertingly plausible even to those who disagree with its contents. ' . . . the march hitherto followed by civilization gives us an idea of the fate which may be reserved for art and poetry in a very distant future. That which originally was the most important occupation of men of full mental development, of the maturest, best, and wisest members of society, becomes little by little a subordinate pastime, and finally a child's amusement. Dancing was formerly an extremely important affair. It was performed on certain grand occasions, as a State function of the first order, with solemn ceremonies, after sacrifices and invocations to the gods, by the leading warriors of the tribe. To-day it is no more than a fleeting pastime for women and youths, and later on its last atavistic survival will be the dancing of children. The fable and the fairy-tale were once the highest productions of the human mind. In them the most hidden wisdom of the tribe and its most precious traditions were expressed. To-day they represent a species of literature only cultivated for the nursery. The verse which by rhythm, figurative expression, and rhyme trebly betrays its origin in the stimulations of rhythmically functioning subordinate organs, in association of ideas working according to external similitudes, and in that working according to consonance, was originally the only form of literature. To-day it is only employed for purely emotional portrayal; for all other purposes it has been conquered by prose, and, indeed, has almost passed into the condition of an atavistic language. Under our very eyes the novel is being increasingly degraded, serious and highly cultivated men scarcely deeming it worthy of attention, and it appeals more and more exclusively to the young and to women. From all these examples, it is fair to conclude that after some centuries art and poetry will have become pure atavisms, and will no longer be cultivated except by the most emotional portion of humanity—by women, by the young, perhaps even by children' (*Degeneration*, 1895, p. 543).

116

mentally ill to-day than it has been for three centuries. Our art and literature are full of mental maladies. Many simple souls are too timid to protest. But such timidity may not be much less dangerous to society than intolerance. Charles II remarked of a popular preacher, 'I suppose his nonsense suits their nonsense': of many artists of our time one can only echo, 'I suppose his neurosis suits their neuroses' (F. L. Lucas).

We must, therefore, beware lest the therapeutic benefits of art are not cancelled out by the social approval, respectability and halo of sophistication lent to a neurotic imagery and a neurotic *Weltanschauung*. So long as abnormal representations in art can, in this way, perpetuate abnormal adjustment conditions, there will be a case against art in general and certain types of art in particular. That this 'seduction' is no paranoid fantasy we have some authoritative testimonies. Oscar Wilde is often quoted as saying, 'Literature seldom imitates life with serious profit, but life imitates literature'. The sway of poetry, and by analogy, of art, over mankind may have been exaggerated by Peacock and Shelley yet it is sobering to allow them to speak now to ensure that we do not become victims of complacency: '. . . thus they (the poets) are not only historians but theologians, moralists, and legislators; delivering their oracles *ex cathedra*, and being indeed often themselves (as Orpheus and Amphion) regarded as portions and emanations of divinity: building cities with a song, and leading brutes with a symphony; which are only metaphors for the faculty of leading multitudes by the nose'.[1] Shelley, elated by the grand significance of his calling, has none of Peacock's scruples, '. . . poets . . . are not only the authors of language and of music, of the dance, and architecture, and statuary, and painting; they are the institutors of laws and the founders of civil society, and the inventors of the arts of life, and the teachers . . .'[2] In other words the whole human culture takes its cue from the poet who, it seems, is the patriarch of all artists and even of all other creators who, needless to say, all have their respective shares in the creation of culture. Peacock would certainly not find the accusation of 'seduction' too strong nor would Shelley question the powerful influence of art on our social institutions, both primary and secondary, as well as on the individual's adjustment. Much is still to be learnt of the

[1] Peacock, *Four Ages of Poetry.*   [2] Shelley, *Defence of Poetry.*

influence of art on life and there is no doubt that the verbal, musical and visual arts vary in their mind-moulding powers. Yet to credit some of these with revolutionizing potency and set aside others as capable of causing no more than private flutter is inaccurate. Wyndham Lewis made an attempt to weaken our apprehension of artistic 'social control' by a discrimination of this sort:

Now it is well to see in the man of words, words that possess so magical a power, the man . . . possessed of a power to shake the earth from one pole to the other. Jean-Jacques Rousseau, with his books, certainly did that—tore up society by the roots. But an oil-painting, or, however beautiful, an ink-drawing, cannot do things of that kind. Paul Cézanne can revolutionize the manner of painting of a generation or two of painters; but it is quite impossible for his canvasses to have any effect outside of the technique of painting. The man who wrote the words of the song used in the French Revolution, *Saint Nicholas a trois clériaux*, can set men chanting with diabolic glee around the guillotine; but a plate of Cézanne's apples could not even stimulate a man's hunger.[1]

Not only do revolutions visit states and whole communities, demolish social structures, and incite to excesses; revolutions can be inspired to take place in man's everyday ways of savouring the trivial realities of his life *without* immediately precipitating revolutions in the larger society. Revolutions of this sort put a new admixture of feeling in the ways of loving a child, of co-operating in marriage, of suffering fools, of trusting nature. No one contemplating Van Gogh's diabolical flora can fail to see the *Weltanschauung* expressed in a plant or a fruit. Cézanne would certainly not have regarded Wyndham Lewis's appraisal of his apples as complimentary. Wyndham Lewis, so much aware of the visual artist's verbal inarticulateness, ought to have known that the verbally handicapped great painter can cram embittered misanthropy or glowing trust and love into an apple. Were it not that the power of this creation enveloped us in so many ways, the totalitarian controllers of art would not have bothered about apples. One further veto must be got out of the way. It may be offered as an explanation that the apprehensions about art's sway over life are caused largely by lack of comprehension or of sensitivity and by a philistine obtuse-

[1] *The Demon of Progress in the Arts*, 1954, pp. 80–1.

ness. We 'don't understand' therefore we should do well 'to pass on without condemning', as Charles Morgan recommended.[1] But the issue is not always that 'one does not understand' but that sometimes one understands only too well and one may or may not approve of what one understands. The absence of approval is not always because of a lack of aesthetic sensitivity but often *in spite* of aesthetic sensitivity.

What matters to us here is that life 'imitates' art and that consequently art cannot escape the jurisdiction of life's positive norm and abnorm. Thus the somewhat tedious argument about aesthetics and morals is to be further endured. Whilst it is true that unhampered aesthetic freedom is a safeguard against the encroachments of the abnorm, it is also true that this aesthetic spontaneity has no way of escaping scrutiny by those who proselytize on behalf of an abnorm or norm. Least of all could art remove itself from the spotlight of science. The two strategic positions in culture, moral spontaneity and moral criticism, are both essential for us to hold, but those who choose to wield the 'moral' weapon, those who attack the moral position of the artist, are in duty bound to define their measure of discord with the artist in terms of positive science unless they are content to match the artist's revelation with their own and relegate the whole dispute to the category of an ideological war. Consider, for instance, the following complaint: 'By their emphasis on Original Sin, the Fall and other concepts which are repressive of emotional truth, Mr. Eliot and others are helping to restore a moral atmosphere which hinders the growth of sanity and indeed of charity. And as far as we can see from contemporary authoritarianism, of poetry also.'[2] Naturally, when the artist is ideologically committed and openly proselytizes he is often and rightly called to account. In cases of this sort the beholder is keenly aware and not rarely apprehensive of seductive intent. But Mrs. Nott mentions the issue of sanity thereby admitting that she is using a positive standard. She would be no less ideologically committed than those whom she castigates unless she defined her position in terms of positive science.

In keeping with the scepticism of this 'antithesis' in my argument I conclude (provisionally and experimentally) that the

[1] *Liberties of the Mind*, 1951, p. 237.
[2] *The Emperor's Clothes*, by Kathleen Nott, 1953, p. 208.

119

demon of artistic passion is born of disbalance, that the very fertility and audacity of artistic creativeness is manured by decomposing matter, that the exhilaration of the beholder is mingled with pride in his misery, that the triumph and sense of achievement in the artist is blended with self-justification. And finally I demonstrated at length that the art of disbalance perpetuates and confirms man's disbalance.

(C) Man has never been fully reconciled to rare and consummate originality. If there is one who can bring this forth, something, some mysterious agent, must be responsible. Man's reverence for the splendid exception has always been ambivalent. First it was the Muse—and madness; then it was divine inspiration—and madness; now it is the genius—and neurosis or psychosis. Adulation and debunking, mystery and misery, are the poles of this ambivalence. One is not ambivalent towards the insignificant and the fiction that genius transcends the ordinary man makes ambivalence inevitable. One detects a clinging to this fiction even in a recipe, like that of Bernard Shaw, according to which the genius is ninety-nine per cent of the same stuff as any other human being.[1] We are conversant with enough chemistry to know that if one per cent of some otherwise harmless matter is an exceedingly potent ingredient the whole mixture may thereby become fatal. Even Shaw's formula is too mystifying. An exception is by definition something outside the rules and nothing engenders resentment more in us than someone's being exempt from rules to which we are all subject. The hero is not to be judged by the science of man; the common measure of man is to be suspended in respect of the hero who is miraculous and unanalysable. The longing of man for a supremely faultless image, for a model of perfection is a longing for proof that the rules can be transcended, that the vulgarity of common human existence is not inevitable. Furthermore, inspiration with the help of hero-images has been a routine practice of communities: the crisis situations, the wretchedness of insecurity, and the violence of the struggle for existence has dictated that we avail ourselves of all the inspiration that can be had. For this reason any objective and unawed analysis of the 'culture hero' is liable to be suspected of envy and of debunking intent. Why should

[1] 'The Sanity of Art, an Exposure of the Current Nonsense about Artists Being Degenerate', by G. B. Shaw, in *Major Critical Essays*, 1932, p. 289.

sociology and psychology escape the charge of jealousy? In these sciences no marginal group of men has been left with the illusion of superior apartness; in the glare of scientific examination the extraterritorial status of the genius is cancelled. In sociological literature today artists are considered as 'an occupational group' with typical 'attitudes', 'standards', 'value-orientations', 'reference group behaviour', and 'professional mores'. If the sociologist escapes the charge of jealousy for having put the artist back into the ranks of common humanity, he will most certainly fall victim to the charge of philistine obtuseness. Sometimes both or one of these charges may be well-founded; yet they are not so frequently well-founded in sociology as outside it where 'the revolt of the masses' is inclined to elevate obscurantism and vulgarity to the level of supreme virtue.

This is one trend only and is the negative side of man's ambivalence towards creative greatness. The positive side is symptomatic of a different need: man also cherishes the extravagance of the artist's nightmare, the refinements of the artist's indigestions, and the exclusiveness of the artist's aristocratic spleen. He treasures the artist's non-conformist courage for it confirms his idea of the scope of his freedom. He is prepared to forgive the artist's reckless provocations and dissent for he grows more aware of his potentialities through the artist's example. One is well advised to remember what archaic intolerances and utopian loyalties may prejudge one's thinking. After this digression I may feel better equipped to match the foregoing thesis and antithesis.

From the Freudian analysis of the primary adjustment process of man we know that disbalance is its universal and inevitable characteristic. The doctrine that the Oedipus complex is a universal nuclear complex of all humanity has been questioned, and since Malinowski's criticism of this doctrine it may seem inadvisable to select this particular stage of human disbalance to illustrate the universality of disbalance. One could, of course, choose the trauma of birth and the infliction of individuality during the first year of life or any of the pre-Oedipal traumata, for these have more far-reaching consequences; yet my choice falls on the Oedipus complex because it has always been nearer to the artistic fantasy of western man than the earlier debacles and triumphs of the artist's orectic history.

It is generally held that successful assimilation of the Oedipal problem does not make man insensible to the artistic representations of this problem in symbolical and dramatized form. A so-called 'resolved Oedipus complex' and an 'unresolved' one are alike in many important ways. Whichever is the individual's lot he will 'resonate' in various degrees to its theme and welcome the socially approved occasions of releasing some of its tension '. . . The Greek myth seizes on a compulsion which everyone recognizes because he has felt traces of it in himself. Every member of the audience was once a budding Oedipus in phantasy, and this dream fulfilment played out in reality causes everyone to recoil in horror, with the full measure of repression which separates his infantile from his present state'.[1] There is a clear continuity between serviceable and unserviceable disbalance. The latter partakes of the hues, tones, and flavours of the former. The artist who succinctly expresses the standard conflicts of man will find an echo in those too whose conflicts are no longer acute, who have successfully assimilated their rupture experiences and whose primary adjustment condition does not issue in syndrome-formation. The malaise of a community, of an era, of a culture, is truly shared by all; the syntax of human conflicts on the primary level is as uniform as the syntax of a language. Any rupture experience of early life is capable of symbolization and will receive the echo of confirmation even from those who have been fortunate enough to steer clear of the more violent and sustained forms of such experiences as these. Even these fortunate ones have had their share of disbalance and hence are sensitized to its artistic representation. The conflicts of childhood are universal, a circumstance which appoints neurosis, i.e. conflict unresolved and deepened, the *lingua franca* of a good deal of human communication and, therefore, of art. The disbalance of our basic needs makes comrades of us all. Hence Oedipus Rex and Hamlet penetrate the marrow of our sympathy not because Sophocles and Shakespeare strove to make capital out of neurosis but because they descended into the common soil from which all human experience springs. *If disbalance is a universal affliction of man, then it is a normal human experience, i.e. normal in the absolute sense.*

[1] *The Origins of Psycho-analysis, Letters to Wilhelm Fliess, Draft and Notes 1887–1902,* by S. Freud, 1954, pp. 223–4 (from the 71st letter, 15 Oct. 1897).

'We have come to view psychological conflict not only as an unavoidable accessory to personality development, but also—within certain limits—as an essential ingredient and incentive,' declares Ernst Kris, and he leads back the whole argument to the issue of 'limits', i.e. what kind of conflict and how much of it? It was indeed difficult to protect the operational limits, suggested in the previous chapter, against the charge of arbitrariness and it is even more difficult to sustain that defence now. Fortunately the fixing of these limits in the present context is not essential to my argument; it is sufficient to say that disbalance, far from being abnormal, is universal and necessary. Some writers have tried to circumvent this by suggesting that disbalance in the creative artist is a very consequence of an initial and exceptional sensitivity and mysterious talent. In this view creative potentialities come first and give rise to a greater disequilibrium than there is in the average. As I. A. Richards put it, '. . . if we knew more about the nervous constitution of the genius we might discover that the instability from which so many people suffer who are at times best able to actualize the possibilities of life, is merely a consequence of their plasticity . . .'[1] We have no reason to think that this constitutional plasticity is more than a potentiality. The range of hereditary variations is a range of potentialities, whereas realities are brought into being through the experiential process of adjustment. One must remember that many are called into being with extraordinary potentialities but few are chosen to use them. Undoubtedly the adjustment process acts as a sieve.

A crucially important aspect of the artistic contribution to the adjustment processes of man is a therapeutic one. That art is therapeutic to both artist and beholder is not an uncommon claim, yet the place of this function of art in aesthetic theory has been inconspicuously small. In the previous section much has been made of the detrimental 'feedback' effects of art and, to do justice to the question which I am now engaged in answering, I must consider the beneficial effects of art; we may find that the latter is not irrelevant to assessing the adjustment condition of the artists who contrive to produce them. In the brief sketch of theory on the dynamics of artistic creation I emphasized that one of its principal sources was the force of cohesion,

[1] *Principles of Literary Criticism*, 1938, p. 59.

123

a force of distinctly social character. The communion which art may call into being is real and effectual when art is therapeutic, cathartic, and syndrome-alleviating both in creator and beholder. Art is therapeutic in as much as it inspires us to follow the artist's transvaluation of his own unserviceable disbalance into a serviceable one. *Der Dicther lebt ihn rettet die Dichtung*— the poet lives, he is saved by poetry—is a half-truth of Goethe's for he could not have been a genuine *Dichter* without also saving the souls of some others as well. This almost utilitarian vein in aesthetics is very likely to be scorned though it is as old as the Aristotelian *Catharsis*. 'No one should turn up his nose in hasty squeamishness at the alleged seduction of aesthetics into the medical realm,'[1] wrote Bernays in 1880, but apart from Tolstoy no one has paid much attention to this kind of aesthetic theory. The therapeutic service discharged by art is a vital ingredient of life in culture. Art is the homoeopathic medicine of cultural man, a medicine which must match its contemporary malaise accurately *or else, in too large doses, it goes over to the other side of illness and instead of fighting it, assists it.* Milton in his Preface to *Samson Agonistes* vividly brought out the medical and therapeutic meaning of Aristotle's *Catharsis*:

Tragedy, as it was antiently composed, hath been ever held the gravest, moralest, and most profitable of all other poems: therefore said Aristotle to be of power by raising pity and fear, or terror, to purge the mind of those and such like passions; that is, to temper and reduce them to just measure with a kind of delight, stirred up by reading or seeing those passions well imitated. Nor is nature wanting in her own effects to make good his assertion; *for so in physic things of melancholy hue and quality are used against melancholy, sour against sour, salt to remove salt humours* [my italics].

It is largely due to the Aristotelian tradition that *Catharsis* in the arts, tragic or not, has not been generally identified: there is no doubt that the therapeutic function of art is not restricted to poetry or drama in a tragic vein. Art is therefore a self-healing expression of man. To say that art has this function is not to

---

[1] '*Möge Niemand in voreiliger Zimpflichkeit die Nase rümpfen über vermeintliches Herabziehen der Aesthetik in das medizinische Gebiet*' *Zwei Abhandlungen über die Aristotelische Theorie des Drama*, Jacob Bernays, 1880, p. 14.

deny that other pursuits in culture have similar destinies; e.g. when Alexander Herzberg wrote of 'the psycho-hygienic value of philosophy' he was referring to a therapeutic role similar to the one just described.[1] Hence a circular argument is created: art springs from disbalance to soothe disbalance. Yet this is not a circle but rather like a spiral changing the form and content of disbalance from age to age. Thus my minimum definition of abnormal adjustment is not made self-stultifying, for the spiral winds away from its base which is the minimum area of abnormality.

In resolving the discord of the first two points I retain some of the scepticism which informed the second and blend it with the trust which was implicit in the first. If man secretes art from his present condition of disbalance, as he has done throughout his short history, then art is a natural and proper antitoxin, a natural and proper allayer of disbalance. Nevertheless the condemnation of excesses in the organism's self-defence is a medical issue, a matter for empirical assessment. We cannot take refuge in a *non possumus* and say, 'a little poison now and then: for that causeth pleasant dreams. And much poison at the last for an easy death'.[2] We cannot agree with Nietzsche who jauntily and irresponsibly suggested that there was no such thing as a 'safe dosage'. The division between 'sharing' and 'invitation to wallow' is something the social psychologist may not shirk exploring. If we cannot imagine inflexible rules for discernment it is because, to our knowledge, no empirical study exists which deals with this matter systematically. In the absence of established generalizations I put it forward that the symbolization and dramatization of disbalance in all forms of art answers a permanent need, for the projection of inner disbalance into artistic form is a relief to creator as well as beholder. At the same time as much of this symbolization and dramatization as is liable to contribute to the volume of abnormal adjustment conditions in a community is an 'invitation to wallow'. The question is, is the feedback of art favourable to the social institutions and usages which are responsible for abnormal adjustment conditions in the individuals? So long as this is left undecided by empirical study we cannot simply say that this work of art

[1] *The Psychology of Philosophers*, by Alexander Herzberg, 1929.
[2] Nietzsche, *Thus Spake Zarathustra*.

is to be castigated and that to be cherished. For the time being I cannot be reproached for saying no more than this:

(a) There is no doubt that artistic creativeness is a product of disequilibrium.

(b) There is no evidence that this disequilibrium *must be* unserviceable from the point of view of my own criteria of abnormal adjustment and unserviceable disbalance.

Thus the thesis of evolutionary relativism—outlined in the first paragraph of this chapter—does not prevail; the definition of abnormal adjustment is not stultified by the alleged formula that the abnormal is essential to a good deal of what is meritorious. Strictly from the point of view of the defence of that definition this would suffice. But more is to be said to strengthen those defences.

In so far as unserviceable qualities prevail over the artistic performance my attitude must be made clearer. In the first place there is no escape from the fact that unserviceable qualities in various magnitudes permeate most of art and are inseparably entangled in its beneficent and therapeutic power. One would be justified in these circumstances in averring that should the sanity of our culture be strengthened the demand for these forms of creative work would abate and the customary association of abnormal adjustment with creative art would fade. 'What does this all come to?' someone may exclaim. 'That times pass and tastes change?' This impression of relativism is precisely the pitfall I am trying to avoid. The anticipated development to which I alluded does not come under the non-committal heading of 'changing tastes'. When a diabetic's greed for carbohydrates is allayed by a shot of insulin he is satisfied with a normal intake of carbohydrates: the biological balance of his organism has been temporarily re-established and it would be facetious to say that 'his tastes have changed'. At the same time it is possible to give a more fundamental interpretation to the anticipated improvement in the level of mental hygiene: one may assume that the very character and intensity of rupture experiences may alter and thus the quality of the human experiences which all genetic psychologies regard as universal. Consequently, in the long run, the correlation between abnormal adjustment and artistic creativeness will become insignificant provided the minimum area of the abnorm is not progressively extended. If

126

it is extended *pari passu* with the improvement in mental hygiene the correlation will remain constant. But let us refrain from pursuing these conjectures about the future. For the time being the student of man, be he a moral philosopher, a sociologist, or a psychologist, may not, without violating consistency, allow extraterritorial immunity to any form of human relationship and thereby to any manner of communication which establishes relationships. Hence this immunity cannot be granted to aesthetic valuations. '. . . True though it certainly is that "there is no arguing about taste", it is unquestionably possible to argue about the human value of those who possess taste,' observes L. L. Schücking,[1] and he goes far enough already for too many people, who deem it a violation of the freedom to be publicly ill when aesthetic performances are judged by other than aesthetic values. They should be reminded of Nietzsche's dictum, 'And ye tell me, friends, that there is no disputing about taste? But all life is a dispute about tastes!' Tastes are indeed not exempt from comparison with the human abnorm. *To make the full weight of this claim felt, in the face of a well-established opposition the greatest prominence should be given to the following; intolerance, dogmatism, and ideological censorship are far more obvious symptoms of abnormal adjustment than the more palpable artistic abortions. The present conclusion is not a concealed Zhdanovism; the freelancing of artists is no more to be limited than the therapeutic and educational work of those who impart information to us about our intellectual and spiritual diet.*

That disbalance is necessary to the meritorious effort is, by now, obvious; that unserviceable disbalance, abnormal adjustment, pervade the creative process in subtle or gross doses has always been suspected; yet I earnestly insist that the abnormal is not essential to the meritorious in art. In some ways at least the artist is, by any definition, emancipated from the conventional in his age, and the intensity, impulsiveness, and oddity of the abnormally adjusted, when he is also an artist, makes his emancipation seem more radical. Whether this enhancement of creative daring is necessary is often debated. I have argued that culture will not sink in inanition and artistic creation will not cease when the vilest forms of personal degradation will no longer contribute to the substance and form of art.

[1] *The Sociology of Literary Taste*, 1944, p. 68.

5. *Political Leadership and the 'Abnorm'*

The second field of human distinction which I propose to examine is political leadership. The questions raised here are the same as those which appeared in the previous section. So far as the answers to be given are similar to those already offered I will avoid repetition. However, it would be superficial to settle the matter with a *mutatis mutandis*. The field of extraordinary achievement in politics is even more immediately and comprehensively vital to us than that which I surveyed above. Furthermore, political achievement has obvious distinctive qualities the analysis of which may profitably supplement my comments on artistic excellence.

I

All political leadership is expressive of the social-cultural climate of the age in which it functions. Notwithstanding the superlative energy and resource displayed by some unique figures of history, they fitted the society which elevated them. They could not differ from their followers and adulators in any essential measure of loyalty or aversion, of loves and hates, of apprehensions and aspirations, for this would have disqualified them from progress to eminence. The leader must always couch his language, attune his emotionalism, and adjust his very manner of domination according to the deep-rooted anticipations of his people. No Hitlerian harangue could have succeeded in evoking unconditional rapture in England and no Churchillian oration would have elicited both support and dogged trust in Germany. In the style of the appeal the personality of the leader makes itself tangible: histrionics, overstated moral purpose, and paranoid extremes of ambivalence in the one, portentous severity, the brilliantly proper phrase chosen with magisterial yet parental care, and the understated passion, in the other, are reflections of two disparate cultures. These two cultures are, in an important sense, as it has now been so often demonstrated, functions of their respective primary institutions. The upshot of the extensive literature on 'culture and personality' is that the nurseries of a nation decide the way

128

in which the citizens of that nation will eventually love and hate. This is a tired theme, yet the fatigue we experience when noting its reiteration should not make us insensitive to its fundamental validity. The evidence has been proliferous and, in most important respects, convincing. Yet, on the one hand, in a modern mass-society it would be futile to expect a high degree of uniformity in the primary institutions and to look for a corresponding uniformity of political orientation. On the other hand, when the predominant types of intrapsychic conflicts in a community persist, they may infuse its secondary institutions as well. It is in this sense that one may speak of 'abnormal cultures'. Both R. Brickner and G. M. Gilbert brought this out effectively with regard to German Culture.[1] There the paranoid core of the culture was largely responsible for the triumph of paranoid leadership. There the abnormality of leadership was not abruptly imposed but was deliberately chosen, elected, and elevated to voice the dynamic and cultural orientations of a people. Yet again it is most significant that Gilbert, who was in an excellent position to make observations, was driven to state that, 'A few, but only a few, of the Nazi leaders showed signs of clinical paranoid tendencies'.[2]

Once again it seems that the abnormality of the leader is no greater than that of the people he leads. Just as in the case of the artist, so in the present context, it does not appear probable that political leadership is quantitatively or qualitatively different in its disbalance from the rest of the community. Every one of the six arguments listed in the foregoing section is valid here as well. The artist, at least, may be at variance with his contemporaries at his own risk and expense and yet remain an artist so long as he can eke out an existence, but the political leader is by definition a 'success' however limited. The political leader cannot deviate from the general moral and emotional tone in more than an insignificant degree. Furthermore, abnormality in leadership has not been demonstrated by research to be more intense or specific than abnormality in other people. Those who deem it to be so, often allow their ideological opposition to a particular leadership, or their distaste at the very

[1] *Is Germany Incurable?* by R. Brickner, 1942, and *The Psychology of Dictatorship*, by G. M. Gilbert.
[2] Gilbert, op. cit., p. 270. Also cf. his *Nürnberg Diary*, 1948.

function of political leadership in general, to influence their judgment. It may be that political action and initiative have all too frequently issued from those leaders whose adjustment was manifestly abnormal. Certainly, history and the present state of the world would readily support such an impression as this. Yet in the field of political action the adjustment character of leadership is representative of the adjustment conditions prevailing in the respective communities. These adjustment conditions are ultimately social-culturally determined and both primary and secondary institutions of society are equally responsible for their normality or abnormality. The stream of the social-cultural process is prior to all other determinants of man's personality. Even the nurseries of a nation are supervised by culturally biased adults. If dogmatism, intolerance, ideological fanaticism are rampant in a community they are the joint products of an authoritarian system of secondary institutions and of a complementary authoritarian system of primary institutions. Leadership must always be in sympathy with the customary ways of symbolizing personal disbalance and these 'customary ways' are implicit in the primary and secondary mores. Of these two the secondary elements of culture prescribe the proper forms our rationalizations of disbalance must take. One is particularly aware of this when one makes comparisons between cultures, for the type of rationalization which a specific culture adopts may differ more sharply than their respective primary institutions. Rebecca West tells us that most of the members of the British Free Corps,—a Nazi military unit recruited by the Germans from Britons,—came from broken homes.[1] But the all too numerous victims of broken homes in Britain do not as a rule rationalize their misery in those political directions. They could not convert their unserviceable disbalance into totalitarian leadership in Britain where this is not the 'customary way' of converting disbalance. The prevailing adjustment conditions in Britain,—themselves the results of a long and complex history—would not allow conversions of this sort. This is not to say that personality is not determined by primary institutions, but that the primary institutions are themselves embedded in a secondary system of institutions which is more manifest and more inflexible. By this I mean that, whereas the

[1] *The Meaning of Treason*, 1952, p. 155.

secondary institutions are fixed for all and demand conformity from all, the primary institutions allow a wider margin of variability. In a distinguished study by Dr. R. E. Money-Kyrle we read the following suggestive hypothesis:

> I have no doubt—though this is an inference rather than an observation—that those in whom the early influence of a humanist home was overlaid by the influence of an authoritarian profession tended to produce homes more authoritarian than they themselves have been brought up in . . . Here then is an example of the effect of social form on individual character.[1]

This must not be construed as a suggestion that an authoritarian state can arise with its multiplicity of authoritarian professions, military, paramilitary, secret police, party, and so on, without being preceded and sustained by a predominance of authoritarian families in that community from which the most active leadership is recruited. So far as we can see the passage quoted merely conjectures that the freedom of a minority from abnormal adjustment conditions may be progressively whittled away in a lasting authoritarian culture. Whether we allot priority to the primary or to the secondary institutions my fundamental thesis remains confirmed, that political leadership is a *feedback* of culture and thereby of adjustment forms. The only defect in this feedback conception is that leaders are often recruited from élites and, although élites 'circulate', the selection of leaders in one epoch is rarely from the total group but rather from a section of it. This sector is usually a social class and there may be some reason to believe that primary institutions vary according to social classes. This variation is now being investigated and it is too early to say whether it is great enough to constitute a hiatus between the primary adjustment condition of the leader and those of the non-élite members of the community. At any rate it is doubtful whether the deviation from the general cultural average is very great. This is borne out by the fact that in democratic as well as totalitarian communities the successful leaders have both the 'gift' and the deliberate intention of appealing to the total community—often in the style of the lowest common denominator, in both feeling and logic.

[1] *Psycho-analysis and Politics*, 1951, p. 14.

131

We need not, therefore, hesitate in saying that the primary adjustment condition of a leader must reflect the prevalent primary adjustment condition of his followers. When one regards the eerie shadows of men such as are depicted in books like Trevor-Roper's *The Last Days of Hitler* or Riess's *Joseph Goebbels* one may feel persuaded that the more concentrated, tangible, and sharply contoured the leader's abnormality the more effective he will be in capturing and retaining power in an abnormal society. Analogously one may also conclude that in societies the cultures of which are not manifestly abnormal leaders are inclined to represent the quintessence of the general disbalance. In other words it may seem that leaders not only reflect a standard disbalance but that they realize it in a concentrated and increased measure. It has been said that their radical abnormality is an asset when they address themselves to multitudes which are of the same bent but less overwhelmed by their illnesses, or that delusion supreme envelopes a delusion hesitant. It is overlooked that something extraneous to the leader's personality creates this apparent difference of degree. The social and statutory position of power, and even the physical or topological position of a platform, are liable to make up this difference. Leadership is self-confirming or as it is expressed in the well-known formula 'power corrupts and absolute power corrupts absolutely'. The social isolation of leadership, coupled with the massive respect it exacts, is at least partly responsible for the more striking abnormalities of leaders. With regard to artistic creativeness my first question was, 'Is the creative artist more abnormally adjusted or abnormally adjusted in a special way?' To that question my answer was negative. A similar question in respect of the political leader receives the same negative answer.

II

But is the political leader dependent on disbalance in scaling the heights although he is no more abnormally adjusted than other people? What has been said before obliges me to suppose that the leader must, at least, simulate the emotional climate, and therefore the disbalance, of his people's culture. But, as it is psychologically improbable that simulation could sustain him through the vicissitudes of political strife, it is not too much to take for granted that those who succeed are spontaneously and sincerely disbalanced in the standard manner of their respective communities.

That the leader is not a saint, a hero, an omnipotent father, a wise and purified mind—at least sometimes, in those cases where we very much approve of his moral philosophy—is not a very palatable thought to many. That the leader must, in fact, draw powerfully on his share of a universal disbalance to achieve leadership and even that we regard that disbalance essential to the necessary effort may be discounted. To voice misgivings on these observations: the reputedly serene elder statesman or the tirelessly efficient family-man-politician with his spotless integrity are surely not instances of disbalanced emotions? Surely, these cannot be said to mirror the average type of man in our communities? Their excellence which secures them their high positions does so by virtue of their being rare and exceptional, integrated and 'balanced', not disbalanced and possibly abnormally adjusted. There are several reasons for reacting to these objections with some scepticism. The overt serenity has often proved in posthumous autobiographical admissions to have been a heroic pose, the puritanic solidity, the fragile shell of a fermenting interior. From the biographical and autobiographical literature of the past to H. D. Lasswell's researches we have an uninterrupted record of disillusionment in leadership which is alleged to be in a miraculously independent and unique sort of way sane. Last but not least, the policies advocated by leaders of this kind entitle us to query the veracity of a picture of unmitigated serenity and unadulterated domestic bliss. Admittedly the analysis of the association between *Psycho-pathology and Politics*,[1] is not as yet as clear as we would wish. One may say that the social psychology of political leadership is in its 'primary process of adjustment' with hypotheses, some of them precariously held, likely to prejudice its 'secondary process'. I can, however, hope to contribute something of use by introducing a certain measure of order into the system of hypotheses and thereby assist their verification.

To begin with it is obvious that not all who share the malaise of their society are able to personify and act out this malaise

[1] This is the title of H. D. Lasswell's first work on this subject. Chicago, 1930.

133

in an equally plausible, emphatic and vivid manner. It is suspected by some that those who have not been able to reduce the underlying conflict and tension of their lives will stand a better chance of having a large enough volume of these available for discharge into political ideologies, rationalized creeds, and, above all, into political action, be it reactionary, or reformist, or revolutionary. The intensity of feeling, the obstinacy of purpose, the one-pointed concentration of intellectual resource cannot be attributed to men who have no amends to make, no self-justification to accomplish. All human ambition may be interpreted in this way and we need have no fear of generalizing when generalizations in this matter are nearer probability than the 'great man theories' with their *Deus ex machina* explanations and with their appeal to the semi-mystical genius-concept. Even the Weberian *Charisma* suffers from this element of mystification. This is how Max Weber defines this well-known sociological catchword. 'The term "charisma" will be applied to a certain quality of an individual personality by virtue of which he is set apart from ordinary men and treated as endowed with supernatural, superhuman, or at least specifically exceptional powers or qualities. These are such as are not accessible to the ordinary person, but are regarded as of divine origin or as exemplary, and on the basis of them the individual concerned is treated as leader.'[1] Weber's very selection of the word Charisma which means '*Gottesgnaden*'—'God's grace', does not conceal Weber's own view on the origin and nature of the qualities which he enumerates. Yet in a telling sentence— alas only one sentence for he did not follow up its implications— he says, 'Charisma . . . may involve a subjective or internal reorientation born out of suffering, conflicts, or enthusiasm'. In other words, the charismatic leader is no other than one whose private misery is an ideal type of the misery prevalent in his culture. I use 'ideal type' in the Weberian sense thus the customary implications of 'ideal' are not present (or are present in an entirely non-moral sense).

When one poses the second question, whether the performance of leadership is possible without the leaders' understanding of man's universal susceptibilities, without, that is, an understanding matured by the experience of disbalance, the

[1] *The Theory of Social and Economic Organization*, by Max Weber, 1947, p. 329.

answer is not controversial. Charisma is indeed a gift of pain and suffering. The rapport of the leader with his followers is through the medium of comradeship in disbalance. I am not forgetful of the non-orectic qualities which are essential to the discharge of leadership functions, neither was I ignorant of these when I reflected on the genesis of the creative artist, but here I am primarily occupied with the dynamic elements of the life-process. This is a preoccupation which must also be justified by the contention that the dynamic factors are *the* decisive ones whereas the others are only incidental accessories.

There are other inherent destinies in the political and the artistic mode of thought which necessitate that a greater share of influence be given to the residues of disbalance. The nature of both political action and of artistic creativeness is such that they can materialize only through the triumph of bias and of sharply astigmatic perception. In every achievement of either we witness a defeat of absolute objectivity. This is indeed a virtue of art which abstracts the personal, the momentary, the subjective; and however faithfully true the result may be to an experience upon which it is based, it is nevertheless an abstraction, a segmental truth, a universal human bias. Its universality is a secret of its success and the condition of its being shared at all. In political action there are fatal consequences to the dictum that objectivity and action are incompatible. Action cannot unfold when a situation is to be reassessed in the light of every new piece of evidence and when it is to take into account all the factors which may have anything to do with decision. Absolute objectivity condemns to interminable hesitation and inaction. We saw how man in the course of history developed quietistic forms of religion, religions of passivity and inaction for he considered action, the violation of absolute objectivity, a humiliating failure, as well as a sinful lapse. And we see now, in the searchlight of modern depth-psychology, the curiously calm refusal to act sweepingly, to arbitrate on momentous and far-reaching matters affecting others, among those whose primary adjustment process refuses to reveal any rupture experiences whatsoever, in other words among the least abnormal members of our society. Whereas the intuitive and religious formulations of the relationship between inaction and truth were escape routes for those who would have been impelled to violate objectivity only too readily,—in the rare specimens of our own society the well-nigh complete absence of inclination to prevail over others, to impose on others, to dominate and exact, i.e. *to act politically*, are the outcome of their negligible abnormality. The contemporary examples of apolitical serenity must not be confused with the better known instances of sceptical or even cynical inactivity apparently producing apolitical objectivity of the same order. These are already rationalizations of abnormal adjustment conditions and possibly even reaction formations to a violently active potential which must be silenced for some reason. The difference between neurotic apathy and apolitical serenity, the difference between an embittered and disillusioned withdrawal on the one hand, and a calm and contented retirement from combatant positiveness on the other, is a difference of adjustment conditions. Whereas it is true that specialization in political and administrative leadership, as well as the greatly increased complexity of state matters, has made conscientious appraisal of policies impossible for the majority, there is a world of difference between the cynical and the stoical citation of these facts when accounting for withdrawal. One presupposes abnormal adjustment, the other does not.[1] There are, of course, blends and intermediate grades, but sociological factors do not change this simple continuum of apolitical behaviour. On the other hand, activism of the political kind must always be sustained by the disequilibrium of life. From disequilibrium political activism may ensue but not necessarily; without it political activism will certainly not appear. For the impulsive termination of reflection and weighing in the moment of political action is not possible without the lifelong bias of the disbalanced. One must warn here that the relationship of bias and disequilibrium is not purely allegorical. The disequilibrium of life dictates that the individual identifies himself from time to time—often with a high frequency of fluctuations—with one or other of the basic principles and hence is 'growth-biased' or 'cohesion-biased', favouring either individualization or socialization: the individual is incapable of coming to a perfect rest at a central posi-

[1] For a stimulating discussion of these sociological factors of political apathy see 'Criteria for Political Apathy', by David Riesman and Nathan Glazer, in *Studies in Leadership*, ed. by A. W. Gouldner, 1950, pp. 505–59.

tion. It is no accident that *all* political ideologies are characterized by the predominance of one or the other of these two principles. Liberalism and conservatism stress the principle of individuation and pay lip-service to the principle of socialization; collectivism, whether socialistic or communistic, gives preeminence to socialization and makes concessions to individuation. It is not too far-fetched to conjecture that the dialectical changes in emphasis from one epoch to another may even correspond to similar changes in the primary institutions of life. For the time being the scarcity of reliable historical data makes it impossible to ascertain this view. Furthermore, the complexity of interaction between generations is only now beginning to be understood.

We may now turn to those features of the leader's disbalance which are echoed by the resolved or unresolved disbalance of the many. These features never operate singly and it is only the more conspicuous presence of one or the other which induces me to make a list of them. Yet I must point out that political action is the function of a tendency more specific than I may have conceded so far. Political ambition aims invariably at the domination of human relationships. The striving to acquire fellowship-bonds through control of, and power over, them, is a manifestation of the principle of cohesion. Power, as a personality attribute, is the awareness of an imagined ability to control the individual's opportunities of 'cohesion', of 'communing', with his fellow-man. That it is fundamentally self-defeating and ineffectual does not alter the nature of motivation. To avoid misunderstanding, this does not make the politician a special kind of neurotic. The constellation of emotions in the background of administrative, artistic, scientific, and other types of ambitions partakes of the same quality in varying degrees. 'Fame' commands respect and thus expands the individual's scope of social participation as well as his access to those 'reference-groups' where he chooses to satisfy his fellowship-needs. *These tendencies widely obtain among people who will never appear in the political arena. Only some will find the path open towards expressing them politically.* The reason for this special luck or misfortune is not orectic (emotional) but pertains to intellectual endowment, special environmental factors, and chance. Now the motivation system which constitutes the drive to domination is characterized by the following three sequences.

(*a*) When frustrations of the principle of cohesion hinder the assimilation of the trauma of birth—the trauma of catastrophic individuation—the reaction to this is an aggressive, rebellious demand that love shall be given unto the individual and that preferably love, approval, and respect shall be at his beck and call. *Love is to be commanded.* That is the only method of securing the individual against repetitions of let-downs, against a recurrence of frustrations.

(*b*) When the aggressive-rebellious reactions on the primary level have gone too far to be simply canalized as such, later in life, they have, in their violence, created an anticipation of danger, an expectation of immediate retaliation. The genesis of guilt is amply set out in psycho-analytical literature and I need not divert my arguments by repeating them. Here *love is to be commanded* for one cannot be free from guilt unless one is constantly reassured of one's worth through being loved by the many, by being acclaimed and respected. The leader obtains respite from doubt through self-justification which is confirmed by the approval of the many.[1]

(*c*) The third type is normally described as issuing from the sado-masochistic tendency. Once again the psycho-analytic interpretations are not at variance with my position except, of course, with regard to metapsychology. Suffice it to say that in this case a fusion took place at an early age between the aggressive reactions of the individual and his cohesive, positive drives. The fusion means that the aggressive tendencies absorb the cohesive energies instead of the other way round. Here the very meaning of *love, which is to be commanded,* changes its character.

These three orientations are intricately mixed in most cases and a sharply defined typology has only a limited practical validity. I am, however, listing them to show that disbalance is inevitably the source of political action, and by italicizing '*love is to be commanded*' in all these three instances I intend to

[1] Cf. 'Our key hypothesis about the power seeker is that he pursues power as a means of compensation against deprivation. *Power is expected to overcome low estimates of the self . . .*' (H. D. Lasswell), *Power and Personality*, 1949, p. 39. Substitute 'politician' for 'power seeker' and my position is adequately represented. Also see S. Freud, 'Civilisation and its Discontents' in *Civilisation, War and Death*, 1953, p. 60.

stress the connection between power and the principle of cohesion.

Once again it is indeed not possible to determine the exact point where power-seeking begins. Karen Horney asked in her *Neurosis and Human Growth*, '. . . who will venture to draw a sharp line and say: "This is where the healthy ends and the neurotic begins?" ' and challenged us to say what the difference is between 'search for glory' and 'healthy human strivings'. I could not set up boundary marks for these two areas. Neither have I suggested that this was possible; on the contrary it has been repeatedly affirmed in these pages that these areas are variable. Notwithstanding I insistently demanded that, in the minimum area of the absolutely abnormal, variability does not obtain.

The manifestations of abnormal adjustment conditions in art escaped an unequivocal censure not so much for a jealous defence of artistic freedom, but rather on account of the therapeutic functions which art of this kind may fulfil. A similar leniency towards the abnormal in politics is impossible. It was deemed sufficient, although regarded as also necessary, that we disseminate knowledge on the genesis of artistic creativeness in general and of abnormal manifestation in art in particular but direct intervention and censure was branded as a symptom of intolerance, itself a manifestation of abnormal adjustment. The dissemination of insight into the genesis of political leadership and of its definitely abnormal types, will eventually be followed up by action and action is not possible without clear specifications as to the minimum area of abnormal adjustment. These specifications would be comprised in the inventories I recommended but the criteria of abnormality are not accessible, or at any rate have rarely been accessible, to the critics of political behaviour. The reasons for this are the following:

(*a*) Political action *qua* action cannot be judged in any other way than against the background of information on facts (political, economic, sociological, and so on), as well as against the background of definitive moral principles. The former, were it possible to command the enormous knowledge it required, also includes information on the relationship between social-political order and adjustment conditions of the individuals. In common parlance one would have to decide what cultures, and more specifically, what political orders are favourable to the avoidance of abnormal adjustment conditions in the citizens. Here the question of a new definition stares us in the face: what is a definitely abnormal political order? The trepidation one inevitably experiences when confronted by this question easily abates when one remembers that social psychological research has already accomplished enough to know where and how to *look for* the answer. Alas, I must satisfy myself with jogging the reader's memory by reminding him of researches carried out on subjects such as 'the authoritarian character', the discrepancy between the number of available places at the top and the credo of competition, the psychological consequences of war, racial, political and religious persecution, the consequences of industrial conflict, of mass-production, of authoritarian education, of a self-righteous penal code, and a score of other subjects. Surely it is not beyond the resources of modern sociology to produce a manual on the *Pathology of Social and Political Institutions*? The precision with which such a manual could be applied to subtle and controversial issues may be energetically questioned; but it is hardly possible to say that political actions cannot be matched to the mental requirements of individual citizens, if it is known what actions are instrumental in producing abnormal adjustment conditions in the individual citizen. It is of no alarming concern to the present argument that such a yardstick as I am offering may not be suitable to settle the contemporary global political differences to which we conveniently attribute all our present misfortunes. No one would receive a hearing if he ventured to disprove the validity of the Christian norm solely by saying that it has failed to resolve those political conflicts to which I have alluded. I am here defending the validity of the human 'abnorm' that island-rock of evil certainty which is perilously within our sailing distance; I contend that we can chart it and hope that at least thereafter all could have a better chance of steering clear of it.

(*b*) Yet is it possible to claim that there are occasions when abnormal adjustment conditions fructify in necessary and meritorious political actions and even that sometimes nothing else could or would suffice to produce these actions? The human predicament contains its quota of inevitable crises, catastrophes and conflicts under any circumstance however

140

utopian. The saving of life and limb, the defence of the 'good of the community', and so on, may be feasible only at the cost of sacrifice or exertion on the part of some individual or individuals. When the sacrifice and exertion is forthcoming the performance is often labelled 'heroic' or 'selfless' and has from the point of view of the species, at the lowest estimate, a survival value. This presents us with the gravest dilemma: if behaviour of this sort in the political sphere as well as elsewhere is to be described as masochistic or guilt-allaying we should be obliged to classify as abnormal a form of behaviour which is of the greatest value to the human species. It may be premature to become disheartened by this impasse in our argument. The zoological parallels, the self-sacrifice of animals for their young and for their congeners, shows that at rock-bottom it is the principle of cohesion which demands this complete renunciation of individual existence, that it is a life-principle which is in command in its naked, primary form and not a circuitous, distorted, compensative self-mortification. But who is to say which self-immolation is primary and which is reactive, secondary, and false? No one can be sure of more than the grosser instances near the extreme of abnormality; and this will have to satisfy us, for my minimum definition is intended to cover just these cases.[1] Yet even so, should the grossest forms of masochistic acts benefit others—and indeed I could not deny that they sometimes do this in our world—I could not retain any justification for my definition of abnormality. I suggest that there is an element of doubt as to the indefinite persistence of a world in which the crisis situations of war, political-economic strife, and social disorganizations of all sorts are unceasing and ubiquitous. There is an obvious link between the irrationality of these predicaments and the human endeavour which they exact from the sacrificial few. If most or all but few of these are relegated to the dark ages, i.e. 'man's history to date', one wonders

[1] The caprice of circumstances makes fair discernment even more difficult. 'Thus one man chusing a proper Juncture, leaps into a gulph, from whence proceeds a Hero, and is called the Saver of his Country; Another atchieves the same Enterprise, but unluckily timing it, has left the Brand of *Madness*, fixt as a Reproach upon his Memory; upon so nice a Distinction are we taught to repeat the Name of *Curtius* with Reverence and Love; that of *Empedocles*, with Hatred and Contempt . . .' From *A Tale of a Tub* by Jonathan Swift. The passage appears in the chapter with the remarkable title, 'A Digression Concerning The Original, The Use and Improvement of Madness in a Commonwealth'.

how much scope would be left to the masochistic hero? Here again our suspicion grows: is it not that the abnormal cultures of our history crave with their moloch-like greed for human sacrifice and that the sacrifice is to be paid by those most faithful carriers of our cultures, the abnormally adjusted individuals? In these circumstances it is not at all surprising that Sir Winston Churchill regarded the use of psychologists and psychiatrists in the fighting services with misgivings.

I am sure [he wrote] it would be sensible to restrict as much as possible the work of these gentlemen, who are capable of doing an immense amount of harm with what may very easily degenerate into charlatanry. The tightest hand should be kept over them, and they should not be allowed to quarter themselves in large numbers upon the Fighting Services at the public's expense![1]

But the values of war are not the eternal values of man. If there are no wars who shall wear the Victoria Crosses, the Congressional Medals, and the Orders of Suvorov and Kutusov? If there are no barricades who shall be the self-abnegating revolutionary idols? If there are no tyrannies who shall be the heroic fighters for freedom? Many will argue that for the time being and for some time to come we shall continue to need men who do the right thing for the wrong reasons, and, so long as this is the case, the abnormality of the reckless few will persist in being an asset of man's survival. According to this view it is harmful to lay bare the motivation of those who fanatically dedicate their lives to a single cause. I cannot reconcile truth with this kind of expediency; neither could I consent to the view that it is necessary to strengthen the ranks of the sane and the just, by enlisting the angrily righteous and the selflessly suicidal. Even today it is *expedient* to exclude the fervour of the latter no matter how ardently these may inspire and lead the former. As for the future, if sanity abolishes the grossest forms of waste no one could step in 'to save the situation' dramatically and in a tragic vein. There is no glory without peril. Yet it will be said that these are idle speculations about a non-perilous and therefore improbable future. But aren't all systems of moral philosophy based on an infinitesimally remote future perfection and on a creed in the perfectibility of man? Isn't it also true that all moral

[1] *The Second World War*, 1951, IV, p. 815.

philosophical systems are idealistic in the ultimate resort? Historical materialism reeks of it, logical-positivism affirms it in its ruthless and supreme logicalness. No apologies are necessary for using the hypothetical future to prise open the secrets of the present: all philosophers indulge in this though few perhaps will admit it. If my basic principles are sound, if they are in harmony with a whole gamut of empirical observations, their immediate and precise practicability does not rest with measuring symptoms of political leaders on the Rotschach and scoring their projections on the T.A.T. If my definition is valid it will not become less so because political leaders are not likely to consent to clinical personality assessment. *If my definition is taken seriously it will, at least, inspire a revolt against relativism and scepticism.* The success of its application to the concrete situation, to the particular individual, will depend on the elaboration of details by research which is already in progress. Let it be said that the whole psycho-therapeutic literature of this age implicitly accepts the doctrine of certainty about the minimum area of abnormality, and there is no prospect of a new scientific discovery destroying this certainty: the evidence in its favour accumulates with compound interest and originates from as widely different fields as brain surgery, endocrinology, experimental psychology, and zoology.

6. *Scientific Achievement and the 'Abnorm'*

It is indeed important that, much as recent developments prompt one, I should not go beyond my allotted task, the vindication of my definition. The purpose of considering the impact of this definition on our attitudes to art and politics was to ensure that facile criticisms regarding the applicability of the human 'abnorm' in these areas should be forestalled. The logical sequence to the foregoing discussion is to meet the charge of *tu quoque*. Alex Comfort phrased this charge aptly when, commenting on the contemporary psycho-pathology of politics, he said, 'The psychiatry which identifies all discontent with society as a manifestation of ill-health, calling for "readjustment", denies its own vocation.'[1] In examining whether this charge can be levelled

---

[1] *Authority and Delinquency in the Modern State*, 1950, p. 88.

against the present synthesis I shall, after art and politics, add my reflections on the relationship between scientific achievement and disbalance. To begin with, 'disbalance' is not the same thing as 'ill-health'. Even more important is it to discriminate between the feedback of disbalance in art, in politics, and in science. We have seen that whereas in art tolerance towards abnormality is not only possible but a case was made out for its therapeutic usefulness, in politics such a tolerance is far less permissible. In science, on the other hand, the risks are even less than they are in art. Whereas politics and art are 'goal-determining' activities, science has always been barred from assuming jurisdiction over goals. Even today the climate of opinion in philosophy is almost everywhere contemptuous of scientific intrusions into the realm of ends and values. The multitude of scientific termites engaged on building their colonies of specialisms are not disturbed by this limitation, for, as 'scientist-men', they are not, in fact, limited and only few of them are 'men-scientists' as well. Many a scientist can accommodate the *Weltanschauung* of an average philistine side by side with the brilliance of some esoteric expertize. Scientific knowledge, with the possible exception of mathematics, is mostly instrumental and involves little commitment, if any, to ends. This brief comment is sufficient to put our minds at rest: much as the unserviceable disbalance may account for extraordinary recluse-like scientific industry and exertion, there is no dangerous feedback here. At the same time there is as yet no easy and reliable way of proving that the disbalance energizing these performances is not sometimes unserviceable. Some twenty odd years ago Hornell Hart and his associates carried out an intensive study of the biographies of 171 well-known English and American inventors of the last three centuries. 'These were found to be characterized especially frequently by persistency, intelligence, insight, eccentricity, timidity, and sensitiveness.'[1] The qualities listed here are hopelessly vague and for our purposes inconclusive. With the exception of intelligence, all the other qualities may be associated with unserviceable disbalance, i.e. with abnormal adjustment conditions; yet even if this was the case several of the qualities could have appeared in a pronounced measure by virtue of the universal disbalance without

[1] *The Technique of Social Progress*, by Hornell Hart, 1931.

144

requiring the latter to be unserviceable. That this is probably a fair assessment of the facts is not countered even by the most sophisticated psycho-analytical demonstrations. A most illuminating example of this, quoted at length, will illustrate this point:

> In the structure of mathematical discovery itself it is often possible to see the imprint, so to speak, of the momentary passage through the barrier of repression. Lobatschewsky, for example, builds a systematic geometry, later expanded by Riemann, upon a negation of sensory reality testing, namely that parallel lines can meet. Non-Euclidean geometry has become an important adjunct to modern physics and astronomy. Cayley's algebra of matrices stood for many years as a kind of bizarre oddity in the field of higher algebra. Beginning with a postulate, in 'paranoic' fashion, which appears to be an absurd negation of the self-evident, namely that the products of 'x' and 'y' are different depending upon the order in which multiplication is performed. From the year 1858, when his first memoir on the subject was written until 1925 the algebra of matrices was a mathematical curiosity. In 1925 Heisenberg recognized in it exactly the tool which he needed for the development of his revolutionary work in quantum mechanics.[1]

It appears then that departures from commonsense, nay, from sanity are instrumental to epoch-making scientific progress. This conclusion inevitably follows from the quoted passage. The hypothesis of a universal disbalance is necessary to eliminate the anomaly of this conclusion. According to this hypothesis *all* harbour in themselves *all* abnormal manifestations, in a rudimentary fashion at least, yet only some translate them into clinically identifiable symptoms. 'Absurd negations' of a speculative, adventurous kind, such as Cayley's, may be the products of these rudimentary structures which are *sufficient* to give rise to intrinsically odd departures. It is of no consequence that many who have given much to science have possessed more than these rudimentary structures and were also clinically classifiable. It is not the 'clinical overspill' of abnormality which is responsible for creativeness, but the universal and basic disbalance from which both creativeness and abnormality may

---

[1] 'On Mathematical "Illumination" and the Mathematical Thought Processes', by Victor H. Rosen, *The Psychoanalytic Study of the Child*, 1953, VIII, pp. 127–54.

issue.[1] This may not be so easily felt in art and politics whereas in science it is certainly plausible.

Nevertheless when we review the position of *social* scientists in general and psychiatrists in particular we come up against a *tu quoque* which is indeed menacing. Ernest Jones writes about this, '. . . no other motive than suffering has yet been found, except in the rarest cases, to induce a human being to submit to any really searching investigation of his own mind.'[2] It is our duty to give the most serious consideration to this testimony. No one should claim to be described as a 'social scientist' unless he has dedicated himself to a searching investigation of this kind. Whereas it is conceivable that a social scientist retains the title, though remaining a mere statistician, it is no longer possible to do any interpretive work in this field without penetrating the innermost nature of the only psyche to which we have access. An understanding of the self is a condition of understanding society. Yet if self-understanding depends on a willing submission to unsparing and exacting probing, and if this submission absolutely presupposes suffering, there would be no escaping the fact that suffering or more precisely, abnormal adjustment would be a prime requisite to the true cultivation of social science. In my opinion it is unnecessary to identify 'suffering' with the universal disbalance of the human condition. That *all* share in this yet but a few will seek radical self-knowledge is a reticence caused by the disbalance itself. Nevertheless this reticence could be appreciably weakened by a culture which would encourage and reward self-examination and which would also provide accessible techniques as well as institutional sheltering against exclusively solitary pre-occupations with the self. If I am to understand that according to Jones neurosis is the only spur to acquiring self-knowledge, I should reply that neurosis is an equally powerful incentive to repudiating self-knowledge. There is no proved correlation between exceptional 'suffering' and a desire to seek the truth about oneself.

This is not to underestimate the danger of neurotic bias in social science and of the feedback effects of this bias. Can

[1] Cf. 'Similar and Divergent Unconscious Determinants Underlying the Sublimations of Pure Art and Pure Science', by Ella Freeman Sharpe, April 1935, XVI, pp. 186–202. Rightly interpreted this paper bears out my conclusions.
[2] *Essays in Applied Psychoanalysis*, 1951, I, p. 124.

social psychiatry—and the present synthesis—reliably free themselves from this danger? They can, for the personal history of the social scientist does not prejudice the validity of his findings if they are otherwise confirmed.

It is now time for a restatement and summing up.

(1) We can no longer persist in judging the achievements of great men by the standards of recorded history. The chief of the robbers is the best among the robbers and the brilliance of a forger is acclaimed by all the forgers; the heavyweight champion, the table-tennis *jongleur*, and the cleverest expert in postage stamps have their excellence recognized by pugilists, table-tennis players, and stamp collectors respectively. The lawyer, the doctor, and the engineer are usually appreciative of a good reputation among their colleagues though they are anxious to be valued by others as well. Though the proof, in their eyes, of professional meritoriousness consists in the praise they receive from their colleagues they are increasingly dependent on the market of the world, on the custom of an age. Not dissimilarly art is first honoured by the connoisseurs and the political leader-candidate is first spotted by the clique, the pressure group, the local association, the party caucus. Eventually both will depend on some non-sectional support and on the concurrence of outsiders. And all the time the achievements in art and politics are judged by minds which are slaves to the heritage of an all too short human history. What has been judged meritorious or necessary we have presumed to know from a few thousand years of human experience. But today, our whole conception of the meritorious is questioned by the findings of social science, as well as by those of the other life sciences. It is, therefore, possible that all the aesthetic distinction and political grandeur, which we know to have been associated with abnormal adjustment conditions, are far more ephemeral accomplishments than we have ever dared to admit. *Hence it is not the conception of abnormality, but rather the image of the meritorious that is ready for revision.*

(2) The disdainful and impatient attitude of the artist towards criticisms other than strictly aesthetic has only a very short-term justification. Whether we argue that all aesthetic experience is really moral experience, or that the converse is true, we

are advocating the view that the valuation of an experience is indivisible. The artist's continued illusion of extraterritoriality is the illusion of the abnormally adjusted, i.e. it is a symptom. Notwithstanding aesthetic opinion from Aristotle to Croce, the artist's art is a moral product and cannot escape being judged as such, for in it man addresses himself to his fellowmen.[1] But let us not stray into ethical language. If artists must be hypersensitive to precepts, and if that hypersensitiveness is a legacy of suffering, of abnormal adjustment, nevertheless we cannot rehabilitate the latter thereby. Sensitivity entails the power of feeling into the vitals of a human experience and if humanity eventually confines the experience of abnormality to the same reserve where smallpox and cholera are held today, sensitivity to the meanings of an abnormal adjustment condition will be irrelevant or at least too marginal, exotic, and too palpably unrepresentative of universal human experience.

On the other hand, disbalance is the essence of life and an artistic representation of it will always have a value in assisting the communion of man. It may be that gross unserviceable disbalance will prevail, and that the ominous signs, the mushroom clouds in the sky, will engulf us; in this case reason will have come to the end of its tether. Otherwise the very fact of continued survival will bring about a transubstantiation of disbalance and the conception of what is meritorious or necessary will assume new meanings. To judge life one must call in as a witness its whole compass: to submit to the definition of the human 'abnorm' one must acquire an evolutionary perspective. The knowledge of history is as woefully inadequate for the understanding of the human condition as familiarity with a zoo is for mastery of contemporary zoology.

---

[1] We cannot, of course, be certain of Aristotle's position. After all, the demand that '. . . the downfall of the utter villain' should be exhibited at all costs (The Poetics, XIII, 1452b–1453a) is not an aesthetic but a moral stipulation. 'Aristotle . . . was the first who attempted to separate the theory of aesthetics from that of morals', observes S. H. Butcher (*Aristotle's Theory of Poetry and Fine Art*, 1895, p. 221). But what other than moral character can be attributed to the rule, 'a perfect tragedy should . . . imitate actions which excite pity and fear . . .'? The whole doctrine of Catharsis has no meaning worth speaking of, if it is not moral. Jacob Bernays (op. cit.) gives Catharsis, 'the purification of passions', the same therapeutic, hygienic meaning I have attached to the whole of artistic experience.

'The root of the plant is not unsightly to science, though for chaplets and festoons we cut the stem short.'

Ralph Waldo Emerson

'The very best that thou dost know thou dar'st not to the striplings show.'

Goethe

'. . . it is a very real psychological question how far human nature, in its present form, is capable of tolerating the truth, the whole truth, and nothing but the truth.'

W. R. D. Fairbairn: *Psychoanalytic Studies of the Personality*, 1952, p. 253.

IV

NORM AND INSIGHT

1. *Some Notes on the Nature of Evidence*

THE philosophical problem of 'other minds' may never be solved yet generalizations on other minds will continue to be made and acted upon. We can no more wait to solve the philosophical problem before we accept these generalizations than Achilles, in his race with the tortoise, could have awaited the solution of Zeno's riddle before overtaking his competitor. Psychologists are always embattled with the critics of psychological method, both sides often failing to see that they argue most of the time from different premises. For example, no one would question the truthfulness of the statement that 'some human beings dream when they are asleep'; the physicist, the mathematician, and the logical positivist (here the 'fallacy of cross-division' is deliberately committed), will all readily admit the truth of this proposition although none has ever experienced anybody else's dreams. The factualness and validity of this statement is not inferior to the factualness and validity of the statements, 'some human beings are darkskinned', or 'some Englishmen are tall'. The difference is in the actual or potential verification of the respective propositions. To verify whether some Englishmen are tall one could rely on the testimony of one's senses and of those of other minds which care to attend. We can all look at the same thing and agree on what we all see. There are, of course, some further difficulties even in this agreement but we can safely ignore them here. At the same time no such simultaneous observation is possible in psychological matters. It has often been pointed out that even behaviourists cannot without converting it into physiology transfer psychology into the ranks of those scientific disciplines which regard

151

simultaneous and repeated observation of the same phenomenon by several people as an essential requirement of their method. The behaviourist observer has, in fact, no right to use a psychological language for he never observes the psyche. Having condemned introspection and thereby *the only psyche* which he could have studied, i.e. his own, he has fatally limited his scope. Nevertheless what behaviourist would dare deny that 'some people dream when they are asleep'? If no one ventures to doubt this it is the outcome of our considerable trust in other people's testimony. Yet clearly we must make use of some additional piece of evidence for otherwise a sizable group of deceived people would easily succeed in convincing us of any absurd thing and we should be defenceless in the face of their unanimous testimony. It may be said, for instance, that our definition of the abnorm is based on just such a spurious agreement as this. How can we vindicate this agreement? Since the discovery of the fundamental connection between the primary adjustment process and adult personality a multitude of testimonies has confirmed this connection. These testimonies are based on each individual's experience of rediscovering this connection by recollecting the primary experience, and realizing its power over his personality. On the other hand we may justifiably question whether the recollection of our experience is a reliable one. We may still say that we are deceived and so are other people who testify that we are not. In respect of the dream example this would mean that no one really dreams at all. But surely this is not acceptable! The vividness of the experience in so many of us forbids us to doubt the veracity of our recollection of having dreamed. Yet there is no proof beyond our testimony and our agreement with other people's testimony.

Let us now consider the following statement, 'human beings express their infantile conflicts in dreams'. Let us also suppose that some of us arrived at this conclusion through self-analysis, namely through a free association of ideas which we allowed to flow from reflection on the dream we had had. The striking vividness and the deeply familiar affect which resulted were accompanied by a sudden recapture of some long forgotten detail of early life. The relationship between the emotional charge of the original experience now recalled was so obvious to us that we would unhesitatingly brush aside the slightest suggestion of scepticism. Needless to say, no other person could have partaken of our experience although some of them, upon hearing of ours, would testify that they made similar discoveries. And others again, engaged in one of the 'reductive' methods of psycho-therapy[1] would corroborate by describing similar discoveries of some of their patients. In an anamnesia one is not in a position to question the validity of the recall, for the recognition of the past event is as overwhelmingly convincing as an immediate present experience would be. Indeed the relief subsequent to these recalls considerably heightens their plausibility.

In a therapeutic analysis, when a repression is completely lifted, both in respect of ideas and emotional charge, and an infantile event is remembered with all its feeling tone, there is never any uncertainty in the analysand's mind as to whether the memory is 'real'. It is believed wholeheartedly, with immediate conviction and no need of proof or reflection. The sense of credibility is an inherent element of the reliving. The analysand, recapturing the full memory, recaptures with it or in it that feeling of reality which characterized the event originally . . .[2]

He has no reason to doubt the authenticity of his recall for it presents him with the account of a long-lost experience which was his *own*. That there have been occasions when parents or others subsequently attested the truthfulness of anamnesias undoubtedly introduces an element of the more traditional type of evidence. Yet upon this we cannot rely overmuch: a consensus between the patient's and the parent's account will, at best, relate to a few externals only. There are also other complications which I cannot consider here.

Basing our evidence on the individual's own recall and its account we may judge his testimony less favourably than our own. This is an incredulity foisted on us by conventional scientific methods which prescribe that we check other people's observations of an object by observing the *same* object. Professor

[1] By 'reductive' therapy we understand a psychological method of healing which recognizes that the adult character structure and adult behaviour are functions of early childhood experiences; these experiences and their affects having been forgotten ('repressed') the method of 'reduction' is used to bring them back into the orbit of conscious reappraisal and control.
[2] *The Psycho-analysis of Elation*, Bertram D. Lewin, 1951, p. 178.

Barbara Wootton's comment on this sums up my position admirably:

The grounds for belief in the sense experiences of other people and the grounds of belief in their primitive psychological experiences are . . . both equally shaky, or equally firm. We derive our conviction that other people experience emotion from the fact that they say so, and from analogies between their behaviour and our own: we derive our conviction that they see and hear from exactly the same evidence.[1]

There is evidently much less discontinuity in empirical verification than one has been led to believe by the critics of certain psychological propositions. The critics who single out certain types of psychological propositions for methodological criticism little suspect that their scepticism may well condemn *all* psychological propositions to the limbo of unverifiable guesses. Professor C. D. Broad writes, for instance:

Of all branches of empirical psychology that which is concerned with what goes on in the minds of babies must, from the nature of the case, be one of the most precarious. Babies, whilst they remain such, cannot tell us what their experiences are; and all statements made by grown persons about their own infantile experiences on the basis of ostensible memory are certainly inadequate and probably distorted. The whole of this part of psychology therefore is, and will always remain, a mere mass of speculations about infantile mental processes, put forward to explain certain features in the lives of grown persons and incapable in principle of any independent check or verification. Such speculations are of the weakest kind known to science.[2]

At what point in the time-scale are we to begin distrusting

[1] *Testament for Social Science*, 1950, p. 9.

[2] *Mind*, 1944, LIII, p. 354. Professor John Wisdom sums up the position about the clamour for 'proofs on utterly conventional lines' in the following words, 'The consequence (of not having such proofs) is that people half feel that astonishing as is the new material psychoanalysts bring forward and impressive as is their reassembling of old material they still never "quite prove" what they say. They are right in a sense. The psychoanalysts' statements in so far as they are not expressed in strict accord with convention will never be proved in strict accord with convention' (*Philosophy and Psycho-analysis*, 1953, p. 271). Even Professor Wisdom—favourably disposed as he is—is unduly cautious, for no *psychologist* ever 'quite proves' in the conventional manner what he puts forward. The predicament is not solely the peculiarity of psychoanalysis. For some further observations on this problem, see 'The Logical Status of Psychoanalysis', by Stephen Toulmin, *Analysis*, 1948–9, IX, pp. 23–9. The same by Herbert Dingle, ibid., pp. 63–6, and 'Psychoanalytic Explanation', by Anthony Flew, *Analysis*, 1949–50, X, pp. 8–15.

human memory? If several trustworthy persons testified having seen a wolf in the forest yesterday would Professor Broad question their testimony and proceed to take his constitutional in that forest? Or would he ignore their report only when it referred to observations made a year ago? All the most respectable empirical observations are committed to memory until they are recorded. And even when they are recorded those who recorded them are expected to confirm the veracity of the records if they are challenged and if they are available to be challenged. The 'perceived' and the 'remembered' are both involved in the empirical. Yet whereas one does not deny that the residues of a perception fade in time, empirical evidence of the kind Professor Broad would approve of must either exclude the element of memory or be conditional on an arbitrary time limit. Moreover length of time and inaccuracy of recall do not absolutely correlate. The childhood episodes in the past of a septuagenarian are often more vividly remembered by him than the exact place where he had deposited his spectacles or pipe a few hours ago. But apart from this matter of an 'ostensible memory', taking shelter under a demand for 'independent checks or verifications' will not do unless we know precisely when checks or verifications are 'independent'. In respect of this Professor Broad must decide whether he regards a psychological science impossible. Let us once and for all face the fact that without subjective testimony only physiological or behaviouristic sciences of man are possible and even these will be only remotely analogous to our subjective experiences. Psychology is a science of subjective experiences or it is not psychology at all. We do not even have a choice in this matter; behaviourism and physiology can produce no meaningful information whatsoever without the aid of subjective testimony. We cannot suspend judgment until a behaviouristic-physiological account furnishes us with further evidence because the proofs thus acquired will not verify anything psychological. This is not to deny that these methods can contribute corroboration, but rather to insist that they cannot furnish checks and verifications. No matter how complementary the physiological and psychological accounts of an experience may yet become, the inner psychological presentation of an experience will never be convertible into a physiological event. Furthermore, no measure of objective precision and detail in the description of an emotion will ever approximate the clarity, immediacy, and completeness with which the experiencing of it informs us of its nature. One of the dangers of contemporary empiricism is its habit of imposing on us skeletal, stereotyped, and highly simplified empirical concepts with a tendency to displace a fuller and richer comprehension of the reality for which the concept stands.[1] We should bear these observations in mind not because it is desirable that we should be distracted from intensive empirical inquiry in favour of some undisciplined reverie but that we should maintain a constant check on the limitations of empirical concepts. It is for this reason that one is tempted to agree with Theodore Reik's statement that, 'Wherever and whenever psychoanalysis makes really important scientific progress, it will be accomplished by an experience in which self-analysis plays the greatest role. No deep insight into human minds is possible without unconscious comparisons with our own experience.'[2] To avoid the danger of a reckless and arbitrary subjectivity one should tirelessly maintain a double empirical guard over the achievements of one's own insight: (1) a comparison with the reported insights of other people, i.e. other people's testimonies about their insights; (2) a preservation of logical consistency and rational unity between psychological insights so established on the one hand and physiological, biological, evolutionary and sociological data on the other. Insight is, however, both the beginning and the end of all psychological observation; without it full comprehension of the observed is impossible.

2. *The Concept of Insight*

To study insight, then, may help to lend further substance and plausibility to the human abnorm which I sought to define. The understanding of the central idea of 'disbalance', the appreciation of the significance of concepts such as 'primary adjustment process', 'rupture experiences', and 'social-sexual inadequacy' depends on the comprehension and awareness of the realities for

---

[1] '*Quaere*, whether or no too great definiteness of terms in any language may not consume too much of the vital and idea creating force in distinct, clear full-made images, and so prevent originality. For original might be distinguished from positive thought' (Samuel Taylor Coleridge in *Anima Poetae*).

[2] *The Inner Experience of a Psycho-analyst*, 1949, p. 18.

which these concepts stand. I would at once suggest a definition as the starting point of discussion. *Insight is the individual's ability to relate the affect of a present experience to that of a past one provided the latter determines the basic quality of the former.* This is a broad definition to allow us an important classification of insights. Two models will be sketched to illustrate the classification I intend to introduce.

Model 1. A young office worker found that he was drawn into irascible and aggressive behaviour while talking to an older man during an ordinary social occasion. After he had detached himself from the conversation he began to wonder why he had been so intensely provoked by one of the man's harmless remarks. The young man suggested that a certain sports event had taken place on such and such a day, upon which the older man observed that he believed the event had taken place on a different day. Our office worker had indignantly repudiated the 'insinuation' that he was careless and superficial or that he pretended to know of this event when he did not. His companion, surprised at the unexpected and unprovoked outburst, had politely steered the conversation away from the subject and broke away from the clerk at the first opportune moment. The clerk, an intelligent though unstable young man, embarrassed by the hardly veiled snub as well as by his own apparently senseless behaviour, collected himself and came to the conclusion that his behaviour had been foolish for he could now see that there was no insinuation whatever in the older man's remark. He allowed himself to be carried away by some inexplicable feeling of animosity towards this chance acquaintance. Some time later, after he had for a while forgotten the unpleasant incident, it came back again with a sudden flash of illumination revealing to him the cause of his odd behaviour. His boss at the office often humiliated him in the presence of others by commenting on his work unfavourably. He felt that at least some of this criticism was unfair, but he thought he could not afford to remonstrate because he was anxious lest such a course of action might endanger his position at the firm, which he wished to retain. Nevertheless the resentment, having accumulated over a number of years, was by now considerable. This chance acquaintance prompted him to release some of this resentment because there was something in the manner in which the older man spoke, in his gesture, in his cool calmness, suggestive of superiority which reminded him of his chief. The connection between the two relationships was so manifest to him now, the 'feel' of the common ground of resentment in the two situations was so direct and tangible that he had no doubt any longer about the immediate cause of his absurd behaviour, i.e. he had some *insight* into its causes and nature.

It is not relevant now whether the realization of insight was followed by a relief from anxiety about his having made himself a fool. As a matter of fact such a relief as this is frequent if not universal: the realization of insight enhances one's self-aware-ness, and consequently one's feeling of self-control, thus re-assuring one that in the future the experience will not recur.

Model 2. Let us now consider that our young man was a markedly disbalanced individual whose syndrome had already obliged him to seek psychological therapy of a reductive type. Let us also suppose that after relating the foregoing incident to his psycho-therapist his relationship towards his office chief was worked through in the course of several sessions. Here it trans-pired that the young man's picture of the reality situation was not accurate, for the reasons he put forward against a firm stand in the face of unfair criticism collapsed under careful examination. There were several instances when he could have defended himself with dignity and without prejudicing his posi-tion. After protracted discussions on this matter and in the course of a lengthy analysis the young man began to realize that his behaviour was masochistic, that he was exposing himself to abuse by authority, that he derived some relief from guilt in this way and that the whole gamut of these affects was a rever-beration of similar affects which had flooded him during early childhood. He recalled the full flavour of certain childhood experiences in which his attachment to and longing for his mother were shamed by his father and whose sarcastic repri-mands he accepted as well-deserved for his illicit desires. Once again the connection between the two relationships was sharply apparent to him. He acquired *insight* into the causes and nature of his present behaviour. Here, however, I cannot truthfully claim that the achievement or otherwise of relief is not relevant to my definition of insight. It is more or less certain that relief is the hall-mark of the genuineness of insight. Without a fusion of primary and secondary affects a complete understanding of his present behaviour would not have been possible and, after all, the fusion of these affects constitutes a relief. Here it is more obvious than in the first model that insight is not merely a cognitive achievement but an orectic one as well. The two are indivisible: they cannot be accomplished separately.

I propose to name the type of insight obtained in the first case (model 1) *secondary insight* for it throws light on the relationship between two experiences both of which occur during the secondary adjustment process, whilst to the insight realized through the recapture of forgotten infantile experiences, briefly sketched in the second model, I shall refer as *primary insight*. It is not at all certain that the realization of primary insight cannot take place outside reductive therapy. The Fliess-correspondence, Ernest Jones's biography of Freud, also Freud's own autobiographical account, as well as a number of other isolated claims for successful self-analysis indicate that there may be other ways. For the time being I leave this issue open and survey further similarities and differences between the two types of insight.

(*a*) Both primary and secondary insights are the outcome of a reductive process. In both cases an affect of the past must be allowed to show itself in two ways: in its original form and in its modified current form. In a sense there are no two affects 'fusing', as I put it before, but one affect appearing side by side in its past nakedness and in its present garb. 'Reduction' consists in retracing the process of 'clothing' but not in the elimination of the present affect and its replacement by its predecessor.

(*b*) Both insights presuppose intelligence, provided that this is conceived to be an ability to discover relationships between ideas or affects. Reductive psycho-therapies are, on the whole, of little benefit to the individual of sub-average intelligence.

(*c*) Both insights result in increased self-control and self-awareness; this can be illustrated through the following parallel. If X is the superior of officials A, B, C, and D one of these, say, A can acquire control over B, C, and D, whilst remaining A as well, that is, by not only being promoted to the position of X but also retaining the function of A. Something like a cabinet minister promoted to the rank of prime minister whilst retaining the portfolio of finance or foreign affairs as well. Similarly the dynamic control of an affect in the present is exercised by an

159

intricate hierarchy of affects stretching back through time and effective through its structural residues in the present. If A, B, C, D are current affects and X is an immediately preceding older parent-affect of A, B, C, and D, then no matter how little control we have had over B, C, D, or even A, we obtain control over all of them when we understand how they are related to X. Thence our control over these four will depend on our control over X. Needless to say, the nearer to the root of the ancestral tree of emotions X lies the larger number of its derivations become controllable through it. It should be noted that the experiences of the primary adjustment process and their residual affects are by no means the ultimate ancestors of our emotional life, and antenatal as well as racial X's may also be taken into account. These are indicated by the Jungian racial unconscious, the Freudian references to racial memory (particularly in *Totem and Taboo*) and by other similar hypotheses. Insights of this depth are, of course, unobtainable and we should be well-advised to adhere to the experience of birth as our starting point for here is the occasion when the individual first becomes aware of a disbalance which could not have existed in the completeness of antenatal union.

(*d*) Laymen often believe that it is possible to grasp a historical and genetic link between affects of the past and those of the present merely 'intellectually', i.e. without thorough affective involvement. Sometimes, even in psychiatric literature, insight is portrayed as an accomplishment of a rational centre or arbiter in the mind; an accomplishment which consists in the extension of the individual's *rational* control over his behaviour hitherto not so controlled. The concept of 'intellectual insight' is a product of this sort of thinking, for it assumes that the 'intellect' can 'understand', and *thereby* control. It ought to be remembered that 'controlling' is a dynamic activity of which the non-dynamic abstraction, intellect, is utterly incapable. Two lessons may be learnt from this. The first is that accurate 'intellectual insight' is possible only if it is supported by dynamic-affective insight with which the individual is familiar from other, simpler experiences, i.e., when it is analogous to dynamic-affective insights already possessed. In other words, insight of this order is never purely 'intellectual'. The second lesson—a somewhat ominous yet inescapable discovery—that the dynamic support may operate from the very opposite direction, that is, 'Some of the signs of insight may result from counterphobic attitudes, reaction-formations, or compulsive identification with the normal.'[1] This is what happens when one accepts an insight from others on trust, as it were, and lives by it without having realized this insight out of the stuff of one's own personal history. Whether this insight is entirely spurious or not it is important to see that even this is not simply 'intellectual'. Nothing in the mind is truly intellectual. Thus I defined insight as an ability of the individual *as a whole* and not an ability of his intellect or reason. Then, if insight pertains to the whole, if it is a quality of the individual's total cognitive-orectic condition it is *ipso facto* a quality of the individual's fundamental disbalance. Insight is disbalance made conscious; and in as much as this 'consciousness' is both self-knowing and self-feeling: insight is disbalance made partially controllable. That there are various degrees of depth to which insight can reach is obvious enough. The available classifications of insight usually set up their categories according to the depth of understanding and control. For example, Reid and Finesinger spoke of three levels of insight, neutral, emotional, and dynamic.[2] The only weakness of this kind of classification is that it implies the dualistic fallacy of 'reason and emotion', that is, of varying measures of supremacy of reason over emotion. My classification by-passes this dualism and regards a temporal division into primary and secondary insights sufficient as well as more realistic.

(*e*) It is a widely held doctrine among reductive therapists that thorough affective anamnesia is impossible without an intimate therapeutic relationship between therapist and patient. There are two diverging lines of reflection we may pursue in this matter. *Firstly*, psycho-analysts are emphatic that a thorough conquest of primary insights is not possible without the co-operative therapeutic relationship between analyst and patient. In this relationship transference is a lever of affects and without transference no repressed affects can be properly unearthed. One cannot acquire primary insights without becoming a child on the

[1] 'The Analysis of the Concept of Insight', by J. Richfield, *The Psychoanalytical Quarterly*, 1954, XXIII, pp. 390–408.
[2] 'The Role of Insight in Psychotherapy', by J. R. Reid and J. E. Finesinger, *Amer. J. Psychiatry*, April 1952, CVIII.

analyst's couch, without transferring to the analyst one's filial and infantile emotions towards one's parents. Furthermore these insights are genuine and effectual only when they are accompanied by the full emotional and even somatic echoes of the original experiences. There is no doubt that for radical therapeutic changes in the personality of the analysand these conditions must be fulfilled. One may add to this that those who engage in reductive psycho-therapy cannot hope to become sensitive to the psycho-genetic casuality in others unless they themselves have undergone reductive psycho-therapy. All these prescriptions are widely known yet there are several reasons why I am obliged to regard them as perfectionistic. The discussion of these reasons brings me to the *second* line of reflection. Those who are concerned with the adjustment conditions of their contemporaries and with the mental hygiene level of their communities cannot view this perfectionism with equanimity. To associate primary insights with those who have undergone analysis and rule out its possibility in all other cases leads to complacency about the analysed and to gross inaccuracy about the unanalysed. H. D. Lasswell rightly observed of the former that,

> Even psycho-analytic experience is not enough since many more or less lengthily analysed persons unwittingly resume old or conventional attitudes after analysis. Continuous support by the environment of the analytical frame of reference is necessary. The task is that of providing a stream of analytic communication which most effectively provides this support. A new culture pattern is called for.[1]

No reductive analysis is ever 'completed'; Freud confirmed this in one of his last publications.[2] The dichotomy of 'analysed-unanalysed' is invalid for the same reasons as the 'normal-abnormal' antithesis is false. We no more know what an 'analysed' person is than we can define a normal individual. To say that an analysed person is alone familiar with the prominent features of his primary adjustment condition is, of course, untrue. Let us not forget that the understanding which the unanalysed Freud managed to acquire *unassisted* was in an important sense vastly more than the insight which scores of

[1] *Power and Personality*, 1949, pp. 14, 253.
[2] 'Analysis Terminable and Interminable', *Collected Papers*, 1952, V, pp. 316-57.

trained and analysed therapists have managed to cull from training-analysis since his time. An obstinate opposition to self-analysis on the part of Freud himself is somewhat of a paradox. On the part of his followers it savours of hero-worship for it concedes success to this method in the case of Freud only. With what sort of insight do these followers credit their un-analysed master? Psycho-analytic intransigence in this respect is absolute; for instance:

> The famous temple of Delphi in Ancient Greece, bore the inscription *Gnothi Seauton*, ascribed to the philosopher Cheilon. This precept, 'know thyself', was just as worthless a few thousand years ago as it is to-day: nobody is capable of knowing himself out of himself. It is as if someone advised: spend a few hours under water. It is true enough that this is possible, but only if you are equipped with a diver's helmet and an air hose. In the same way, with a psychic diving apparatus—the help of a trained psychoanalyst—the dive below the psychic surface is possible—and rewarding. . . . Objectivity toward oneself is impossible outside of analysis, and is not practised at all.[1]

Psycho-analysts will agree that objectivity towards others is impossible without objectivity towards the self; according to this pronouncement of Bergler's Freud could not have possessed either of these two objectivities for he never underwent analysis.

Another reason for scepticism in the face of this dichotomy, i.e. 'analysed-unanalysed', is sociological. It is often contended that primary insight in the therapist is sufficient for the understanding of the primary processes of others. Analysts are inclined to be contemptuous of regard for reality situations and for sociological factors. It is irrelevant according to many whether their patient, over and above being a neurotic, is also a victim of parental penury, racial persecution, hereditary or acquired physical defect, or cultural abnormality and conflict. It is often held that no matter how little the psycho-analyst is acquainted with the reality situation of his patients the analyst's training in the dynamics of the primary adjustment process is sufficient; the analyst should be able to reconstruct the patient's reality situation from the patient's account and he will require no

[1] 'The Mirror of Self-knowledge', by Edmund Bergler, in *Psycho-analysis and Culture, Essays in Honor of Geza Roheim*, 1951, pp. 320, 322.

other information. As analysts mostly treat patients whose cultural background is not very different from their own, the complacency of this attitude has not been adequately appreciated. Yet it is at least probable that sociological ignorance, and obtuseness in the face of cultural variations of background, and a lack of insight into the mechanism of social causation, are the limitations of a strictly individual-genetic understanding. Needless to say the same limitation would obtain in all unassisted realizations of insight: it is frequently suggested, for instance, that Freud was a victim of a narrow Viennese middle class mentality. These pitfalls, however, can be avoided by a sociological reassessment of the primary insights one manages to acquire. That this reassessment does not always take place is very probable. 'Some psycho-analysts discover that their own psycho-analysis did not free them from compulsive acceptance of many symbols and practices of the culture in which they happen to be reared.'[1] Yet another reason for scepticism in the face of the notorious dichotomy of 'analysed-unanalysed' springs from a commonsense condemnation of the costly reductive therapy which has by now become a privilege of an élite of some opulence or at least of comfortable means. Meanwhile it appears that no 'short-cut methods' or 'cheap editions' of reductive psycho-therapy are free from arbitrary interference with the integrity of the individual. In this respect Lindner's apprehensions were indeed well-founded.[2] The middle-class professionals are not to be trusted with suggestive therapies! In these circumstances the 'analysed-unanalysed' dichotomy assumes an ominous quality of class-differences. It may be that this quality is also implicit in the intelligence requirements of reductive therapy. No one below a certain level of intelligence could benefit from this technique and thus insight would join intelligence in qualifying the 'scientific caste-system' of the future. Be that as it may, for the time being the correlation of class and intelligence has already been established and our anxiety about class-bias in analytic insight is probably justified.

Recent findings tend to deepen our apprehensions; for example:

Psychotherapeutic methods are applied in disproportionately high

---

[1] *The Analysis of Political Behaviour*, by H. D. Lasswell, 1947, p. 292.
[2] Cf. Chapter III, Section 2.

degree to the upper social levels. Organic therapies tend to be applied most often to the small business, white-collar, skilled and semi-skilled workers of social classes III and IV (Hollingshead's classification). Custodial care shows a consistent inverse relationship to psychotherapeutic methods and is given in largest measure to patients representing the lowest social status positions.[1]

Although the investigators managed to control the economic factors in this investigation the factor of intelligence was not controlled. Naturally, if intelligence is hereditary and if reductive insights are the privilege of the intelligent one would be forced to draw curious conclusions as to the future of a mental health movement which awards top-prize to the perfectionist and interminable reductive therapies. For the time being there are far too many hypotheses involved in this apprehension; I should, however, examine the exacting stipulations of reductive therapy in the area in which they can be already observed, i.e. among intellectuals.

Those who are in sympathy with this concern and have attacked the perfectionism of some reductive systems have been searching for other methods of solution. H. D. Lasswell calls attention to these partially unassisted methods of seeking primary insights, 'The acquisition of skill in self-analysis by the route of psycho-analysis is becoming more common among social scientists.' He also advocates a certain measure of weaning from the co-operative therapeutic solution, for example:—

Persistent self-examination can go a very considerable distance in enlarging the part of the personality whose resources are made available for the ends sought. There was a time when insight researchers were disposed to pooh-pooh the idea that very much could be accomplished through insight outside the prolonged psycho-analytic interview situation. But in recent years there are abundant signs that this sectarian viewpoint is much relaxed . . . There are doubtless debits as well as credits in the account, but from the standpoint of clarity of human understanding the complications that come from partial insight are to be preferred to the complications of innocence.[2]

The 'abundant signs' to which Lasswell refers are, presumably, not only the self-analytic extensions of co-operative therapy but

[1] 'Social Structure and Psychiatric Treatment', by H. A. Robinson, F. C. Redlich, and J. K. Myers, *Amer. J. Orthopsychiatry*, April 1954, XXIV.
[2] *Power and Personality*, pp. 198–9.

also the promising results of group-methods as well as the insight-giving features of the press, cinema, wireless, and television.[1] The perfectionists are particularly suspicious of the so-called mass-media of communication when they are used for purposes of insight-giving. I shall have occasion to explore the insight-giving potentialities of these media. For the time being we must decide whether or not it is possible in however small a measure to realize primary insights outside the affective relationship called transference. We have reason to believe that the therapeutic relationship no longer retains the monopoly of insight-giving which is attributed to it. That insight-giving is not possible outside a co-operative therapeutic situation I do not see proved. If I continue to think in terms of assisted and unassisted primary insights I do so with the assumption that both are possible. At the same time one must yield the credit of greater effectiveness to the therapeutically assisted insights for we are as yet far removed from the 'new culture patterns' for which Lasswell calls and are so much steeped in a culture of deceptions that without the discipline of a therapeutic co-operative analysis we cannot aim at more than a modest measure of the primary insights available. For this reason one cannot deny that the possibility of 'affective reliving' without the lever of transference is somewhat doubtful in our culture.

So long as we seek no more than a minimum definition of abnormality, so long as we restrict the sphere within which both assisted and unassisted insights join to define the area of abnormal adjustment conditions, a consensus of a much wider kind could be assured by allowing equal say in these matters to social scientists trained or self-trained in reductive psychology. One may fear that the larger the number of those who agree the

[1] This is suggestively commented upon in the famous work, *The Authoritarian Personality* (by T. W. Adorno, E. Frenkel-Brunswick, D. J. Levinson, R. Nevitt Sanford, 1950, p. 976), where in connection with the problem of ethnocentric prejudice the following passage appears, 'Although it cannot be claimed that psychological insight is any guarantee of insight into society, there is ample evidence that people who have the greatest difficulty in facing themselves are the least able to see the way the world is made. Resistance to self-insight and resistance to social facts are contrived, most essentially, of the same stuff. *Techniques for overcoming resistance, developed mainly in the field of individual psychotherapy, can be improved and adapted for use with groups and even for use on a mass scale.* Let it be admitted that such techniques could hardly be effective with the extreme ethnocentrist, but it may be remembered that the majority of the population are not extreme but . . . "middle" ' [italics mine].

narrower will be the scope of their agreement, or that the advocacy of a minimum definition of their agreement will produce no more than an eclectic compromise. Apprehensions concerning this have often been voiced, for instance:

... although it is too soon to observe the influence on the lay public of professional efforts to consolidate psychological theory, it is safe to assume that the attitude of the average reader will be receptive to the new eclecticism. And this means in effect that with the passage of time, the most comforting theories will tend to resume their earlier sway. This tendency will no doubt be sedulously fostered by the Churches.[1]

Once again this is the voice of perfectionism. I believe that by making explicit the shared views of the several genetic psychologies we should certainly exert a more immediate and beneficial influence on man and his societies than psychological understanding has made possible so far.

Notwithstanding an agreement—a minimum agreement—on insights, the crucial issue in the minds of most sceptical people will remain this: the conventional methods of investigation have established relatively little so far to entitle us to demand the acceptance of this minimum agreement. I should have comparatively little difficulty in making my first inventory accepted by reductive psychologists, but those outside this category will continue to insist that empirical evidence be supplied before they considered my proposition seriously.

Not wishing to be indifferent to empirical verification I must stress the need for continuing the attempts at furnishing 'proofs' of the conventional kind. At the present juncture there is no danger that this work is going to be neglected; as it is, it is difficult to distinguish at a glance many a contemporary journal on psychology from one on mathematics. A new statistical summary is wanted, a new tabulation of deep-psychological insights into rupture experiences and syndromes from which we could glean a minimum agreement for our two inventories. The nature of the evidence thus produced need not cause us apprehension. It would be ridiculous to raise methodological objections in the face of the international, and therefore intercultural, unanimity thus reached by thousands of observers. It

---

[1] Edward Glover, *Freud or Jung*, 1950, pp. 16–17.

will be of no avail to object, when the minimum agreement is supported by innumerable testimonies on primary insights from areas as different as middle class Vienna, the Central Australian Arunta, proletarian Paris, upper class London or New York. For me the minimum agreement on primary insights is an ultimate verification which cannot be displaced by any form of conventional empirical proof. The latter has one function only —and admittedly an important one—it is the strongest weapon with which we can combat all resistance to insight.

The concept of 'resistance' is well-known as a key-concept in psycho-therapy. Practising analysts know that the imparting of insight to patients is a risky and slow affair. Often, when an interpretation is easily available to the analyst he withholds it until the patient is ready to receive and assimilate it. A premature interpretation may stiffen the patient's resistance making further therapy more difficult or even impossible. It is very likely that in trying to give insights to those who are not patients, but parents, educators, child-care workers, and so on, we may merely enhance their resistance. For this reason the following reflections on resistance to insight are included for the benefit of those who are entirely unfamiliar with the experience of primary insights. The few paragraphs which follow are not intended to be a contribution to the clinical study of 'resistance' but are offered to the general reader as a stimulus to self-questioning. The clinical specialist may regard the following discussion as a summary of rationalizations which most frequently cover the mechanism of resistance in both clinical and non-clinical situations. For the purposes of my present study I define resistance as an attitude of disbelief in the 'primary' determination of personality as well as a repudiation of the doctrine that defence mechanism against unconscious motivations are universal.

3. Resistance to Insight

'You would pluck out the heart of my mystery!' Hamlet reproaches one of the King's courtiers. Two of these, Rosenkranz and Guildenstern, were charged by the King to find out why Hamlet was moody and depressed. There is a note of hurt vanity in Hamlet's reproach; his melancholy he calls a 'mystery', and

to attempt to unravel this mystery is a presumption. The cour-
tier was guilty of underrating the noble Prince's profundity.

Hamlet's depression appears to him as a sublime condition
of despair; its hates are righteous indignations, its suspicions,
clever, resourceful observations, its loves, holy devotions. And
the tragic tangle of it all is a *mystery* to be nursed, fostered and
ripened to a grand climax. To harbour such a mystery as this
with steadfast perseverance is a source of security. One feels
that this mystery—(or shall we call it misery?)—is not unmingled
with conceit about its apparent complexity. It is not just a plain,
pedestrian misery which besets us—it is something unique, something very personal and original. Of this no one should dare
to deprive us. We shall fight our would-be helpers, healers
and interpreters. Their offer of insight in exchange for our
intriguing misery is an insult to our self-esteem.

To resist insight is easy. We have accustomed ourselves
throughout the years to love and hate in certain specific ways
and all we have to do is to continue. When a river's course is
blocked by a landslide it breaks through at the weakest point
of resistance which may not be some sector of this new barrier.
It may be a good way further up, where the banks are low and
the land beyond is lower still. And so it happens that the river
abandons its original course for a new one. If a return to the
old course is to be effected by human effort, it could be accomplished only by planning, resource and many months of toil.
The vast bulk of water, flowing through the newly carved course,
would sweep away any half-hearted, flimsy intervention. The
river has, by now, accustomed itself to the new course and will
refuse to be coaxed back into the original one.

No matter what name we select for the steady flow of life's
energies—no matter whether we call them a stream of instincts,
desires, drives, sexual libido, *élan vital*, will-to-power, or the
principles of growth and cohesion—these energies, in their
totality, will run the same obstinate course as our diverted river.
It is a common-place of modern psychology that the major
blockages and diversions of energy occur in early childhood.
Much has been written and said about this matter and almost
as much has been resolutely and even fanatically resisted. The
objectors, nearly all of them, cling to a dogma or to a consolidated doubt. When one tells them, to quote one example, that

loving and hating the same person near and dear to us is merely a revival or a continuation of an earlier 'lovehating'—and when one tells them—that this lovehating was directed originally towards the providing as well as prohibiting parents, they fervently object. And their objections are fed by their unconscious fears of being found out. In the course of their lives they all tackled this emotional landslide in one way or another. They found a new course, or to depart from my simile, they effected an adjustment. The jealous defence of this adjustment is, after all, very understandable. It is, in fact, an everyday experience. Take, for instance, the case of the overgenerous husband who buys that unsolicited present for his wife because he is at times weary of her, yet loving her, as he does, feels that he has to atone for his guilty thoughts. If our interpretation reminds him of such spurious motives as these feelings of guilt, he may reject it. And he may battle against the interpretation with the determination of one who wishes to convince himself at least as much as he wishes to silence the interpreter.

Or consider the rebel, the self-righteous protagonist of some cause. He will charge his rhetorics with such fervour as cannot be explained by saying that he is, after all, right in what he says. It is not enough to say that the selfless protector of the oppressed or the heroic rebel against tyranny are fired by the spectacle of an injustice and the vision of restitution. Some people, equally intelligent and also sensitive to these injustices, may not react with the fury of a wounded beast, whilst others would be only too glad to gnash their teeth. The complacent thinker will, no doubt, say that these are temperamental differences. He will imply that variety is a good thing and there is nothing we can do about this—even if we wished—for we are born with these differences. A simple-sounding explanation—but it won't do. We know a great deal more of acquired temperamental differences than of hereditary ones, and it is somewhat doubtful whether hereditary differences are decisive enough in this matter. The fury of rebellion is the fury of grievance, that is, of experience and not of heredity. Neither is this fury fanned by the cold intellectual appraisal of an injustice or by the perfectly natural compassion for its victims. For the fury to flame, love is not enough: sympathy for and identification with the victims presupposes some experience which is similar to

170

that of the victims. In other words we must have been real or imagined victims too in the past, perhaps in a very ancient past of our individual history. If there is insight, that is to say, if there is, at least, an intuitive understanding of one's personal aggressiveness, of one's personal rebelliousness, there is always a good chance for the evolutionary instead of revolutionary solution of an intolerable situation. Herein lies the greatest significance of insight at the present juncture of human history. Unfortunately, such an insight as this will be resisted. The grievance is old and painful, and it is good to rebel and retaliate.

One more example. I am thinking of the stubborn intellectual certainty which is usually associated with resolute actions. It is the kind of 'either-or' thinking the relentlessness of which invariably leads to some suffering, especially when political leaders indulge in this logical disjunction. Now, to affirm something unconditionally, and often blindly, is a form of aggressive defence. It amounts to saying that 'this much I know for certain and this certainty is my fortress in which I can withstand my own doubts and the hostility of others'. This is what Nietzsche meant when he said that 'the object is not to know but to schematize'. That is to say, we get hold of a certainty not because it is an absolute and objective certainty but because we need the subjective experience of being certain. We don't always discover features of order in the universe, we impose the order, that is we schematize. Once again, insight could save us from the arbitrariness and falsehood of this condition. But no, insight will be only too often resisted because it deprives us of our makeshift fortress of certainty. At the same time, of course, we must be wary not to deny all certainties on account of their being certainties. Such an intellectual nihilism as this defies itself and is meaningless. The certainty of which I am apprehensive is the uncompromising, fanatic certainty of unconscious despair.

The resistance to insight always assumes some reasonable looking disguise which seems to suit the occasion admirably. Psycho-analysts call these disguises 'rationalizations'. There are several forms which these disguises or rationalizations may take.

The *first* of these is the protest which comes from those who cannot suffer the determinism of modern psychology. For these, the belief in a uniquely free moral initiative is an essential part of human dignity and self-assurance. Surely, they say, not *all* our morally relevant decisions are mere ripples of a river the course of which is determined by the emotional landslides of childhood? We cannot see why an affirmative answer to this question should be disillusioning. However, it is not my task to seek for a formula of consolation if the truth seems disconcerting to some.

The *second* form of rationalization complains of 'debunking'. It suspects that the world-wide agreement among psychologists is a conspiracy of decadent thinkers. Those who voice this rationalization would say that psychologists and psychiatrists drag down into the mud all that is noble and sublime. Assuredly, their wicked practices ought to be exposed. These objectors are particularly agitated at the hearing of such terms as 'sublimation'. The objectors consider the widespread vogue of these terms as well as the acceptance of their meaning the end of man's spirituality. What these objectors fail to see is that the noble and the sublime are permanent attributes of a healthy humanity, a humanity of sane mind as well as of sound body. They fail to observe that it is their accusation which degrades perfectly natural impulses of humanity by calling them 'lower', in distinction from the 'higher' things which the psychologists are supposed to be debunking. These objectors are unable to sense the noble potentialities of a spontaneously conducted life, of a healthy and of a not abnormally adjusted personality. They seem to have a stake in their stale, artificial and enforced nobility which they jealously guard against closer examination. They resist insight because they do not believe in its moral dignity.

The *third* type of rationalization is an apparently mild and tolerant one. It is the bemused, sometimes flippant irony of the sceptic. He resists insight for the sake of affirming his independence, for the sake of cultivating a fastidiousness in the face of unwieldy certainties and senseless facts. One is reminded of those who aspire to a state of mind called by Keats Negative Capability. This is a condition in which '. . . a man is capable of being in uncertainties, mysteries, doubts, without any irritable reaching after fact and reason'. A man in this state of mind holds no brief for a dogma or revealed inspiration, he is just himself—a unique person—who rebels against being fitted into any generalization whatsoever. Sometimes he displays a sense of humour which would readily make a caricature of everything including health. The delightful cartoons, funny stories, and so on, which nowadays circulate at the expense of modern psychiatry are largely the creation of this mood.

'During the twenties [wrote F. C. Redlich] caricatures of psychiatrists in popular magazines were too rare to be counted. During the thirties only one of a thousand cartoons dealt with psychiatry. During the past few years, however, one to two out of 100 cartoons of the *Saturday Evening Post* and the *New Yorker* have dealt with psychiatrists and their patients. Psychiatric cartoons have become more frequent than cartoons about general practitioners and ministers.'[1]

Most of the time these are harmless enough reactions to the grotesque in human disbalance; nevertheless they are both expressions and inspirations of resistance. Humour, however, is a marginal form of this resistance. The resister who urges that humanity is far more complicated than the limited number of generalizations would allow often speaks with a less tolerant tongue than we should expect from one otherwise so sensitive and discerning. Writing one of his weekly notes in *The Observer*, Harold Nicolson lamented, '. . . psychology, with its ever-branching tributaries and rivulets, has become at this stage one of the world's worst bores'.[2] The satiety which prompted this wail was surely not caused by the psychologizing novel—upon which he was commenting—nor was it brought about by a solicitous impatience with multiple schisms in modern psychology. The nausea had deeper sources: it is the impatience of one who cannot forgive reductive psychology the impudence of having stolen the thunder from much artistic and intuitive characterization. It is the impatience of one who is put off by the austerity of psychological categories and by the uniformity of psychological portraiture. Sometimes the peculiarity of an art-form or the recurrence of a theme in a novelist's works can be better understood by means of modern clinical insights; yet, should one make an attempt to apply these insights to such characters of fiction as Hamlet or Heathcliff, the sceptic would receive the attempt with raised eyebrows—a customary reaction to irrelevancies and oddities. It is perfectly useless to me to know—he

---

[1] 'The Psychiatrist in Caricature: an Analysis of Unconscious Attitudes towards Psychiatry', *Amer. J. Orthopsychiatry*, July 1950, XX, pp. 560–71.
[2] London, 29 August 1954.

would exclaim—that Marcel Proust's exquisite melancholy was rooted in an unresolved Oedipus Complex. If what you say is true—the sceptic would protest—then millions must suffer of the same afflictions, yet there is only one Proust. In this the sceptic is right, of course. Unfortunately, by implication, he seems to affirm that the 'One Proust' rose above the common ailment and made it irrelevant to his genius. Proust most certainly did not accomplish that. We should know much less of art than we do and even less of the artist if we ignored modern clinical generalizations. Sir Herbert Read, whose authority and competence in these matters is not often questioned, wrote, '. . . I believe that knowledge which comes from a complete understanding of a poet's personality is the best basis for the appreciation of his poetry. For it is not a belief in the ideas or dogmas of a poet that is essential for the reader's poetic "assent" but rather a sympathy with his personality.'[1] He also declared this understanding to be fundamental to all aesthetic criticism:

. . . the only kind of criticism which is basic, and therefore complementary not only to technical exegesis but also to ethical, theological, philosophical and every other kind of ideological criticism, is ontogenetic criticism, by which I mean criticism which traces the origins of the work of art in the psychology of the individual and in the economic structure of society.

Although the present work does not concern itself with the economic structure of society, in its last chapter, it points to the way in which the 'abnorm' may be related to all sociological problems. Here, I am embattled with the view that the most essential traits of the artist's personality are inscrutable to science and those of his dynamic qualities which can be known and systematized are not decisively relevant to the appreciation of his art. In an age of disillusionment all explanation of the kind I suggest is suspect. The artist, as well as the public which is attuned to him, cling to the only remaining respectable sort of mysticism represented by the utterly inexplicable and sublime genius-role. The sceptic of psychological 'regimentation' often expostulates to defend this last of all illusions. Sometimes it is probably true that the sceptic-resister leaves an element of

---

[1] 'In Defence of Shelley' in the volume, *The True Voice of Feeling*, 1953, p. 246.

doubt in us whether he intends to resist at all. When he listens to our clinical interpretations and peppers our pauses with sarcastic asides, he may perhaps be wallowing in a resignation to the relative simplicity and uniformity of man's predicament. His sarcasm may mean, for all we know, that he agrees with us but he is bitter about it. As if he said, 'Aren't we wretchedly stereotyped creatures?'

The *fourth* type of rationalization is that of the addict to some other determinism, usually of an economic or social-cultural brand. The resister who indulges in this type of rationalization sits in a neatly compact ideological nest from which he throws out everything which may disturb his comfort. If one offers him a new explanation, or perhaps merely a supplement to his own explanations, he turns suspicious and even hostile. His ideology which is, as a rule, a political one, is a haven, a refuge for him, and anything that does not fit in smoothly or cannot be made to serve this ideology he regards as treacherous. Even when the new knowledge is unquestionably valid, it is described as hair-splitting 'objectivism' and useless punctiliousness. Hence it happens that the political fanatic and the mystic cannot tolerate the new psychological insights.

There is yet *another* kind of resister, perhaps the most difficult of all: he is the scientist. Not that all who bear the name 'scientist' would refuse to entertain a thesis when it cannot be demonstrated in the physical or chemical laboratory or when it cannot be measured. But there are only too many scientists whose ideas on proofs and evidence are still in the Aristotelian backwoods. These people cannot grasp the necessity of new scientific methods which, for the time being—if not for ever—must remain non-mathematical. When science is confronted with some utterly unassimilable and baffling material, some experience which is indubitably real yet scientifically inexplicable, e.g. hypnosis, extra-sensory perception, and in fact all the common psychological phenomena, it simply by-passes the *terra incognita* with the complacent assumption that the well-tried empirical methods of science will eventually explore those territories as well. It is only a question of time. 'The hatred against the discoverers of a phenomenon which threatened to undo cherished beliefs of science was as bitter and inexorable as that of the religious persecutors. . . . It was, in fact, of the same character.'[1] We must be on our guard, for the triumphant advance of the natural sciences and the consequent attitude among scientists towards yet greater technological feats has served to veil scientific dogmatism. Today, the scientist is most liberally ready to receive new substantive knowledge provided its methodological credentials are in order. Except in countries where science is ideologically censored the scientist enjoys the reputation of being the freest man from bias in the face of new substantive information. What is much less realized is that he opposes non-substantive, methodological deviations with the same medieval fervour which characterized the persecutors of Galileo. It is in this sense that Professor Polanyi's observation is valid even in our day.[2]

Surprisingly, the same methodological dogmatism is sometimes voiced by social scientists whose resistance to insight is by no means manifest. Margaret Mead writes, for instance:

> Exaggerated and poorly supported claims of the importance of the mother as a single figure in the infant's life . . . as Hilde Bruch has cogently pointed out, is a new subtle form of antifeminism in which men—under the guise of exalting the importance of maternity —are tying women more tightly to their children than has been thought necessary since the invention of bottle feeding and baby carriages.[3]

Margaret Mead asks us to bear in mind that so long as our aim is to breed mother-fixated sons to ensure monogamy this is the right policy; but, she implies, that objective might not answer the absolute bio-psychological needs of men. Here again, as so frequently elsewhere, the cry goes, 'Not enough evidence!' Evidence of what kind? I believe that the first section of the present chapter treated this problem with as much consideration as is possible at the present time and that the conclusions reached there will have to silence our doubts unless, of course, we prefer the conclusion that psychological knowledge is impossible.

In addition to these five types there is the clinically trained resister who has learnt about the new psychological insights

[1] Michael Polanyi, *The Logic of Liberty*, 1951, p. 15.

[2] For a somewhat brief yet stimulating paper on these issues, cf. 'Anti-Psycho-analytical Forces in the Development of Western Civilization', by Silvano Arieti, *Amer. J. Psychotherapy*, Jan. 1952, VI, pp. 63–78.

[3] 'Some Theoretical Considerations on the Problem of Mother-Child Separation', *Amer. J. Orthopsychiatry*, July 1954, XXIV, pp. 471–83.

and has intellectually accepted them all—even those which the more sober observer or clinical worker may describe as somewhat extravagant. This resister, of course, would know of the phenomenon of resistance. His unquestioning, enthusiastic acceptance of a reductive psychological theory may provide him with valid interpretations of behaviour and personality but, alas, these interpretations only superficially apply to him who so vehemently adopted them. One sort of defence this resister may take to is well described by Bertram D. Lewin in the following report:

> I . . . assumed that the condition which evokes a denial during analysis, namely intellectual insight without emotional self-commitment, is also provocative of elation or depression, especially the former, and that similar insight or near insight in ordinary life might have the same effect.

Nothing is more suspect than the so-called psychiatric utopianism of the mental hygienist. The present thesis, affirming as it does that the disbalance of man is universal and inevitable, is far from being utopianistic. It is only too true that '. . . exaggerated belief covers a profound unbelief'.[1] At the same time, when he assesses others, we must not judge this resister on the basis of his motives; here he may still be accurate though his self-assessment is open to criticism.

4. *'The Ethics of Insight-Giving'*

These resistances to insight should be viewed against the background of a multitude of reports from authoritative sources which tell us of the incidence of neurotic disorders (abnormal primary adjustment conditions) in our modern communities. It is, of course, not suggested here that insight-giving is a simple medicine for this condition. But prevention, effective, long-term prevention, is well-nigh impossible without adding to the insight of those in particular who are in charge of children. A good deal of our large-scale measures—those, for instance, which are incorporated in the Education Act and the Children's Act in Britain—are weakened because the administration and execution of those measures are largely in the hands of people

---

[1] Melitta Schmiedeberg, op. cit., p. 128.

who have little or no insight. Such people as these may thrive on any of the available rationalizations and gain added fervour from them for their obsolete convictions. But insight-giving is not a matter of simple instruction, a matter of handing out information. I have sufficiently stressed that a lack of insight is most frequently coupled with a rationalization which is a source of security to the individual. Take away the man's cataract and the glaring conflicts of his world will promptly make him shut his eyes. It is obvious, therefore, that insight-giving, if it is to be beneficial to the recipient, must obey certain technical rules without which it is nothing much else than pro-vocation and aggression, though unconscious, on the part of the insight-giver. Before I continue developing this theme it is advisable to bear in mind that I am not here concerned with the technique of insight-giving in reductive psycho-therapy. The literature of psycho-therapy amply caters for those who are engaged in 'insight-giving' as part of their healing work. A much more momentous issue is the disseminating of primary insights *outside* the clinical routine for the purpose of creating a new cultural atmosphere in which both preventive and large-scale attenuating measures could be increased. The social welfare measures of the modern states include a substantial number of provisions for this very end without an adequate preparation of either personnel or technique. My analysis of the problems of insight-giving in this area may interest the practising therapist as a citizen, but can hardly benefit him as a clinical practitioner.

It is still generally believed that there are two reasons for inquiring into the condition of man: the quest may be impelled by the curiosity to find out what is true about man or it may be inspired and sustained by the desire to lighten the burden of man's existence. In the ultimate resort the first motive is spurious; upon examination it usually turns out to be the second. Also we have learnt by now that not every find, in the kind of search for knowledge which claims the first motive, is an addition to our happiness. As it is, every increase in our understanding has to earn its place among the benefits which make human life endurable. The *a priori* affirmation of 'truth for truth's sake' can lead to dangerous idealism. Contributions to human welfare are often mingled with a subtle element of deception. In the non-clinical dissemination of primary insights the rift between truth and goodness unashamedly widens when appropriate technical rules of dissemination are not available or when the available rules are ignored. Now the conflict between truth and goodness is a rather hackneyed topic of ethical textbooks. The sort of thing one reads there is too gross and too palpable to guide us with insight-giving. For example, '. . . to save a friend's life at the cost of concealing bad news by a lie would be a less evil than the voluntary causing of his death by speaking the truth'.[1] Compare this with the following clinical examples: 'To achieve my aim I exaggerated the possible gravity of a symptom, and frightened the patient.'[2] Or, 'He (August Aichorn) shows them (young delinquents) how well he understands them and humbly he even goes the length of assuring them (and somewhat infringes on veracity for the sake of a positive transference) that he would have acted the same way in their place',[3] i.e. he would have stolen, played truant, and so on. Insight-giving on these clinical occasions may proceed with greater moral licence for through the close relationship between therapist and patient the latter is likely to arrive at the truth eventually. Freud himself seemed to justify this when he quoted Polonius saying 'Our bait of falsehood has taken a carp of truth'. Clearly this licence is not permissible outside the clinical situation. In education, general welfare work, in the insight-giving ventures of the press, theatre, wireless, cinema, television —ruse, disguise, and deception cannot operate without grave risks. In these fields the insight-givers remain impersonal, distant agents and there is no consolidated, lasting personal relationship in which to work through towards truth. For this reason it is regrettable that no systematic study has yet been written on the techniques of mass-insight-giving, an omission which is becoming increasingly evident. In commenting on Lawrence Frank's book, *Society as the Patient*, Margaret Mead writes:

. . . Individual Americans reading a book about American society are not themselves patients voluntarily come to a consulting room, where as they are treated they are also protected against insights that

[1] Hastings Rashdall, *The Theory of Good and Evil*, 1924, p. 92.
[2] Anna Freud, *The Psychoanalytical Treatment of Children*, 1946, p. 15.
[3] *Searchlight on Delinquency*, 1949, 'Therapy and Ethics in August Aichorn's Treatment of Wayward Youth', by Oskar Pfister, p. 37.

crowd too fast upon them. Just because the aberrations of the maladjusted are systematically related to the best behaviour of the well-
adjusted, discussion of these aspects of culture may have undesirable
effects in given contexts.[1]

Margaret Mead is anxious lest unguarded insight-giving should
result only in the strengthening of certain rigid moral defences
and lead to a 'destructive crusade' by some who could accomplish this against those who would merely turn out to be
weaker.

. . . For those whose cultural adjustment is precarious [she goes
on], such discussion may even be dangerous . . . When one writes
in a way that is easily accessible to all interested citizens [she is
referring to the Kinsey Report], I believe one should put oneself in
those readers' place, and not force them either to accept or reject
interpretations the implications of which they would not have
chosen to hear had they been fully aware of them . . . We must also,
at least as the world is organized to-day, push away such detailed
knowledge . . .

In case the complexity of the subject may conceal it I may as
well make the gist of this plea bluntly explicit: the truth must
not be unreservedly published for there may be many who
would not benefit from it. Margaret Mead entitles her chapter
on these matters, 'The Ethics of Insight-Giving', and indeed
this is a fundamental ethical problem which demands close
attention. On the one hand I sympathize with the view according
to which the individual's integrity should sometimes be protected from his would-be saviours, but the indiscriminate advocacy of such policies as these is even more dangerous. How are
we to ward off the next wave of obscurantism? How are we to
shield ourselves against the last wave which has not yet receded?
Karl Mannheim who seemed to share Mead's anxieties regarded
opposition between the analytic truths of psychology and the
communing with the grandeur of total reality as irreconcilable
and fatal. In his view the piecemeal perception of our motives
and feelings results in their disintegration.

Frequently what is a gain for scientific knowledge is a loss for
integration of personality and social cohesion . . . Here it is no
longer the obscurant who protests because he fears the dissemina-

[1] *Male and Female*, 1949, p. 448.

tion of knowledge, it is the educator seeing the dissolution of those basic images of our fantasy—the core of our everyday experience and the light in which we co-operate.[1]

In this our age we have irrevocably renounced the consolations of ignorance; we have also become all but insensible to the naïve peace of ingenuousness. Although we have so far failed to produce an easy formula by which we could unite innocence with knowledge it is not because we have lost the capacity for innocence but because we have not acquired enough knowledge. One wonders how 'those basic images of our fantasy' so often the source of much obscurantism could rescue us from obscurantism. If certain unifying images come naturally to a sane life the science which dispels them is not scientific enough.[2] Man has always viewed the acquisition of knowledge with apprehension and the foregoing instances of this attitude are not novel signs, e.g. 'He that increaseth knowledge increaseth sorrow' (Eccles. i. 18). From time to time one comes across this ostrich-philosophy in all sorts of contexts; a typical instance of this is the following, '. . . from the human standpoint, the important thing is less that man's will should be free than that man should think it is free.'[3] Meanwhile the problem is not how to protect people against insight but how to procure it for them. There is no doubt that insight which harms is not insight for it will be resisted by a redoubled deception. I cannot shirk the trouble of examining in some greater detail those features of the clinical process which have their counterpart in non-clinical insight-giving. In the course of the brief study which follows I shall find that some at least of Mead's apprehensions and Mannheim's concerns may be allayed. The method I propose to employ is to follow up the insight-giving process in three representative situations graded in such a way that the closeness of the personal relationship between insight-giver and recipient is progressively lessened.

(1) A distracted mother of three children consults a psychiatric social worker in a child guidance clinic and complains to her that her eldest child, a boy of eleven, is unmanageable. He steals,

---

[1] *Freedom, Power and Democratic Planning*, 1951, p. 290.

[2] Though relying exclusively on a Jungian psychology this is well shown by P. W. Martin in *Experiment in Depth*, 1955.

[3] Sir Charles Sherrington in *Man on His Nature*, p. 230.

lies, plays truant and is destructive. She says that she is at the end of her tether and, though she finds it painful to confess, she admits that she has come to hate the boy. She also tells the psychiatric social worker that she has divorced her first husband, the boy's father, who deserted her. Since then she has remarried and the other two children are by her second husband. When she speaks of her first husband she condemns his character with insincere firmness. It appears from what she lets drop in the course of some of her interviews with the psychiatric social worker that the growing boy's physical features strongly remind her of her first husband and engender in her a violent hostility towards the boy. After some prolonged interviews the psychiatric social worker concludes that the mother's moral condemnation of her first husband is a reaction-formation, for she is still in love with her first husband and is dissatisfied with her second. Although the clinical worker sees this constellation clearly and understands the recent sequences in the secondary process, she has little knowledge, if any, of the primary factors which preceded them. This is, after all, not a full-scale psycho-analytical procedure and, in spite of some resemblances, i.e. transference, free-association, and after some sessions, in favourable circumstances, even anamnesia, the technique is often desultory and the relationship short-lived. In clinical interviews of this nature primary insights are harder to come by than in protracted individual psycho-therapy. Nevertheless in both these situations neither psycho-analyst nor psychiatric social worker would turn upon the patient and present her with an interpretation as soon as it is available. Should they do so, the patient may break contact with therapist or clinic and stay away, perhaps even more disturbed than she was before. In our case the clinical worker's purpose is to save the boy and with him the adequate functioning of the family as a whole. She knows that this can be achieved only if the mother gains the insight and develops the will to change her attitude towards the boy. The worker, therefore, starts by expressing sympathy for the mother and by encouraging her to come regularly and talk to the worker about her worries and difficulties. In the course of many meetings she leads the mother very gradually on to the discovery of some of her motives. Eventually the mother acquires some insight into the secondary motives of her condition and may develop a more tolerant as well as less rejecting attitude towards her son. There are, of course, other techniques which may accompany this treatment, the disturbed boy may be receiving treatment too; but here I am not concerned with the clinical procedure in its entirety; it is the handling of the mother under such conditions as I have described that yields us the first technical principle of insight-giving. This principle applies to *all* therapeutic situations and in its simplest form appears to be the following: *Don't tell the truth, but help others to discover it for themselves.* One must, however, realize that there are exceptions to this rule; e.g. sometimes immediate 'shock-interpretations' may be effective not so much because they are time-saving but because the personality of the patient may respond to these favourably. It is true that often these shock-interpretations are coupled with suggestions, persuasions, and ethical or even religious inspiration; one should not hesitate to insist that the cause of insight-giving, that is to say, of self-knowledge, is not furthered by these appreciably. On the whole, the co-operative, piecemeal recovery of truth is the only thoroughly effective method of insight-giving. The rate of progress will depend on the insight-tolerance of the patient which is impressionistically assessed by the therapist.

(2) Let us now suppose that a lecturer in psychology is confronted with a class of social workers, medical students, or teachers. His relationship with his students is, as a rule, somewhat ephemeral and consists of addressing them from the impersonal distance of the lecture-platform over a limited number of occasions. He may also work with the students in more informal tutorial or seminar sessions, but even here the students will not normally contribute personal material to the discussion; the average academic environment would not encourage communicativeness of this nature although cultural differences may allow more personal testimony in some communities than in others. If the lecturer possesses some insight—and one would not like to think that he does not—he will discuss personality development at some length. He will be obliged to describe, for instance, as imaginatively and thoroughly as he is capable, the far-reaching consequences of an early separation of mother and child, to use a random example. He will point to certain personality traits in the adult which are the signs of acute disbalance,

and link this with the experience of having been abandoned or rejected by the mother in infancy or early childhood. Now there may be some students in his class who have had such an experience as this and whose so far well-controlled anxiety is aroused by the lecturer's discussion. Mischief may be caused by teaching of this nature in a number of ways. To illustrate one of these: many young people find it difficult to control their resentment against their parents. It is a resentment which they cannot allow fully to enter their consciousness. As the lecture course will necessarily cover the whole range of primary disbalance it is likely that a goodly number of students will always readily identify themselves with the heroes and heroines of case-histories presumably included in the discussion. One repercussion of this may be that they will release some of the resentment harboured by them against their parents and will feel deeply justified in doing so, for they now 'know' that their parents are to be blamed for mistakes which they have committed in their early upbringing. One may say that this outcome is salutary and a discharge of resentment clears the air, yet it is by no means certain that the frictions created thereby can be discounted. At any rate the teacher of the subject of personality development is in duty bound to define his point of view in the face of such repercussions as these. Of course, the hypochondriac medical student who believes he has the symptom of that physical disease which he happens to be studying, receives no protection. No one would seriously consider sheltering the medical student from anxieties of this nature by withholding certain information from him. There is, however, a very different attitude shown by people who object to an intensive instruction in personality development to young students of education, of social work, of psychology, and so on. They are afraid that the deep-lying conflicts of students will only be raked up by an instruction which gives merely an analysis of their conflicts and disbalances, and supplements it with no inspiration for a synthesis of their personalities. They are afraid that students will adopt an introspective, self-centred preoccupation, blaming for all their shortcomings the ignorance and negligence of their parents and shifting all their responsibilities on to causes outside their control. Notwithstanding these misgivings the people who have them or give them expression often pay lip-service to the teaching of psychology to doctors, educators, social workers and others, and it is with their explicit agreement, or, at least, with their tolerance, that some kind of psychology is in fact included in almost all these courses. But on closer examination one usually finds that lecturers and tutors steer clear of the reductive theories of personality development and teach a very much bowderlized psychology. It is not that they advocate the first technical rule of insight-giving, as stated above, but that they themselves are anxious to avoid reactivating their own primary disbalance through any measure of preoccupation with that subject.

Those who in the future come under the care of our educators, social workers, doctors and others, have the right to a well-instructed and well-informed treatment. Insight in the teacher, social worker, and doctor is an essential condition of such treatment. Preventive steps against unserviceable disbalance cannot be restricted to the clinical consulting room. That way lies eventual failure for the mental hygiene movement. Nor may we any longer leave the acquisition of insight to the benevolent chances of life experience. It is no longer permissible to rely on the future experience of the student to bridge all the gaps of his training, nor is it any more permissible to expect him to refrain from pathogenic influence on others because he has undergone the approved religious or ideological conversion. In short, we may not say with a clear conscience that we cannot teach or must not attempt to teach self-knowledge.

The policies nowadays drafted for the training of personnel in the various fields of child-care, to take one example, teem with unresolved contradictions and a pious verbosity. The cause of all the hesitation and confusion is in this: no one has attempted to face the task of defining the rules of insight-giving in an area like this and almost all is left to momentary intuition or to the discretion of those who are in charge. One can find examples of indecision on the highest levels. In a report of a joint *WHO-UNESCO* Expert Meeting[1] we find some passages which repay careful analysis. Writing of the role of the nursery-school teacher the Report states, 'A young nursery-school teacher is not orientated biologically to any one child, *except indirectly through identification with a mother figure*' [italics mine]. A little further

[1] *Mental Hygiene in the Nursery School*, Unesco, Paris, 1951.

down we read 'On the assumption that the nursery school supplements and extends in certain directions the functions of the good home, the nursery school teacher naturally takes over some of the attributes and duties of the mother for the school period, *without however seeking out of her own needs to develop a maternal emotional bond*' [italics mine]. The italicized passages contain advice which reflects a hesitation on the part of the authors whether they should or should not discuss the true motives of women for seeking employment as nursery-school teachers. The report, an admirably sound document in many respects, shirks decision on insight-giving, for although it advocates a mental hygiene bias it continues to speak of the 'normal' problem of childhood and of the 'gross psycho-pathological disorders' of childhood as of two separate themes. With regard to the latter the Report observes:

This aspect of child study, especially if it is backed by much first-hand experience of clinical case work may lead to wrong emphasis, and is in any case liable to attract the potential nursery school teacher away from the work for which she is training towards the field of child guidance. It is wisest, therefore, to base the teaching chiefly on the clinical study of the 'normal' problems of childhood rather than the grossly abnormal.

So long as this recommendation is taken to mean that teaching material should correspond to what the nursery-school teacher will meet in her work it suffers from the following shortcomings:

(*a*) The writers of the Report should have known that the resistance of those to whom the Report is addressed will inevitably dilute a recommendation of this sort. They should have been more specific.

(*b*) The persistent dualism of 'normal-abnormal' merely reinforces the popular ideology and conceals the principle of continuity which characterizes human disbalance. No insight-giving is effective without the clear and effective demonstration of this continuity. Neither is a unified mental hygiene philosophy possible without the understanding of this continuity.

The emphatic insistence on teaching unreservedly a unified theory of personality development and of communicating the entire outline of what is known is my second technical rule. It appears, therefore, that the restraints and delays which are expedient in clinical therapy do not apply here. There are, however, important qualifications to be added to this rule. We must explore new ways in which teaching could be made less impersonal and study the conditions under which tutorials, including personal aid and counsel could supplement class teaching. There is nothing unprecedented in demanding so much as this from the teacher of educators, social workers, and the like. The ancient conception, and I might add the true conception of the philosopher-teacher, included the functions of friendship and guidance. It is only in a degraded mass-teaching process that the true meaning of education is lost and impersonal indoctrination takes its place. Meanwhile, in the classroom, the lecturer or teacher should vividly portray the great ennobling virtue of insight and link its pursuit to the ultimate value of truth. It is time that we sought to remove the notorious connotation of 'debunking' from the concept of insight-giving and replace it with the meaning of 'truth-seeking'. Herein lies the distinctly ethical inspiration which justifies my technical rule even according to traditional moral orientation. Admittedly a small number of students in these courses of teaching may react all too negatively to instruction such as I am advocating here; also we may find that some of these may become too disturbed to gain from further training; yet it is not too calculating to suppose that, if they give up their training it will, at least, save those who would have been their future charges from the ministrations of abnormally adjusted individuals.[1]

(3) Having discussed the technical issues of insight-giving in the consulting room and in the lecture theatre or class room I now turn to the contemporary media of mass-communication. Whereas patient and student come into the orbit of a systematic guidance, broadly speaking, from their own choice, this cannot be said of the average wireless listener, television-viewer, cinema and theatre audience, or newspaper reader. Furthermore, the key-word 'systematic' in the foregoing sentence decisively separates the general public from the first two categories. An uncontrolled, planless, and unreserved dissemination of insights in this area is to be rejected for it is simply inexpedient and even

[1] Cf. 'The Training of Social Workers and the Teaching of Psychology', by Paul Halmos, *Social Work*, Jan. 1949.

demonstrably pathogenic. Nevertheless mass-communication media represent a most effectual arm of the mental hygiene strategy. So far the manipulation of these instruments has resembled guerilla warfare with a goodly number of outlaws, brigands, and looters, masquerading as patriotic guerillas. Although the discrimination of these is sometimes comparatively easy, even for the average intelligent person, in many cases he cannot escape being misled.

The dramatic representation of psychological problems and healing methods are frequent features of broadcasting these days. One example of such programmes is the graphic account of the work of child guidance clinics. A clinical worker told the present writer some years ago that her clinic's attendance had noticeably increased because mothers who had listened to the broadcasts eagerly followed them up by hurrying to the place where great things would be done for their difficult children. As it is, even now, there are not enough child guidance clinics to deal with all abnormally adjusted parents and children. The clinical worker's conclusion was that an otherwise informative broadcast might lead to disappointments when it did not give a comprehensive picture of the inadequacies of institutional provisions, of personnel, and of therapeutic techniques. In her view disappointments also arise from another almost inevitable characteristic of this sort of publicity. Programmes of this kind set out to explain highly complicated personality problems in a simplified manner—not infrequently attempting to induce confidence by reporting the more attractive success stories—and thus raise hopes which neither the institutional provisions nor the present efficacy of treatment methods may subsequently fulfil. On the other hand the complacency and superficiality of some of the 'let-me-help-you' columns, the useless sentimentality of so many journalistic features, the thinly veiled pornography, and the horrific portraiture of abnormal adjustment, are so palpably outside the sphere of insight-giving that they can be repudiated without further examination. The third rule of insight-giving is pertinent to the field of mass-communication. It is to be derived from extensive research into the impact of these media on the primary institutions of a community, and especially from research into their insight-giving potentialities. Yet even before these research results are available I would advance the simple rule that what is harmful is not insight-giving. I exempted the second area from this simple rule because harm caused there to the immediate recipient is cancelled out by the avoidance of harm to future charges of these recipients. In the third area the simple rule is unconditionally valid. By 'harm' I understand an increase in unserviceable disbalance. Whether the mass-media of communication operate harmfully in this respect is to be ascertained as far as possible with the help of research. Pending investigations of this nature the third rule is: *disseminate insights so long as you can be reasonably certain that the majority receive them as such.*

A further step in my discussion of these processes is necessary if I am to avoid giving a superficial impression of what really happens. Unless a personal therapeutic advantage is gained by the recipients it is somewhat fanciful to think that primary insights are, in fact, gained. One may take it for granted that in the third area it would be most exceptional if more than secondary insights materialized. In the second area much depends on the teaching methods and their subsidiaries (group-discussions, tutorials, and so on) yet even here primary insights would open up only infrequently. It is in the first area of insight-giving that primary insights are deliberately sought. This is, of course, truer of individual psycho-therapy than of child guidance work with mothers. Clearly in the second and third area, much of the work done definitely aims at an objective which I must separate even from secondary insights. The importance of this objective in any community is in inverse ratio to the insights of the average man. This objective is *preventive instruction.* If, for example, a student of child-care is taught imaginatively enough to understand that on the whole 'a bad mother is better than a good institution' no matter how little primary insight, if any, materializes from this understanding the acceptance of the slogan will prevent the student from taking overhasty administrative action eventually when she is called upon to decide whether or not she should arrange to send a child to an institution. It is, of course, not the slogan which will ensure her circumspection and a careful weighing of all available information but the theory and research evidence on the mother-child relationship which she has been taught unreservedly. If an article in some women's journal explains that we must tell an adopted child about his adoptive origin before he finds out about it from others, we are again witnessing preventive instruction and only incidentally insight-giving. Being instructed in matters of personality development is sometimes referred to as 'intellectual insight'. This is a misnomer. Intellectual insight is not insight: it is a logical construction the premises of which are accepted on trust. Nevertheless without this spearhead of the mental hygiene strategy we can do almost nothing to reduce unserviceable disbalance in contemporary man. Unfortunately the literature of personality development, and particularly psycho-analytical sources, are not sufficiently appreciative of the value of preventive instruction. The sort of thing one reads is, for instance, '. . . we know that even if parents have insight on an intellectual level and do not *do* anything harmful to the child, but are highly neurotic, the child has but small chance of normal development'.[1] Similar arguments are often related to the positions of the educator, the social worker, and the like. One wonders whether the profound scepticism of this view is understood by those who hold it? It is also a demonstrably misleading view: 'not doing anything harmful' to the child goes a very long way. Neurotic parents who don't do anything harmful to the child are very much preferable to those neurotic parents who are also ignorant into the bargain and consequently do a lot of harm. There is a large scope for preventive instruction in the three areas particularly in the second and third.

Yet preventive instruction is all too often a precarious affair. Among several others Theodore Reik complained rather forcibly about the anomalies created by instruction without insight-giving:

I am afraid of the ease and facility with which they put labels on very complicated human developments. Such throwing around of technical terms can conceal a void full of pretensions. It can easily be confused with a penetrating comprehension of unconscious processes. It can lead to a false show of knowledge that remains peripheral. It can seduce a man into thinking in psychoanalytical clichés and in terms of a card-index science instead of one of personal experience.

People learn the shibboleths with surprising avidity; it is a

[1] 'Incentives to Development and Means of Early Education', by L. E. Peller, *Psychoanalytical Study of the Child*, 1946, II, p. 398.

short-cut to the complacent awareness of being in the know. This is regrettable yet not altogether harmful. It is conceivable that a parrotlike memorization of do's and don't's in antenatal care, in parental guidance, and even in certain phases of student training fetches returns of no mean value. We cannot afford to be fastidious and reject minor attenuating methods out of perfectionist scrupulousness. Preventive instruction, even of the mechanical kind, has always the potentiality of turning into insight eventually, although this is not to be taken for granted. Much of our general education makes use of this sort of anticipation. For example, the uncommonness of literary and artistic appreciation in the young does not withhold us from the teaching of the arts and many are the instances of people discovering the inner sense of a work of art with which they have originally formed a soulless acquaintance.

There is a well-known objection to the dissemination of insights which I should also include in my scrutiny. It is believed that the so-called instinctual spontaneity of man is worth far more than any amount of articulate self-knowledge we may assist him to attain. The *Docta Ignorantia* of Nicolaus Cusanus is an early although typical formula of this; even earlier is the teaching of Plotinus and his followers to whom reason of any kind was suspect and a useless burden. The theme of 'Blessed are the poor in spirit: for theirs is the kingdom of heaven' (Matthew v. 2) lingers on and appears in modern forms like, 'Appalling is the condition of man; there is no drop of happiness in his lot but has its source in ignorance.'[1] An echo of this is audible in contemporary psychological and psychiatric opinion which justly puts a great deal of trust in instinctive feeling whilst regrettably giving no credit to articulate and conscious knowledge, and does so in the face of disappointing evidence to the contrary. A good specimen of this tendency occurs in the *WHO-UNESCO* Report. 'A mother need not have intellectual understanding of her job because she is fitted for it in its essentials by her biological orientation to her own baby. It is the fact of her devotion to her own baby rather than her self-conscious knowledge that makes her good enough to be successful in the early stages of infant-nurture.' Now there are a good many reasons why an emphasis on instinctual spontaneity is out of

[1] Balzac, *Eugénie Grandet.*

191

place at this time. Firstly we may consider that '. . . in the year 1944/45 alone no less than 107,312 children coming from 41,050 different families were dealt with by the National Society for Prevention of Cruelty to Children . . .'[1]; it is simply not true that this large scale break-down was caused exclusively by a 'faulty biological orientation' in respect of babies, or for that matter, of children. Secondly, mothers belong to the species of 'cultural man' and not of 'instinctual man', that is to say, their instinctual spontaneity is already canalized in cultural channels most of which may be leading away from an increasingly parched region of life, motherhood. The haste to go out to work, in order to get the satisfaction of companionship (cohesion) in the workplace, or to increase the family income for higher cultural standards which may be secured thereby, or the comparative ease with which this 'instinctual spontaneity' may be sent hibernating while the upper-middle and upper class mother goes away for a holiday and leaves her under-fives in the care of grandmother or of frequently changing nannies—all these make us sceptical of spontaneity. The many other forms in which cultural standards envelop the 'instinctual' mother and divert her from her 'biological orientation' no longer permit us to depend on spontaneity. Both insight-giving and preventive instruction, which are after all complementary, are culturally devised to counteract the deviations from biological orientations. A hankering for primitive spontaneity is incompatible with the culture in which we are obliged to live. This reliance on the spontaneous love of the mother is reinforced by a psychiatric scepticism which is becoming more and more articulate these days. Clinical specialists often advise against insight-giving because they regard it as useless or downright harmful, e.g. '. . . personality disturbances in children and adolescents may develop in spite of, and even on account of, the psychological indoctrination to which their parents had been subjected'.[2] I have no doubt that they may so develop yet this statement is only partially true and as such it is reactionary. That '. . . injudicious parent education may overburden parents with guilt

---

[1] *The Neglected Child and his Family*, 1948, p. 13.

[2] 'Parent Education or the Illusion of Omnipotence', by Hilde Bruch, *Amer. J. Orthopsychiatry*, Oct. 1954, XXIV, pp. 723–32. Also cf. *Don't Be Afraid of Your Child*, by Hilde Bruch, 1952.

and anxiety' is by now well-known. It is, however, noticeable that without a precise indication as to what is and what is not injudicious, authoritative pronouncements of this sort are already having undesirable consequences. It is one thing to rail against 'experts' who 'bully' parents and against the feelings of 'morbid consciousness' as well as of 'fear of incompetence' created in parents by these experts, and another thing to undermine the mental hygiene movement by alleging that parents and teachers have been 'too much impressed by the *supposed modern scientific knowledge* of how children should be brought up' [italics mine].[1] So we see that the otherwise salutary scepticism of the clinically experienced and reductively trained psychologists and psychiatrists is now being put to work for resistances with which we have long been familiar. This psychiatric scepticism, apart from being sobering and moderating, also accommodates a few fallacies. In the first place it ignores the difference which, according to psycho-analysis, exists between the so-called traumatic neuroses and character neuroses. It is particularly the former, which are largely the consequence of specifiable shock experiences, that preventive instruction will indubitably affect. That rupture experiences are of two kinds, i.e. episodic, isolable, distinct and biographically conspicuous on the one hand, and protracted, systematic, largely concealed, and sustained by the parent's own abnormal adjustment condition, is ignored by this newly awakened scepticism. Surely, the effectiveness of preventive instruction is not deserving of the same scepticism in the first case as it is in the second? And even in the second instance, is it not true that a character neurosis can be fatally aggravated and complicated by traumatic experiences which do not follow from the parent's abnormal adjustment but from his plain ignorance of what is right? Those who are most emphatic in their scepticism usually proceed by attributing fantastic assumptions to the advocates of preventive instruction. For instance, Hilde Bruch attacks the

... assumption of parent education, namely, that telling people what to do will change their behaviour and emotional attitude. It is fallacious to assume that psychological prescriptions can be carried out in this way. Whatever the psychological advice, one can be sure that it will be put into practice in as many ways as there are parents.

[1] *The Times*, 30 Dec. 1954.

Instructing parents in 'right feelings and attitudes' neglects the fundamental tenet of psycho-analysis, namely that most of what is going on in the emotional interplay between parents and children is more or less outside simple verbal instruction. Children respond to the genuine, though often unconscious emotional attitudes of their parents and are not fooled by intellectualized and pretended feelings.

It is wise and proper to bear these things in mind and not to expect too much from preventive instruction. Yet it is injudicious to allow these arguments to assist the hardening of resistance to insight. Furthermore, it is wrong to attribute these assumptions to those workers who know that nothing more than a piecemeal betterment can be accomplished through preventive instruction and who are well aware that basic personality changes cannot be brought about through 'instruction'. One suspects that the energy with which views of this sceptical nature are put abroad these days is inspired by the disappointment in the effectiveness of the new insights. These disappointments are more bitter when the initial trust and expectation are greater. It is probable that the explanation for the spirited warnings of some psycho-analysts may be found in the libidinal dialectics of their own careers, and not in a strictly rational assessment of the situation. It is also possible that an understandable impatience with piece-meal betterment conceals the remaining benefits of preventive instruction and induces the sceptic to seek a solution somewhere else altogether. Or, perhaps, it is an unconscious attempt at securing an almost extraterritorial apartness and superiority to the clinical analytic situation with which, presumably, no other situation is really comparable. As if there was a possibility of impoverishing the prestige of the consulting room by exporting some of its techniques in appropriately modified form to less privately closeted human relationships. The ancestry of these apprehensions goes back to Freud who, of course, could not be blamed for not extending his already many-sided interests and researches to the sociological problems of insight-giving. Writing of interpretations which do not register affectively in the patient, he explains:

We have increased his (the patient's) knowledge but effected no other change in his mind. We have much the same situation when people read psycho-analytical writings. The reader is 'stimulated'

194

only by those passages which he feels apply to himself, i.e. which refer to conflicts that are active in him. Everything else leaves him cold. I think we have a similar experience when we enlighten children on matters of sex. I am far from maintaining that this is a harmful or unnecessary thing to do, but it is clear that the prophylactic effect of this liberal measure has been vastly over-estimated . . . For a long time after they have been enlightened on these subjects they behave like primitive races who have had Christianity thrust upon them and continue in secret to worship their old idols.[1]

Once again the truth is more succinctly expressed in Freud's metaphor than in his reflections: the ancient Teutons, Gauls, and Britons were primitive races who had 'Christianity thrust upon them'; and eventually the slow and merciless power of the moral truths in Christianity have squeezed out most of the pagan morality and practices of the European peoples. By all means see to it that no immediate returns are expected from preventive instruction but take note that no return of any kind will be secured without it. Preventive instruction is an instrument of progressive social betterment, not of revolution.

There can be little doubt that even the mother who loves her child unreservedly—without being oversolicitous—is also constantly exposed to normative control by society. In all ages and in all communities the primary institutions of life, the specific rules of child-care, have been ready-made for mothers no matter whether their own adjustment condition was normal or abnormal. To say in these circumstances that preventive instruction is useless because the mother's spontaneous love for the child is all that is wanted is unrealistic. In a book by a psychiatrist and a sociologist it is suggested that beyond an emotional acceptance of the child there is little more for the mother to do.

She may, without serious consequences ignore every precept laid down in every book on child care, being guided solely by her love and by the reactions of gratification or distress in her child. But, out of her deep love, she is ever eager to accept common-sense advice, such as offered in books to-day, in the past offered by older women. As in modern circumstances, she usually finds it difficult to establish such contact with women who have had children, she is forced very

---

[1] 'Analysis Terminable and Interminable' (1937), *Collected Papers*, 1952, V, p. 336.

often to rely on books, magazines, lectures and newspapers. But no amount of guidance by books or physicians can be a substitute for her inflexible love.[1]

We readily agree that instruction cannot make up for the lack of maternal affection. Yet the obvious truth of this may harbour the fallacy of a fatalistic attitude. In the first place it is by no means certain that the inspirational value of instruction is negligible in terms of increased maternal love. Secondly, as I have already explained, preventive instruction can reduce the occasions of severe rupture thereby setting up moderate 'virtuous circles' in the mother-child relationship. And thirdly, it is most illogical to spread scepticism about the hygienic value of preventive instruction when as a matter of historical and sociological fact all communities have always engaged in prescribing for the mother and hampering her spontaneity. The 'loving mother' does not exist in a cultural vacuum; indeed she will wish to do well for her child by tapping all the maternity lore of her culture. To shelter the well-disposed mother from adopting rules which are harmful a well-informed preventive instruction is essential. To oppose this would mean that we are content to say that, 'people have as much insight as they have and we can do nothing to increase it'. The fallacy of this fatalism is too obvious to be laboured any further.[2] Another form opposition sometimes takes is to construe instruction as invariably pathogenic when it falls short of genuine insight-giving. It is believed that with this kind of instruction the recipient's ego is furnished with the Davy-lamp of 'intellectual insight' without the mask to protect him against the subterranean fumes of aggression and guilt. Norman Reider provides us with a clinical illustration of the inaccuracy of this apprehension. He tells us of a compulsive character who acquires an intellectual understanding of the nature of his behaviour and thereupon develops a compensative irregularity and disorderliness to protect himself against what he now understands to be a symptom. Reider re-

[1] *The Modern Woman, the Lost Sex*, by F. Lundberg and M. F. Farnham, 1947, p. 487.

[2] That the charge of fatalism has some substance is already being recognized by leading psycho-analysts, e.g. 'It is our job to express . . . insight in terms that will arouse parents' initiative and not to express it in a form that will induce a fatalistic attitude' (E. H. Erikson in *Symposium on the Healthy Personality*, ed. M. J. E. Senn, 1950, p. 56).

marks that this is now '. . . a great reassurance to him since it is "normal" ',[1] i.e. statistically normal. Reider calls this condition 'pseudo-normality' and claims that it 'works'; that is to say it aids the compulsive individual to develop more self-confidence and assists him in his adjustment to his immediate environment. If preventive instruction to the not so well-disposed mothers achieves no more than a pseudo-normality in certain sectors of their personality, the beneficial modification of the mother-child relationship, in however modest a measure, cannot be questioned.

Yet another form of opposition to preventive instruction appears in a moral guise. This consists in the demand to refrain from self-examination, equating the latter with selfishness. This obscurantism is especially ominous when put forward as a life-philosophy.

Self-forgetfulness [wrote the late C. E. M. Joad], herein lies the justification of my description of the self as a little pit of vanity and desire from which it is our duty, so far as possible, to avert our eyes. The Greeks advocated knowledge of the self as the end of life, and the psycho-analysts have given to their advocacy a pseudo-scientific backing, bidding us perpetually to dig up the seeds of our nature that we may better attend to the growth of the plant. For my part, I would praise not self-knowledge but self-forgetfulness. Such happiness as I have known has resulted not from preoccupation with myself, but from oblivion of myself in concentration upon some external thing.[2]

The difficulty of countering this inducement is that it contains a half-truth. Indeed it is a sign of comparative freedom from abnormal adjustment when we *can* forget ourselves and concentrate upon some external thing or person but so long as this is in the nature of an *escape* it also involves an escape from the truth. Abnormal adjustment is not amended in this way, it merely gets encysted.

The relationship between insight and 'abnorm' is, as we have gathered, an important one. Yet I must hasten to combat the doctrine that the possession of insight is the essence of normality

[1] 'The Concept of Normality', *The Psychoanalytical Quarterly*, 1950, XIX, pp. 43–51.
[2] *The Book of Joad*, 1943, p. 224.

whatever the latter may seem. Money-Kyrle defines an integrated person as one '. . . whose mind has nothing permanently hidden from itself, and who is rational in the sense that the belief-systems governing his behaviour are true within the range of his experience because they have been consciously tested. . . .' To equate the norm with the level of insight is, in my view, mistaken for the following reasons, firstly, the definition of the 'normal' is not possible; the case against an attempt to derive the norm from positive science was amply set out in Chapter II.

Secondly, the definition of the abnorm cannot use insight as a *definiens*, for abnormal adjustment is a comprehensive condition of which a certain defective state of insight is a mere component, a corollary, perhaps a symptom. We cannot equate an adjustment condition with the condition of insight for the latter is *less* than the former. It is another matter altogether that there may be an absolute positive correlation between deficient insight and abnormal adjustment but, even so, one cannot be defined in terms of the other.

At the same time I agree that insight plays the most essential role both in the prevention and in the therapy of abnormal adjustment conditions. This seems to commit me to a conventional kind of rationalism which is taken amiss from the contemporary social psychologist and sociologist. It is charged that modern social scientists, and in particular modern psychologists, have been, at least partly, responsible for the contemporary scepticism towards reason. Modern psychologists, we are told, are the very people who never tire of showing reason's subservience to instinct and desire. Some people would put all the blame on the psychologist for the undermining of the prestige of reason. This charge is derived from a misunderstanding. The psychologist of orexis neglects reason for he is bent on specializing in what has so far been neglected by reason. But he does not relegate reason to a second place. In fact, he is engaged in rehabilitating reason by showing the ways in which the Bergsonian antithesis of 'instinct-intelligence' can be resolved in a new synthesis. In man reason is the axis of disbalance; through this axis the opposing forces exert their influence on each other according to specified rules which the nature of this axis implies.

We may insist as much as we like that human intellect is weak in comparison with human instinct, and be right in doing so. But nevertheless there is something peculiar about this weakness. The voice of the intellect is a soft one but it does not rest until it has gained a hearing. Ultimately, after endlessly repeated rebuffs, it succeeds.[1]

It is a great pity that Freud never demonstrated how this consoling conclusion was to be related to the psycho-analytic theory. Reason is not—as one writer put it—a mere cork floating on the waves of instinct and desire: it has evolved into a great and powerful vessel equipped with the most sensitive instruments and capable of riding out the storms of oceanic instincts. I shall put this simile to further service by saying that it is not the function of ships to subjugate the seas, but to sail through them, that it is to sail through the seas with the help of the seas and in spite of their unruliness. Similarly it is not the function of reason to subject the instincts and desires but to ride them out, and to harness them. Keeping to its steady course reason can deliver its spiritual cargo only because there are those eternally restless waves on which to travel. How could one of those sailing ships accomplish its task on a permanently becalmed sea? The very winds which scourged the waters into perilous waves were a source of its locomotion. And so it is with reason: it needs the elemental forces of instinct and desire to affirm itself and perform its task. Yet even this tempting simile is fundamentally unsound, for it continues to encourage a dualistic psychology of 'orexis' and 'cognition' as well as a moral philosophy harping on the conflicts of 'will' and 'knowledge'. Reason is not apart from or above disbalance, it is a function of disbalance, its attribute, yet also its self-engendered mediator.

To understand our own perplexity, or a fellow-being's plight, the cold calculus of logic is not sufficient. Insight as we experience it today is a fusion of logic and feeling. When we speak of reason we no longer think of the *intellectus siccus* of the rationalists but rather of the ancient conception of *Wisdom*. This I would define as reason steeped in self-experience and in a condition which is relatively free from the symptoms of abnormal adjustment.

One would hardly be taken seriously if one claimed that the abnorm as defined is a sufficient guide to moral and political

[1] *The Future of an Illusion*, by S. Freud, 1928, p. 93.

philosophy. Even if no attention is paid to the obvious logical difficulties which beset the translation of a positive norm into a normative precept it would be fatal to assume that the foregoing reflections were intended to be more than a plea for ridding contemporary scientific objectivity of the etiquette of 'no certainty' in human affairs. This etiquette or convention becomes an obsession and an evil when its perfectionist scruples *prevent* the consolidation of even the most plausible interpretation of evil. A perfectionism which delays the stocktaking of a sociological synthesis today because the business of ideas and the commerce of empirical facts is booming and because the stocks will presumably be higher and richer tomorrow, will have to meet the inevitable slump with unbalanced books and unmarketable reserves. The critic should ponder before he opens the sluices of sceptical invective; if my definition of abnormal adjustment is not acceptable to him, on what grounds does he approve of, or even tolerate, widespread social welfare measures which have been designed to protect the child against rupture experiences and not only against destitution or physical harm? Is he content that these modern refinements of Christian moral philosophy are autonomous extensions of Christian and humanistic concerns, or does he underwrite social action in these fields because he knows that we have come by a new knowledge which all must respect? But if he shares our respect for the new knowledge what reason can he give for calling a halt to his continuing acceptance of the insights—which inspired those measures—when confronted with a systematic deployment of these insights? That the abnorm needs specification, that its casuistry must have quantitative—though operational—criteria with ever increasing precision, that the writing-large of individual abnorm to social and cultural abnorm demands a fantastic volume of painstaking research and thought, all these are squarely faced. Even so, none of these can be even conceived, let alone launched, unless the principles set out above are received, at least, with the benefit of the doubt.

Then virtue, it appears, will be a kind of health and beauty, and good habit of the soul, and vice will be a disease, and deformity, and sickness of it.

The Republic of Plato, Book IV, 444.

'There seems to be an untested and optimistic premise that social scientists have an *indefinite time* at their disposal in which to perfect their researches and bring them, when fully formed, to practical uses. No doubt the full period of gestation is most comfortable for mother and child alike— but there are times when Caesareans, induced artificial labor, or forceps must be used to safeguard both. It does not appear alarmist to maintain that this is the situation of present-day social science. It must either attempt to fructify democratic action with whatever imperfect concepts and generalization are now available, or risk delivery of a fully developed discipline, which, if not dead at birth, will be born orphaned. Bereft of the democratic culture which conceived it, this social science will be unable to mature.'

Alvin W. Gouldner in
Studies in Leadership,
1950, pp. 13–14.

'. . . man is stricken deaf and dumb and blind,
For intellect no longer knows
Is from the *ought*, or *knower* from the *known*—'

W. B. Yeats,
'A Dialogue of Self and Soul'.

V

THE NORM AND

SOCIOLOGICAL THEORY

1. *Ethics and the 'Abnorm'*

WHEN I asked a bus conductor whether it was worth my while to get on a bus to reach the High Street he replied, 'You don't want to do that, you can walk it in two minutes!' Instead of pleading with me that I 'shouldn't', 'mustn't', or 'oughtn't to' board a bus he observed that I 'didn't want to' do such a thing. Instead of telling me that the walk would do me good, and both laziness and throwing away twopence were unvirtuous according to some rule extraneous to me and my nature, he reminded me of what *I really wanted* to do, he enjoined me to consider my true needs, my true nature. Instead of the imperative of moral persuasion he used the indicative of psychology. Now I do not wish to engage in an elaborate logical analysis to prove that all indicatives and imperatives are mutually convertible. The parable about the bus conductor is offered merely to show that a statement of fact and a moral command have a good deal more in common than logical analysts generally admit. Similarly I shall show that the cultivation of social science and that of moral philosophy are much less divorced pursuits than most would concede. And as in this book I sought for a moral measure of man so in the following pages I, a social psychologist and sociologist, must explain why I regard myself as free from the charge of trespass.

(1) The only scientific discipline which deals with the total field of human relations and human conduct is sociology. It seems, therefore, proper that if a scientific appraisal of the rules of conduct be made it should be made by a sociologist. In other

words, should a naturalistic moral philosophy be feasible, that is, should we contrive to rid that philosophy of its well-known logical difficulties its sole legitimate sire could be no other than sociology. Past attempts at affiliating a naturalistic moral philosophy to theology, biology, or psychology have failed partly because none of these enjoys co-ownership with moral philosophy of the *total* area of human behaviour and relations. There is no doubt in my mind that only an integrative study of human relations and conduct, such as sociology, is eligible for this role.

At the same time my perseverance in regarding psychological and even biological knowledge as the only hard currency in sociological budgeting is bound to be received with some surprise—especially now that I have allotted a central position to sociology. Surely, it will be observed, enough has been said of the fallacies of 'pan-psychism'—the doctrine according to which the universe is all psyche—and of the fallacies of a 'psychologistic bias' in sociology—the view that social causation is ultimately psychological causation—to restrain anyone from regarding psychology as a sufficient guide in human affairs. In view of this it is understandable that the economist, the historian, and the sociologist too, do not take kindly to a psychological guardianship which they consider narrow. These social sciences have always striven to keep themselves free from outside tutelage, aspiring, as they have all done, to the status of independent scientific disciplines. Whilst they all deal with human nature in one way or another, they have persisted in claiming self-sufficiency and autarchy, at any rate, in respect of psychological incursions. I do not wish to argue that there is nothing 'social', 'historical', or 'economic' left after the psychological has been subtracted from Sociology, History, and Economics respectively. Nevertheless even this purely sociological, historical, and economic 'remainder' can be evaluated only in terms of the psychological impact it makes on the individual. This is not to deny that there is such a thing as a social reality nor to insist that all the reality of human experience is convertible into psychology; rather, I should like to stress again, it means that the understanding of the remainder and of its relation to man's needs is not possible without a psychological appraisal.

Accordingly, I devoted this volume to the search for a psychological norm without which a sociological norm cannot be discovered. A search for the latter presupposes success in the former. Thus my first task was psychological: the discovery of the fundamental needs of man, the definition of normal conduct and normal personality, or in default of these the definition of the minimum area of abnormality. To me, the psychological abnorm is simultaneously a moral abnorm: it tells me what man shall not be. Thus the psychologically positive will assume a moral content yet without the translation of the abnorm into sociological terms this moral content will remain tentative and sketchy. In other words, knowing what is right for man must include the knowledge of what sort of society, of social order, is appropriate to man's fundamental needs. Unfortunately this translation could not be made in the present study and will have to be postponed until my conclusions on the psychological abnorm are tested and refined by the criticism they will draw.

Admittedly, perfect knowledge of the fundamental and true needs of man or of the ways in which they could be most consistently satisfied is not available and possibly will never be available. I too have been obliged to conclude that 'normality' as an absolute measure of man is not definable, yet I have shown that a minimum area of 'abnormal adjustment' is already the subject of a substantial agreement. Whilst the absolute measure psychology can give at this stage, the abnorm, can tell us no more than what we should avoid, the niggardliness of this measure is no excuse for repudiating it and denying it the authority which, I believe, is its due.

(2) Meanwhile the tweedledum-tweedledee dualism between the indicative and the imperative continues to hamper us: what is the good of defining a positive norm or abnorm when even a definition will not make these obligatory? The logical gap between the positive and the normative appears to remain unbridged. It is one thing to tell a man that smoking will injure his health and another that it is his moral duty to stop smoking. An ever growing number of medical men claim that they can prove the former, but does that verify the latter? Does anything verify the latter? I believe that human thinking is at the mercy of its grammar and this is why we have not been able to see that in fact there is only one statement to be verified here but it is neither the first nor the second, it is some kind of a merger of

the two. In other words, there may seem to be two different meanings yet there is only one reality which is both positive and normative at the same time. The fallacy of linguistic analysis is that it expects language to increase understanding when in fact the categorical structure of language is too hidebound and unwieldy to ensure this. Yet it is by no means impossible to explain clearly what is to be understood by this merger of the positive and of the normative. A most concise explanation of this union was given by Gregory Bateson in the following:

Whatever communication we consider, be it the transmission of impulses in a neural system or the transmission of words in a conversation, it is evident that every message in transit has two sorts of 'meaning'. On the one hand, the message is a statement or report about events at a previous moment, on the other hand, it is a command—a cause or stimulus for events at a later moment. Consider the case of three neurons, A, B, and C, in series, so that the firing of A leads to the firing of B, and the firing of B leads to the firing of C. Even in this extremely simple case, the message transmitted by B has two sorts of meanings referred to above. On the one hand it can be regarded as a 'report' to the effect that A fired at a previous moment and on the other hand it is a 'command' or cause for C's later firing. The same thing is true of all verbal communications whatsoever.[1]

I think that this passage shows ably why we should not succumb to grammatical tyranny: information and command, indicative and imperative merge here in a single process of communication. There is only one communication but we stubbornly attach two distinct meanings to it. Whether the bus conductor informs me about the true nature of my needs and intentions or he exhorts me to have certain intentions he communicates very much the same thing to me notwithstanding the difference in the style of the communication. So it is that 'this is white' and 'this is good' are both normative and positive communications. In this sense all communications are both normative and positive at the same time. In this light the logician's talk about 'emotive' and 'non-emotive' statements becomes suspect and possibly superfluous. This unity of value-qualities and fact-qualities in communication is manifest at both ends of the line

[1] *Communication*, by Jurgen Ruesch and Gregory Bateson, 1951, p. 179.

of communication: the person who communicates transmits a blend of fact and affect simultaneously whereas the person who receives the communication absorbs information and suggestion at the same time. For a long time it was taken for granted that perception begins with affectless cognition; this fallacy of 'cognitive priority' in perception was sometimes matched with its opposite, the fallacy of orectic or 'value priority'; Max Scheler furnishes an example of the latter, '. . . the *value*-qualities of objects are already given *in advance* at a level where their imaged and conceptual features are not yet vouchsafed for us, and hence the apprehension of values is the basis of our subsequent apprehension of objects.'[1] The truth is that there is no priority: information and exhortation are simultaneous and are two facets of the selfsame thing, communication. This is not the first time that artificially separated categories are reunited: the Helmholtzian division in physics between structure and dynamics is no longer apposite in modern physical theory and the arbitrary division of psychological processes into conative, affective, and cognitive processes had to be abandoned in modern psychological theory. Similarly, I hope that the grammatical division of indicative and imperative statements will no longer be allowed to suggest that they constitute two essentially different kinds of communication.

If the definition of the abnorm is a task for psychology the psychologist who communicates this definition and the sociologist who translates it into the terms of social structure and function can no longer plead the neutrality of scientists, for no matter what psychological or sociological information is imparted it cannot fail to be either an inspiration to or a veto upon some individual conduct or social action. For this reason I look upon the role, 'social scientist', as co-extensive with the role, 'social philosopher'. '*Je ne propose rien, je ne suppose rien, je n'impose rien . . . J'expose,*' bears the marks of conceit as well as deception.[2]

(3) But if psychological and sociological 'intelligence' is normative, which I believe it is, what can I reply to the objection that a moral judgment cannot be derived from mere knowledge of man? As Professor Ginsberg put it, '. . . the moral judgment

[1] *The Nature of Sympathy*, London, 1954, pp. 57–8.
[2] Cf. *Historical Inevitability*, by Isaiah Berlin, 1954, p. 58.

207

itself would still have to be made independently and could not be deduced without remainder from psychological and sociological facts.'[1] The gist of this objection is that familiarity with the nature of facts does not oblige us; that moral obligation does not spring forth from knowledge and that social science because it is a science and therefore deals with facts entails no moral obligations. In the language of the moralist: the knowledge of good and evil does not suffice to make us will the former and eschew the latter. But if psychologists have been obliged to abandon the division of the mind into 'knowing and willing' parts, why do moral philosophers persist in relying on these arbitrary categories? The truth is that knowledge that has no power over the will is not knowledge of good and evil; knowledge of good implies the power, the skill, the knowledge of doing good. Paul's 'For the good that I would I do not; but the evil which I would not, that I do' (Romans vii. 19) is the impasse of an outmoded psychology. There is only one kind of awareness, which we have always split into two false categories. My insistence on their reunification is not just an old-fashioned rationalism patched up once again to conceal its notorious weaknesses. The very division into rational and irrational processes is a regrettable error, there are no two such streams as these. That this division is untenable is well shown by such of its inevitable curiosities as that 'we have a non-rational desire for rationality'. What we have is a desire for the mastery over our fundamentally anomalous nature and that desire is alone responsible for our moral aspirations.

Further just as the fusion of the rational and of the irrational does not end in the revival of an outmoded rationalism so the merger of psychology and ethics will not spell a reduction of the normative to the positive. The synthesis of the positive-normative aspects of existence is not a reduction of one aspect to the other. This is not a matter of converting 'ethical propositions' into 'non-ethical propositions' as Professor Broad explained[2] but an interpretation according to which all propositions are *communicative propositions*. Thus this is not a new species of 'debunking', or of disillusionment; on the contrary, my con-

---

[1] 'Durkheim's Ethical Theory', by Morris Ginsberg, *Brit. J. Sociol.*, III, pp. 210–18.
[2] Cf. *Five Types of Ethical Theory*, by C. D. Broad, 1930, p. 258.

ception of knowledge as 'insight' restores more moral dignity to man than my analysis may have whittled away. The fourth chapter of this book contains much to make this claim plausible. It is not my intention to 'reduce' ethics to something less sublime. We must remember that the ultimate psychological entelechies—the fundamental psychological forces—are themselves rooted in universal principles which are *not* psychological. Even though one may superficially talk of 'converting' ethics to psychology what in fact one does is not converting but leading back ethics via psychology to its true mother-soil, metaphysics. To complain that this conversion of ethics destroys the distinctive character of ethics, of a legitimately specialized discipline, is to ignore the fact that all sciences are in the process of being so converted.

(4) Sociological and psychological knowledge truly understood comprises *insight*, a novel concept developed by psychology. This insight unites the so-called 'knowing' and 'willing' faculties of the mind. Because this understanding has so long eluded us we have allowed the mysterious and extraneous something called 'moral obligation' to confuse the issues. Let us suppose that the injunction, 'you ought to be charitable', is examined with a view to discovering where it obtains its ultimate authority. If we obey the command we do so because of one or more of the following reasons, firstly, because we feel the need of being charitable, that is, we are desirous of having the experience of being charitable; secondly, because we feel the need of social or divine approval usually given to or supposed to be given to and, therefore, expected by charitable people; thirdly, because we feel the need of escaping the censure to which uncharitable people may be exposed. In all these instances our acceptance of the moral precept, 'be charitable', depends on our feeling some need. Without this feeling the moral precept would assuredly be disobeyed or only accidentally conformed to. Though the moral precept cited by others and addressed to us may carry with it the idea of a command, of threats, or rewards, it will not be effective unless it allies itself with an internal need. If a man hearing the exhortation acts charitably whereas without the exhortation he would not have acted so, the exhortation is merely (*a*) a reminder to the individual that he was about to ignore or misjudge his fundamental needs, (*b*) a reminder or

information as to what the exhorter regards to be the funda-mental needs of the individual he addresses, (c) a communica-tion that one of the exhorter's needs is to exhort on this or such occasions. None of these carries with it moral authority: the authority of the precept is within the man to whom the exhor-tation was addressed. In this respect I could hardly improve on Carritt's conclusion that, 'You cannot prove to a man that he has duties, or should do his duty, or that justice is duty . . . all you can do is to get him to imagine the situation again and repeat the act of moral thinking with greater attention.'[1]

The man who utters the 'ought' or the 'should' does so him-self because he experiences a need to communicate his discovery of a need and his preference for the satisfaction of that need. The nature of this fundamental need to communicate is perhaps explained by saying that one likes to share and to be confirmed in one's loyalties and aversions. Therefore, 'you ought to do this' comprises two statements both of which are *psychological*: one is, 'I wish you'd do this', the other is, 'you *really* prefer to do this', i.e. if you comply with your true nature. One of these is a statement about the speaker's mind and the other is a state-ment about the mind of the listener. As Radhakamal Mukerjee put it, 'morality is not an external binder of society', that is, morality has a psychological reality and not a social one. Morality like gravitation does not act as an external coupling but as an internal attribute of those which are coupled. In a moral command no obligation is really conveyed: the obligation is in the mind of the recipient. A moral command or a moral judgment is a communication which may act as a stimulus to the recipient to reassess his own desires and preferences; simi-larly, psychological or sociological propositions may have the same effect. Thus psychological or sociological communication is always moral in both its motives and in its impact. No amount of neutrality-pleading can alter this. At any rate, after the errors of the past and in the uncertainty of the present it is hopeless to pretend that reflection on human affairs can be dissociated from a craving for betterment in our condition.

(5) When philosophers ask questions such as 'why be good?' 'why be rational?' or 'why avoid being abnormal?' Many insist that these questions cannot be answered without reference to a

---

[1] *The Theory of Morals*, by E. F. Carritt, 1928, pp. 71–2.

moral obligation which is ultimately extraneous to man's psyche. Meanwhile such questions as these are no more meaningful than the question, 'why live?' or 'why love your mother?' or 'why love your child?' It is simply not true that we have a moral obligation to do these things. That external dictates may have a persuasive or an inspiring effect in these matters is not a moral fact but a social one, much as education or propaganda are social facts. Nothing moral can be predicated about this relationship of 'enjoining' or 'persuading' or 'exhorting'. Man alone is moral and his social relationships can be morally judged only by relating them to the values inherent in the fundamental needs of man. So long as it does not occur to us to ask, 'why love your mother?' or 'why love your child?' or indeed, 'why live?', that is, ask questions to which there is only one sensible answer, that 'we must by virtue of our nature', we have no reason to doubt that all the other similar why's would be adequately answered in the same way. Let us not think that the 'must' or 'ought' disappears from this sort of thinking altogether; it is still there but it is a 'truly I must' or 'truly I ought' and not a 'you must' or 'you ought'. There is therefore no spurious 'ought phobia' in my thinking[1] and the 'ought obsession' which mars much of moral philosophy is obviously not particularly noticeable in it either.

2. Scepticism

Can the cripple of moral philosophy lean on sociological crutches? Is sociology sturdy enough to support the aged and venerable weight? At first one is scarcely encouraged to place much trust in sociology. The science of sociology is the child of disillusionment and the father of a promise. The doctrines of the so-called 'nothing but' theories revealed their weakness as history put them to the test. Their veneer of masterly simplicity wore off but not before we had paid a price for our credulity. At times the ghostly figure of the 'economic man' still haunts us but we have learnt to recognize him for what he is. The evolutionary man, who was getting better and better in spite of himself, and the apocalyptic man who did away with himself at the

[2] Cf. 'Psychoanalysis and Ethics', by Morris Ginsberg, *Brit. J. Sociol.*, III, pp. 287–304.

end of neatly constructed cycles or stages of history, were similar abstractions. To meet our disillusionment with these and other schemes of interpretation modern sociology emerged. Its point of view, its method, required the dispassionate, almost indifferent, neutrality which had been a condition of success in the natural sciences. At the same time sociologists, who were now in possession, displayed a single-mindedness and even optimism as to the eventual outcome of their labours. They invited us to look forward to an objective and total comprehension of social living. The disillusionment was salutary but the promise is yet to be fulfilled.

The discrediting of 'single cause' explanations had, at least, one becalming effect on the navigators in search for social truth: simplicity and monistic accounts became a taboo. Painstaking objectivism obliged the sociologist to take 'multiple causation' in all social phenomena for granted. This was an understandable reaction from the earlier over-simplifications. The integration of causes into unitary systems grew suspect on account of its tidiness and compactness, for this was out of keeping with the bewildering complexity of social life. It is held today that very few things are absolutely certain and that we must not expect to obtain comprehensive principles from the study of the contemporary social scene or, for that matter, from the examination of its historical antecedents, '. . . At this stage the vain hope of discovering truth in a form which is independent of an historically and socially determined set of meanings will have to be given up.'[1] Thus the late Karl Mannheim, whose work remarkably fused the notes of disillusionment and promise. While he never ceased to relate sociological theory to the social context from which it emerged, and while he always warned against the ideological nature of all social thought, he also seemed confident that by the synthesis of our discoveries in the social sciences we might attain to a lasting and valid insight into the complexities of the social process. He advised that from the failures of the intellectualist as well as anti-intellectualist 'certainties' of the past we should derive humility and caution which would yield us more truth than we ever dared hope to possess: 'Only when we are thoroughly aware of the limited scope of every point of view are we on the road to the sought-for com-

[1] *Ideology and Utopia*, 1946, p. 71.

prehension of the whole.' He seemed to have it both ways: with a gesture of ascetic resignation, or rather of wise restraint, he abstained from the search for a perennial logos; at the same time he lured us towards the very treasure which he had himself abandoned. That he has never been acquitted on the charge of scepticism is well brought out by Paul Kecskeméti, the editor of Mannheim's posthumously published essays on the sociology of knowledge.[1] The theory of socially determined thought, *Seinsverbundenes Wissen* (knowledge determined by existence), omits to tell us what this *Wissen* must be by virtue of being human. Man's values may be socially created or bolstered up, they may be socially inhibited and our awareness of them socially phrased for us; but what is here socially articulated and standardized for us was always real, universal, and absolute before culture and society left their mark on it. There may be innumerable variations in culture and in social order yet the contravention of man's bio-psychological needs by them cannot persist indefinitely: there is a core of the socially necessary which these variations must respect. Indeed it may be possible to argue that the very violations of this essential core are necessary themselves, that society perfects itself by lessons learnt from errors. So long as the failure of a society, of a civilization, is a regional failure and new beginnings can come about on the ruins of the old this 'trial and error philosophy' has had ample historical justification. *But in a global civilization error may well amount to suicide when the power of technological tools surpasses the recuperative power of life itself.* This, as is too well known, obtains today. As the 'trial and error philosophy' grows feebler—for the danger of a catastrophic error ever increases—the commanding need for the definition of what is absolutely essential to society for its survival simply does not allow further procrastination. Let it be that social thought is a function of the society which thinks it; let it be that the whole categorical structure of a science, any science, may be socially determined, yet at this time we are irrevocably obliged to commit ourselves and to define the essentials of survival in the terms we understand at the present or else we, the agents of understanding, will not be here tomorrow to revise the conclusions we reach today.

[1] Cf. *Essays on the Sociology of Knowledge*, by Karl Mannheim, 1952, pp. 27–32.

Furthermore, it is about time that we examined the psychological content of objectivity and demonstrated its freedom from fundamental scepticism. Objectivity, in its conscientious and scrupulous discipline, is idealistic and not sceptical. Dedication to objectivity begins with dedication and not objectivity, whereas scepticism is the withering away of all dedication. If objectivity is turned back upon this dedication with a view to discrediting it the outcome is meaningless.

3. *Positive Norm and Normative Precept*

Whether scepticism or confident anticipation shall inform our attitude towards the discovery of social truth we may gain from making explicit one of its essential qualities. The possession of knowledge about social living is, always and inevitably, more than mere comprehension. It is inconceivable that an increment in our understanding should have no effect whatsoever on our conduct. The perennial social truths do not consist in positive formulae of social structure and function; these truths are not simply answers to questions like, 'How does society work?' or 'What does society consist of?' These truths are also final and irrevocable rules about what society cannot be if it is to continue in being. In an important sense they are also directives as to what society 'ought to' be, 'should' be, or 'must' be although—as we have seen—the 'thou shalt not' issues with much greater specificity from general principles than the 'thou shalt'.

Also it is a commonplace in sociology that publicly defining a situation alters that situation. Just as the act of observation becomes part of the environment of the observed so much the more the publication of the observation affects that environment. In physics this limitation was clearly recognized when Heisenberg formulated the Principle of Indeterminacy. The scope of this principle widens as one ascends the hierarchy of sciences from physics to the life-sciences. Larger and larger units of substance succumb to this limitation as we proceed from physics through chemistry, biology, psychology, to sociology. Yet whereas the physical generalization retains its statistical validity above the atomic and sub-atomic levels the sociological generalization is capable of invalidating the statistical totals as

214

well if and when these generalizations are publicized. Hence positive statements in the life-sciences—provided that they are communicated to their subjects—become increasingly normative, and they reach full normative status in sociology. To deny this inevitable normative function or even to belittle it is bad sociology. In the age of mass-communications the principal features of sociological 'intelligence' cannot be kept confidential. Every sociological enunciation is automatically a moral injunction.

It is a well-known complaint that deriving the obligatory from the inevitable is a *tour de force* of logic.[1] We are told that it is no use for sociologists, psychologists or biologists to exert themselves in search of universal positive norms for even if there could be an agreement on these we could still not claim that there was an obligation to realize these positive norms. We read in a sociological journal that even if there was an agreement, say, with regard to the concept of mental ill health, '. . . the old disagreement would re-emerge . . . whether *all* mental sickness, so defined, and (those) cases in particular, which are agreed to fall under its definition, ought to be cured'.[2] Professor Flew doubts that there could be a universally valid 'abnorm' in the realm of the mental and declares that even if there was such a thing as this we should not be ethically bound to do away with the conditions which it designates. In the face of this one could, of course, take the attitude that the latter is a philosophical objection which is irrelevant to the validity or otherwise of a positive norm. One may say, for instance, that unless the sociologist trespasses and presumes to claim moral authority for his positive norm it is not his duty to meet this objection. I may as well confess that I have no intention of taking up this attitude.

Philosophers, on the whole, have made two fruitless attempts to unify the positive and normative hemispheres of human knowledge; on the one hand naturalistic moral philosophy failed to bridge the logical chasm between the two worlds; on the other, the logical-positivist elimination of the dualism consisted in demonstrating that there was no bridge to be built, for there was no chasm, no duality—only positive science. These

[1] Cf. *Ethics and Language*, by C. L. Stevenson, 1950, p. 325.
[2] 'Crime and Disease', by A. G. N. Flew, *Brit. J. Sociol.*, March 1954, V.

NORM AND SOCIOLOGICAL THEORY

two failures overshadowed all hopes for a rational and scientific control of human behaviour, and for a systematic application of understanding to conduct. Nevertheless the sociologist can afford to ignore the bleak philosophical prospects of his labours towards a synthesis. To him it is by no means certain that human knowledge is anything less than positive and normative *at the same time*. One is naturally aware of the difference between the statements 'sociological "intelligence" *is in fact* normative', and 'sociological "intelligence" *ought to be* normative'. The first of these needs little documentation. In the modern age—if not already before its beginning—side by side with the unfolding of scientific knowledge, man has behaved increasingly *as if* he had been committed to a naturalistic moral philosophy, or more precisely, *as if* he could not divorce his understanding from his moral judgment. The history of penal reform, our changing moral principles relating to responsibility, our consequent treatment of the poor, the criminal, the coward, the sexual pervert, and so on, on the one hand, and our appraisal of the great man, the hero, the patriot, the mystic, on the other, have become, to say the least, coloured by the discoveries of the social sciences. To assert that these are merely changes in the *forms* of perennial moral principles without the principles themselves undergoing change is as inane as saying that the advance in medicine signifies no change in the human condition for we are still not immortal. The thesis that certain perennial moral principles do not change no matter how much and what kind of factual information is forthcoming is in harmony with my way of thinking; if there are bio-psychological constants it is logical that there should be perennial moral principles, for the latter could not persist without the former. My definition of a perennial 'abnorm' is in keeping with the belief in the lasting moral qualities of the human species. Yet every time we apply psycho-therapy to a juvenile delinquent instead of flogging him, or deporting him, or locking him up in 'solitary' we effect a moral revolution, we create new derivative principles from the perennial general principles of tolerance, forgiveness, or love. It is important to bear in mind that we have been able to do this because we have changed our diagnosis of the facts, because we have allowed psychological and sociological discoveries to bring about a change in our moral judgments. This is an historical

216

fact and not a moral-philosophical thesis. There is then no doubt in our minds that sociological 'intelligence' is normative, but can we also claim with the same facility that it *ought to be* normative? Past historical sequences though verified cannot impose obligations on us now or in the future. Some may doubt whether the historical process in which understanding is always converted into precept will continue indefinitely. I readily admit the hypothetical nature of such an expectation as this—not being blind to the regressions of recent history—yet I justify this expectation by saying that a full-stop in the expansion of science is unthinkable, that human curiosity about the nature of the universe is a bio-psychological constant, and that no schism between understanding and conduct can be maintained for long: the continued existence of man would be fatally threatened by a condition which would deny unity to man's mind. But all this proves no more than that the process of naturalistic determination in moral conduct and judgment will continue, that is to say that the process is *inevitable*. But is there a gratuitous force, the so-called moral obligation which is supposed to assist the inevitable? Here I am not prepared to conduct a full-dress logical analysis of this problem and content myself with stating that sociological awareness and psychological insight are new and unique features in the history of the inevitable; that sociology is a record of social man's self-awareness and this record is an increasingly potent variable of the socially inevitable; and finally, that the moral obligation to make the record and the moral obligation to heed it are not extraneous to the inevitable but are inevitable themselves. To me there are no two questions such as 'Is sociology in fact normative?' and 'Ought sociology to be normative?' There is only one question which remains unverbalized for our linguistic poverty permits of no compromise between the indicative and the imperative. If all that exists also commands, if the concept of an inert structure is a fallacious abstraction, for all that exists is dynamic, then no violation of logic is perpetrated in insisting that moral obligation is both inevitable and desirable. A logical analysis along these lines, as well as with the help of parables such as the one presented earlier, will be undertaken elsewhere. For the time being I cannot go beyond these brief remarks. If philosophers trespass into the pages of sociological journals telling us that our search for positive norms is futile, they should not be surprised at a sociologist's temerity in threatening to return the compliment.

Nonetheless this is not to suggest naïvely that the positive study of psychology and sociology will at once replace moral philosophy altogether. The minimum definition of abnormal adjustment does not tell us what a 'normal society' is, that is to say, the abnorm cannot sketch Utopia for us. In many ways I am in sympathy with Professor Ginsberg's warning that

> Ethics . . . is not identical with the comparative study of moral obligation. This is not to say that these latter studies are not important. They are, on the contrary, of great value, firstly as parts of the sociology of culture, and secondly as affording important data to ethics proper. In this latter respect they are especially valuable because they serve to inculcate a critical attitude towards our moral intuitions by revealing the great diversity of moral beliefs and practices. But such studies do not take the place of ethics proper any more than the history and psychology of thought constitutes logic.[1]

Yet if the result of this critical attitude is the discrediting of a moral principle and its replacement by another one, who or what was responsible for this change in valuation if not 'the comparative study of moral obligation'? It is indeed possible to deny psychology and sociology the right to take over the function of normative direction, but then is it also possible to say that these positive sciences have not, in fact, assumed any normative direction at all? In an important passage Professor Ginsberg points to the key to this riddle though unfortunately neither he nor others have cared to use this key. He writes,

> . . . the study of fact and the study of values should be kept distinct, though in a final synthesis the two types of inquiry must be brought together. Confusion is likely to arise if their distinctness is not recognized, *but also if they never meet at all. A complete study of human life thus involves a synthesis but not a fusion, of social science and social philosophy* [italics mine].

If this passage means in the words of Frederick the Great *Zertrennt marschieren und vereint schlagen* (to march separately and to strike together) the question is, who should command the unified forces, the sociologist or the philosopher? This is not a rhetorical question for a 'complete study of human life' is presumably to be cultivated by someone. Is it to be the philosophical sociologist, the social philosopher, or the social psychologist? We could, of course, content ourselves with the knowledge that such a study as this will be cultivated anyway even though the precise nature of this affiliation remains undecided. But this complacency would not quite do in an age when some sociologists have, in fact, shown that they were alone qualified to assume a total scientific control over the study of human social life. Yet whilst sociologists are alone competent to give a balanced account of a social situation or process they recoil from the task and its responsibilities. The contemporary climate of opinion among them is well illustrated by the remarks of F. Stuart Chapin who addressing young American sociologists said, 'You should seek to become known as a social scientist in the field of your speciality. Do not be misled by resistance to overspecialization. True integrations which fill interstitial areas between older specialities, themselves become new specialities.'[1] Of course, theoretically there is no limit to finding new 'interstitial areas' and creating new specialities out of them, but is this the proper message of inspiration at this time when the fragmentation of sociological knowledge has cast most items of it beyond the reach of a central meaning? Would it not be more auspicious to reflect on special techniques of synthesis as well as encourage 'specialization in synthesis'? The advocate of specialization may perhaps be tempted, if he is reminded that important analytical insights often spring from new syntheses.

Whether there is such a thing as a 'scientifically validated moral philosophy' or not, the sociologist cannot but proceed with the assumption that nothing else could adequately justify his demands for a hearing or, for that matter, his existence. Yet sociology has so far neglected the problem of the Human Norm, unless the recurrent notes of scepticism as to the possibility of its definition are to be counted as contributions to this work. Since Durkheim's inconclusive reflections there has been nothing systematic attempted in this subject. Whether it is a Human Norm or Human Abnorm which we succeed in

[1] *Amer. Sociol. Rev.*, Dec. 1953, XVIII, p. 599.

isolating, it is clear that the whole structure of sociology would have to be reorganized according to its specifications.

It is almost certain that these expectations—pronounced with some confidence—will be received with scepticism. To shield myself with conclusions reached by others and similar to mine does not amount to furnishing proofs; yet when reputable sociologists find themselves obliged to concede the legitimacy of schemes such as mine I believe I may, at least, proceed with enhanced assurance. Georg Simmel, for instance, comes intriguingly near to my line of thought in the following:

> . . . nature not only is what really alone exists—the substance of all historical oscillations and shifts—but also, at the same time, it is what ought to be, the ideal with whose growing realization all men must be concerned. To say that what truly exists is, at the same time, an aim that must yet be reached, sounds contradictory. Yet actually, these two propositions are two sides of a consistent psychological position which is taken in regard to more than one value complex. We can simply not express it otherwise than in this logically contradictory dualism . . . We feel in ourselves an ultimate reality which forms the essence of our nature, but which is yet only very imperfectly represented by our empirical reality. But it is by no means merely a fantasy-like ideal which hovers above this empirical reality; for, in some shape it already exists, traced in ideal lines, as it were, into our existence; and yet it contains the *norm* for this existence, and only requires to be fully worked out and elaborated in the material of our existence.[1]

The co-existence of the positive and normative elements of reality is recognized here to be of a significance which the sociologist cannot ignore. Simmel deems it the sociologist's duty to locate and define the norm immanent in this reality. There is a most instructive follow-up of these ideas in a more recent sociological work.[2] H. D. Lasswell and A. Kaplan approaching the problem with caution state:

> It must be emphasized . . . that a scientific interest in political inquiry need not exclude a political interest in its outcome and applications. Inquiry has not only a creative role in the formation of policy—serving as a means of self-orientation in a flow of events of

[1] *The Sociology of Georg Simmel*, ed. Kurt H. Wolff, 1950, p. 71.
[2] *Power and Society*, by H. D. Lasswell and A. Kaplan, 1952.

changing significance—but also an instrumental role in implementing policy. Thus the purport of inquiry is not necessarily 'theoretical' rather than 'practical'; both manipulative and contemplative standpoints may be adopted.

Although these writers admit that the two types of inquiries are 'intertranslatable' they insist that we must not lose sight of the difference between the two standpoints. They warn that

. . . to rely exclusively on the manipulative approach—thus limiting inquiry to a consideration of ways and means—is to court the danger of interfering with inquiry if it has implications contrary to antecedently fixed policy (ends). The purely contemplative standpoint, on the other hand, fails to maximize the relevance of inquiry to the richest potentialities and most pressing needs of society in the given situation. This is what is sound about the emphasis on 'unity of theory and practice' in pragmatism and the traditional literature of Marxism.

Lasswell and Kaplan do not consider whether the contemplative method could discover anything substantial and practical about the potentialities and needs of *all* situations—not only of a 'given situation'. Had they done so they would have found even less difficulty in unifying the two methods, an approach which they clearly recommend, 'The adoption of both manipulative and contemplative standpoints in inquiry we designate the *principle of configurative analysis*. The deliberate use of both standpoints is of value for both theory and practice. The functions of the scientist overlap and interact with those of the policy maker.' And as they are not unmindful that 'the social scientist may affect the phenomena he observes to a much more significant degree than is true of the physical sciences . . .' one begins to wonder whether this does not in the ultimate resort reduce all contemplative work to manipulation. Indeed the difference between these two standpoints seems much rather a difference in the manner in which the sociologist manipulates society and not a difference between his manipulating it or not. After all, if we assume that the sociologist's findings are *communicated*, that people are informed of these findings, the influence thus exerted will not fall short of manipulation. In the introduction of a recently published work on problems of social mobility we read, 'Such problems are central to the study of

221

social structure; they are of direct concern both for the development of sociological theory *and for the formulation of social policy*' [italics mine].[1] Here it appears that communicated sociological thought is manipulative and that this consequence is honestly recognized by a sociologist who is empirically minded and whose objectivity is scrupulous. Sociologists are fond of prefacing their treatises with remarks of the following kind. 'Nothing concerns me but the truth. Sociology is a science, it deals with what *is* and not what *ought to be*.' Then they invariably slip in a piece of self-justification such as this, 'At the same time I hope that my findings will be of value in solving such and such a social problem.' Of course, they have no intention of determining human values, they merely wish to provide us with a more precise tool of knowledge with which we should shape our future in pursuit of our own ends. Sociologists protest that it is not their business to fix these ends. Protesting they forget that the concept of a social 'end' is inseparable from that of social means. An 'end' clearly sets a terminal stage to our pursuits which—at least in the social sense—we never reach. Perhaps the pair, 'values and means' instead of 'ends and means', would let us off this difficulty. But then values would be set apart from, if not set against, means which one hardly finds permissible. Means, in fact, partake of values; and human life, indeed the social process as a whole, consists of an unending series of means. We realize our values in using means: as social reformers and administrators this is the only kind of moral activity we can engage in. The moral end in social action is moral in its pursuit only, for its terminal position ever recedes. The sociologists' plea that his concern is with means not with ends is somewhat spurious. For one thing, his insistence on being heard and heeded commits him in the choice of means: he manifestly demands that the means must be sociological and scientific, not revealed, inspired, and impressionistic. Secondly, we must include the value of 'survival' among the values of social reformers for, at the present time, without this central value all other values are vain presumptions. Now it is a matter for positive science to determine what impediments must be removed from our way if we are to cultivate those other values which are consistent with this central value. The opposition to

[1] D. V. Glass in *Social Mobility in Britain*, 1954, p. 3.

these ideas is expressed with enviable certainty by Stanislav Andrezejewski:

> ... my supreme goal is to find the truth and I have tried to the best of my ability to uphold every true scientist's credo of facing the facts, whether they are pleasant or not. I am convinced that, far from being a useless pastime, such disinterested pursuit of truth is the best way in which a social scientist can serve the welfare of humanity. Science, being ethically neutral, cannot indicate the ultimate goals of human endeavour.[1]

Thus we are presented with the 'ideal type' if not the *ideal* of a sociologist who serves the welfare of humanity without being able to say anything definitive about what is certainly inimical to the welfare of humanity.

> Sociology cannot prove that one ought to love one's neighbour, any more than optics can prove that a painting is beautiful ... Chemistry can teach us how to cure, but also how to poison. Psychology can teach us how to rehabilitate juvenile delinquents, but also how to mislead by clever propaganda. Science, in short, is no substitute for ethics: it can only indicate means, never ultimate ends.

On the one hand the sociologist and psychologist asks for recognition as scientists who contribute to the welfare of humanity, on the other hand it is entirely fortuitous—so far as their contribution is concerned—whether the truth will be used for the curing of criminals or the committing of crimes.

> Nevertheless, social sciences have an essential contribution to make. So far, social reformers have resembled more sorcerers than modern physicians. Knowing neither the causes of a disease nor the effective remedies, they tried and still try to cure by incantation; often trying to exorcise the evil by denying its existence. Modern medical science came into existence only after discoveries, which at the time seemed completely remote and useless, were made by men motivated only by the disinterested search for truth. Similarly, social science may give to social reformers the knowledge of the means by which they can attain their ends.

The analogy between medicine and social science is particularly helpful to me. Medicine, we understand, is a science. It is a science which tells us how to discern a disease and how to cure it. The social sciences and sociology on the other hand

[1] *Military Organization and Society*, 1954, pp. 1–2.

are not to assume the authority of determining when and whether a society or any of its organs is diseased and the competence of prescribing how one should go about curing such diseases. If sociology is to make 'an essential contribution to the welfare of humanity'—which is a recurrent theme of moral justification in sociological writings—it must also show the difference between the uses of sociological knowledge in the service of conflicting ends, such as, for instance, the difference between using sociology for oppression and using it for freedom. To hand over sociology to social reformers as 'a means by which they can attain their ends' is no more a contribution to the welfare of humanity than handing over nuclear fission to political and military leaders. If the gulf between sociology and ethics continues to be industriously widened, at least, let there be an end to the sociologist's high-sounding claims of 'contributions to the welfare of humanity'.

The sociologist is a kind of architect who should not be expected to provide blueprints according to the whims of customers. The architect is not going to pander to the caprice of his clients if it meant that the house built according to the client's specifications would collapse in a few years' time. If he is an honest member of his profession the architect would try to enforce the basic principles of his speciality or abandon the commission. The code of the sociologist is no less exacting. The ends or values of reformers and administrators are socially realized; this process of 'socially realizing values' has its own positive norms; of these we are now beginning to understand a few negative imperatives; these the sociologist cannot disown without committing himself to a moral and philosophical scepticism which is incompatible with his scrupulousness and scientific honesty.

Accordingly, much more of the 'formulation of social policy' falls within the scope of the sociologist than he has so far dared to claim openly. The sociologist is most reluctant to make this claim for fear of being banished from the bright uplands of science into the misty valleys of philosophy. To illustrate briefly how this claim could be made I select a problem discussed in the work on social mobility to which I referred earlier.

'. . . Though we may infer from other studies that the individual

224

manual worker in the three countries (Britain, France, and U.S.A.) differs in his view of the desirability of upward social mobility— that, for example, the French syndicalist may regard such personal mobility as being "treason" to his class, whereas for the American worker the idea of upward movement is part of the accepted set of aspirations in his society—we cannot say whether such differences actually affect the rigidity of the social structure.'

Here I find the sociologist studying and recording relationships of the following kinds: firstly, differences in the attitudes of workers to a social phenomenon, upward mobility; secondly, as yet a query, but it is implied that the sociologist studies and describes it—the effects of these attitudes on the social structure. Though it is not included in the passage quoted one may add a third item of study, namely the impact of mobility or rigidity on the personality structure of the individual. The third item would, as it were, close the circuit individual-society-individual. Now it is obvious that such studies as these have no anchorage in anything permanent, as the generalizations at which they can arrive are applicable only to particular situations and times. That the French attitude is this and the American attitude is that at a particular period of history and that one or the other attitude would favour a flexible social structure in given circum- stances and, finally, that a mobile or non-mobile social structure has certain effects on the personality are all propositions which concern unique historical situations. Generalizations on these matters are indeed valuable, nay, indispensable for the under- standing of the social process at particular times and in par- ticular places, but this is no longer sufficient to justify the labour and expenditure which sociological investigations involve. A fourth item of study is now to be included; this will relate the first three and particularly the third to a system of principles which survive all historical changes. Having defined the abnorm of adjustment we may now proceed to match this abnorm with the social structure and ask, for instance, whether the incidence of abnormal adjustment is favoured by the flexibility or rigidity of the social structure. According to an hypothesis advanced by A. B. Hollingshead and F. C. Redlich, 'Mobility in the class structure is neurotogenic.'[1] In my view, rigidity in the class

[1] 'Social Stratification and Psychiatric Disorders', *Amer. Sociol. Rev.*, April 1953, XVIII, pp. 163-9.

structure may also contribute to abnormal adjustment if compensatory outlets are lacking. It may seem that this matter of 'compensatory outlets' would hopelessly complicate the fourth study I am recommending; one may say that cultural forms, structures, and institutions which are not directly connected with social class may counteract and even cancel out the pathogenesis caused by social class; and one may conclude that the matching of the abnorm to a single institution such as social class is bound to be an unreliable method of assessing the abnormality of a social institution. Yet I believe that to isolate all these variables and match every one of them in a given situation against a universal abnorm of adjustment would not be too great a task of systematic assessment. If, for instance, a certain type of religion were used to provide compensations for failure in upward mobility one could at least try to compare the abnorm with effects of the religious precepts outside the institution of class and say whether what was gained on the swings was not being lost on the roundabouts. I do not deny that this sort of comparison would entail a stupendous amount of painstaking work and some amount of reliance on quantitative methods; nevertheless the difficulties are not crippling and they do not justify continued scepticism.

In the example quoted the study of social mobility is not related to constants such as my abnorm. Consequently the results of each and even of those of the three together remain apart from and, let us face it, unrelated to sociological studies in neighbouring fields.

In these days there has been a tiresome repetition of pleas for 'synthesis' in sociology. Tiresome, for these pleas do not indicate whether the synthesis should be ontological-substantive or conceptual-linguistic, or both. An ontological synthesis is an integration of meaning or, to be more specific, it is the development of a central norm through which it becomes possible to make all partial meanings commensurate with a central meaning. If, for instance, a rigid social structure (i.e. the absence of upward social mobility) is combined with religious institutions proffering mystical and otherworldly compensations, the two, rigidity and compensations, are truly commensurable only on the level of individual psychology. On this level the significance of each can be expressed in a common psycho-

226

logical currency the value of which could be fixed by an agreed psychological abnorm. Herein lies the essence of the much coveted sociological synthesis. Without this procedure onto-logical synthesis will continue to flounder in the mire of ideo-logies and dogmas, for these alone have tried to offer social thought a central meaning with which all part-meanings are commensurate.

In a paper published before the appearance of his *Social System* Talcott Parsons remarked about empirical research that, '. . . the most disappointing single thing about it has been the degree to which the results of this work have failed to be cumulative.'[1] Now he and others have been deeply committed to assist 'cumulation' by creating a new conceptual scheme for sociology. Parsons observes that '. . . a common conceptual scheme' would make 'the work of different investigators in a specific sub-field and those in different sub-fields commensur-able'.[2] But how can conceptual uniformity 'cumulate' diverse and incommensurable material? A conceptual scheme can never transform incommensurable entities and processes into com-mensurable entities and processes. At worst, a scheme of this kind may consist in the spreading of universals like umbrellas sheltering ill-matched phenomena; at best, the scheme may serve as a merger of duplicated concepts in general use and thus lead to a certain economy of thought. Agreement on con-cepts is indeed helpful when thinking is to be dovetailed, but in itself it constitutes no progress towards establishing increase in substantive social knowledge.[3] The refinement of conceptual tools does not introduce a new element of understanding of social meanings when the older concepts, in all their multi-plicity, have often maintained closer relationships with those meanings. One cannot help feeling that this kind of theoretical work has been all scaffolding and no building. Furthermore one must protest that the abstract conceptual schemes so far produced are no less diffuse and unco-ordinated than the social thinking to which they were intended to apply. In short, we cannot establish a coherence of meaning by designing a new

[1] 'The Prospects of Sociological Theory', *Amer. Sociol. Rev.*, Feb. 1950, XV, pp. 3–16.
[2] Ibid.
[3] Cf. 'The Present Status of Social Theory', by Theodore Abel, *Amer. Sociol. Rev.*, April 1952, XVII, pp. 156–64.

sociological *lingua franca* if what we are translating does not possess a coherence of meaning.

At this point the idea of commensurability introduces a new and important issue. If all sociological information is organized around a norm, if all social phenomena become commensurable then, as well as a substantive and ontological synthesis, we have arrived simultaneously at a teleological synthesis.[1] Even if we know no more than the minimum area of abnormal adjustment—the 'abnorm'—we should be able to catch a glimpse of the broad direction towards which the social process must continue if it is to continue at all. Without commensurability, talk about synthesis is futile; with it the cautious sociologist may have more thrust upon him than he originally wished for. Also as commensurability means 'unified measure' along a single continuum which is both positive and normative at the same time it is inevitable that certain areas of this continuum will be designated as 'normal' and 'abnormal' or, in ethical parlance, as 'good' and 'evil'. The point at issue is this: without synthesis sociology is condemned to remain a *melée* of disparate pieces of information and not a coherent scientific discipline; with synthesis it becomes both a scientific discipline and a social philosophy. This predicament is by no means peculiar to sociology, all the life sciences share this fate in some measure, in particular psychology and biology. In all these, the norm and abnorm of being amounts to the norm and abnorm of becoming, and the latter, as I suggested above, is the only source of a social philosophy we, as scientists, are capable of assimilating.

The idea of commensurability is similar to what R. K. Merton called 'functional alternatives, equivalents, or substitutes',[2] except for this: from the point of view of a central norm no two functional alternatives are equivalent. For example the religious compensation for an absence of upward mobility may be a functional alternative but it is not an equivalent or even a substitute. Whereas £5 and £10 are commensurable they are not equivalent. To illustrate further, political fanaticism issuing from the cultural forms of party, doctrines, symbols, and so on,

---

[1] This is not unrelated to Professor Ginsberg's remark that '. . . institutions can only be understood teleologically . . .' *The Psychology of Society*, 1944, p. 123.

[2] Cf. *Social Theory and Social Structure*, 1949, p. 52.

may have a self-transcending function for the individual not unlike the functions offered by a pietistic religion. However an appeal to a central norm would soon destroy the illusion of 'equivalence'. All this may strike the reader as if I confidently anticipated a time when all these functions would become exhaustively measurable. That some residual and tangible effects of these functions will become increasingly quantifiable is certain but the exhaustive quantification of the realities which make up these functions is probably impossible. It may be sobering to consider in this connection the following: '. . . the developing scientific outlook owed its main features to the predilections of the mathematicians, and the main assumption of the philosophy accompanying this scientific achievement is that the real may be identified with the quantitative.'[1] This shrewd observation ought to be drummed into the heads of all budding arithmetically minded sociologists.

4. The Minimum Certainty is Psychological

It seems reasonably well established [writes Talcott Parsons] that there are minimum conditions of socialization with respect for instance to the relation between affectional support and security, without which a functioning personality cannot be built up . . . These minimum needs of individual actors constitute a set of conditions to which the social system must be adapted.[2]

He calls these minima 'functional prerequisites'. This is a significant statement which subsequently gets lost in the ensuing conceptual analysis. It drew no fire from critics who, presumably, took no notice of it. That there is a minimum certainty of this nature is quietly admitted at times and hastily qualified by saying that the minimum is too paltry, too ineffectual for us to specify the proper outcome of the many vital issues of social living, and too vague as well.

The concept of functional requirements (needs, prerequisites) [writes R. K. Merton], . . . remains one of the cloudiest and empirically most debatable concepts in functional theory, as utilized by sociologists, the concept of functional requirement tends to be tautological or *ex post facto*; it tends to be confined to conditions of

[1] J. W. N. Sullivan, *Limitations of Science*, 1938, p. 177.
[2] *The Social System*, 1952, p. 28.

229

'survival' of a given system; it tends, as in the work of Malinowski, to include biological as well as social 'needs'.

Indeed it has not been obvious how and where to find the distinguishing marks of these functional needs. The sociologist stubbornly intent on deriving the vital needs of social existence from sociology alone or even primarily from sociology will never get anywhere near finding them. Notice Merton's criticism of Malinowski for the extravagance of including in the concept of functional needs 'biological as well as social needs'. But what is wrong with commencing our sociological theory with biological and psychological postulates? What is wrong with reaffirming that the substratum of society is the living man whose bio-psychological imperatives continue to prevail in a social existence? The condemnation of a biological frame of reference has outlived its purpose. The anti-Spencerian reaction against organismic analogies was salutary in its time, for this eliminated some of the most misleading importations into sociology from biology. But recognizing the weakness of biological analogies with social structure does not entail refusing to learn what we can from biology about either the individuals who make up that social structure, or their functions within it. In fact, it is simply not true that the decisively substantive information on functional needs can come from any other quarter than biology via psychology. The second misgivings about this minimum certainty was recently reiterated by Professor W. J. H. Sprott:

. . . there are what one might call psychophysiological imperatives. Every social system must satisfy certain basic needs of its members. The trouble here is that beyond such obvious needs as the provision of sufficient nourishment we hardly know what these basic needs are. If, however, we could get some agreed criteria of what is pathological, we might be able to find out what pressures different role systems bring to bear upon their actors, and what compensatory reliefs they are likely to seek.[1]

Thus, while the minimum certainty about the normal is trivial, a definition of what is pathological could dispose of this predicament. This is precisely what the present work has attempted to

---

[1] *Science and Social Action*, 1954, p. 138.

accomplish. I have considered whether the minimum certainty furnished to us by bio-psychological constants is really so insignificant as to be of no immediate use to the various fields of human action in which sociological knowledge can be applied. And now I conclude that the definition of abnormal adjustment may well become a guide to the reformers of our primary and secondary institutions.

Claims of this sort place on me the responsibility of defining the way in which, in my view, psychology and sociology are related. An outline of this relationship nearest to my conception is given by Talcott Parsons:

It is not possible simply to 'extrapolate' from the personality mechanisms of the one to those of the many as participants in the social system . . . These considerations should not, however, give the impression that what are ordinarily called 'psychological' concepts have no relevance to sociological theory . . . it is of the greatest importance that motivational categories should play a central role in sociological theory. Essentially the dynamic elements of personalities and of social systems are made up of the same 'stuff'!

Parsons time and again stresses his objection to treating the social systems as 'resultants' of personality systems.[1] There are some incompatibilities in Parsons' position and some of these appear in the passage quoted. Firstly, I should make it clear that the writing large of individual dynamics into social dynamics *is* an extrapolation; this is a difficult task and no one expects to obtain social norms by 'simply' extrapolating. Secondly, it is well known that Parsons makes 'action' the ultimate element of the social system—but then on his own showing the social system consists of bio-psychological occurrences, events. After all, systems of action are systems of psychological phenomena in the ultimate resort. Thirdly, if as Parsons concedes 'motivational categories should play a central role in sociological theory' he presumably admits that they are causally more decisive than relational or social categories.

I am very well aware of the importance of social causes which are not psychological: both physical and social factors affect motivations; but when motivations are so affected they are affected psychologically. And just as the social exerts its influence on the individual psychologically so does the psychology

[1] For instance, op. cit., pp. 14, 18, 202, 249, 539, 542, 543, 548.

of the individual imprint itself on its physical and social environment: society, its institutions, symbols, and so on, are all projected psychological vehicles, carriers of psychological meaning. Society is a bio-psychological creation and no matter how far in culture it may have receded from its bio-psychological origins it cannot be divorced from them. It is for this reason that we must count on biology and psychology to furnish the fundamental principles of the socially normal or abnormal.

To ensure that this claim is not misunderstood one further explanation is added. If we ask the question, 'how does a particular social value arise?' it is obvious that an exclusively psychological account will not be sufficient for an answer. If, on the other hand, we ask, 'what sort of values are most appropriate to the bio-psychological nature of man?' it is certain that we should explore *that nature and nothing else* to obtain the first principles of this 'appropriateness'. The present study aims at making the first hazardous step towards solving the problem of appropriate values. It is only later that the truly sociological questions as to the social norm or abnorm can be raised, that is questions such as, 'what sort of social organization (institutions, symbols, etc.), are most appropriate for the sustenance of values which in turn are most appropriate to the bio-psychological nature of man?' In fact, I have done no more than define the individually inappropriate, the abnorm, from which the socially inappropriate is as yet to be obtained through laborious extrapolation. Instead of positive functional needs, instead of a positive norm, I sought for the absolute minimum area of abnormal adjustment, for a positive 'abnorm'. Clearly without an agreement at least in this matter we cannot proceed to matching values with the abnorm and rejecting those values which countenance the abnorm. Even less could we pass on to the question of what is an inappropriate social organization, institution, symbol, and so on. The extrapolation of the individual abnorm will require separate studies each possibly far more extensive than the present one. It is often suggested that even if we had clearly defined psychological norms or abnorms they could not be simply converted into sociological norms and abnorms without combining them with *sui generis* sociological norms and abnorms. Whilst it is true that the conversion is by no means simple there is no such thing as a *sui generis* sociological norm. People defending the sociological point of view sometimes argue that there are *sui generis* laws of chemistry which are not reducible to laws in physics. The comparison is fallacious; a norm or abnorm has no meaning unless it pertains to bio-psychological entities such as human beings. A human group as such is not a bio-psychological entity. Even if there is such a thing as a social law or sociological law a *sociological norm* remains an extrapolated psychological norm.

I conclude (to make use of my earlier example), that if a society affords more affectional support to those higher up on the social ladder then the seeking of affectional support will inevitably express itself in a hankering for upward social mobility. I also conclude that if frustration is caused by the limited room towards the apex of the social pyramid, without this frustration being forestalled or countered by commensurable satisfactions, society would be in a condition in which the basic human need for affectional support would be chronically frustrated. Should we declare this predicament of individual human beings 'abnormal' there is no reason why we should hesitate to describe the society which has given rise to this predicament in the majority of individuals as an abnormal society. So long as we agree that no commensurable solutions are equivalent we should be able to eliminate those at least which are definitely responsible for abnormal individual conditions. Much as in our age we deeply suspect settlements of political or sociological disputes by the verdict, 'this is human nature', the fact remains that all disputes are so settled in the ultimate resort. It is therefore one of the sociologist's more urgent tasks to relate psychological abnorms to social structure. 'There are at least words that are shorthand for criteria in the case of individuals', remarked Crane Brinton, 'health and disease, normality and abnormality, sanity and insanity. I think that those of you who work with individuals really do know concretely —operationally—what you mean by those terms. For collectivities, there simply are no such terms.'[1] I do not indeed expect that individual norms lend themselves to easy and smooth extrapolation. Yet isn't it true that, in this very day, investigations are conducted into the problems of restructuring organizations

---

[1] 'Individual Therapy and Collective Reform: A Historian's View', *Amer. J. Orthopsychiatry*, July 1950, XX, pp. 453–5.

and communities with a view to securing the realization of implicit and sometimes explicit individual norms? Isn't it true to say that all reform movements commence and continue with the assumption that such extrapolations are possible? And finally isn't it the case that all sociological thinking is inspired by this very assumption? Consider projects such as 'action researches'[1] which mean, we understand, investigations into the causes and nature of a social situation or phenomenon alongside their *treatment* according to some criteria of health, normality, or adaptability. It is astonishing that the action researchers have managed to shirk the task of declaring what their standards for collectivities really were and how they carried out the business of extrapolating their individual norms. An eminent example of the sort of thing these action researchers, or 'social therapists', do is furnished by a publication[2] which contains the record of a team of consultants attached to a London factory (Glacier) for the purpose of assisting the management and the workers in developing a smooth consultative and executive machinery as well as a specific kind of morale deemed by the consultants to be desirable. The writer of the report, Dr. Jaques, remarks in his introduction that action research which is carried out '. . . without regard to the needs of the client . . . (is) . . . a breach of the professional role of the research workers. . . .' This application of normal medical ethics to social research would have been laudable if the sociologists had been as definite and explicit about what was to be considered a social abnorm as the medical practitioner or researcher is explicit about a physiological abnorm. Instead of this we were treated to the following equivocation:

To solve immediately practical problems for the factory was therefore inconsistent with the aim of the project, concerned as this was with developing methods of assisting groups to deal with such problems for themselves, so that the organization as a whole could become a more adaptive and self-dependent industrial community . . . It will be some time . . . before it can be determined how far the present work-through methods have gone towards creating that

---

[1] Cf. 'Implications of Medical Practice and Soc ial Case-work for Action Research', by A. T. M. Wilson, *Journal of Social Issues*, Spring, 1947, III, No. 2.

[2] *The Changing Culture of a Factory*, by Elliot Jaques, 1951.

degree of insight which will allow a higher degree of conscious determination of policy to be regularly maintained . . . The fundamental problem confronting Glacier as a factory is not merely to ride the difficulties of the moment, but to maintain a social structure, culture, and corpus of personnel, which will allow it successfully to meet the changes demanded of it in a future, in a changing society. *Our definition of social health in an industrial community would picture a factory not so much free of problems, as one capable of tackling in a realistic way whatever technical, economic, and social problems it may encounter* [italics mine].

There is no doubt that the work carried out by Dr. Jaques and his colleagues was useful and its record interesting. These workers cannot be called to account for the obvious equivocation of the foregoing conclusion because they had not been furnished with a method and a unified conceptual scheme whereby they could have extrapolated their mental hygiene bias. As it is, the collectivity which came under their microscope could not properly be measured with the help of any norm and their valiant attempt to formulate one failed. What does it mean to 'maintain a social structure, culture, and corpus of personnel, which will allow it successfully to meet the changes demanded of it in a future, in a changing society'? Isn't this the individual norm of adaptability writ large? We have had occasion to see that this individual norm is useless but even if it were not it would be a downright reactionary thesis that an individual or a collectivity must seek flexibility and adaptation at all costs. It is a commonplace that often it is a more conclusive sign of great vigour when the individual or collectivity clashes with its environment to adapt the latter instead of adapting itself or when a collectivity dissolves itself altogether to be replaced by more adequate collectivities. The gratuitous essay at formulating norms for collectivities in this breezy manner fully justifies Crane Brinton's scepticism about such norms as these. We know that the simple 'writing large' of psychological norms into social norms will not do and that each institution as well as each system of institutions will have to be matched carefully to the psychological norm which we may contrive to isolate. '. . . The mental health movement seems increasingly unwilling to furnish the public with chapter and verse regarding the institutional threats to mental health . . .'

writes Dallas Pratt[1] and he strangely surprises us with the obvious for we have become accustomed to keep religiously clear of norms, be they psychological or social. The responsibility for this rests with contemporary sociology and not with the mental health movement; the latter constitutes organized social action which would readily follow the guidance and inspiration of a sociological critique of institutions. In a critique of this nature the social institution of the family would become the axis of a 'normative' sociology. By this I mean that the condition of extrapolating the psychological norm is that we constantly relate the main features of such institutions as class, property, justice, religion, and so on to the central institution of family. In more explicit language—and in keeping with my selected example—a certain class system will be judged by the influence it exerts on the socialization of the mother and child, by how far it helps or hinders the individual in the smooth transmutation of unserviceable disbalance. Extrapolation will mean that conclusions—with various degrees of specificity—will be reached and couched in terms such as the following: 'a social order which seduces the mother from discharging her bio-psychological functions is abnormal', or 'a culture which attaches prestige to the independence and professional activities of mothers of under-fives is abnormal', or 'a fiscal policy which encourages mothers of under-fives to leave their families and go out to work is abnormal', and so on.

It is somewhat of an anticlimax when I admit that I do not intend to deal with the problem of extrapolating individual abnorms and formulating social ones. My justification for evading this task is that extrapolation presupposes agreement on the psychological abnorm. The definition of the latter must occupy all my attention, for a positive-normative synthesis of sociology depends completely on this. I must emphasize that this plea for 'psychological priority' has nothing to do with the psychologistic theories of social causation. The point at issue is this: we must distinguish a 'sociological law' from a so-called 'sociological norm or abnorm'. Sociological laws, such as those, for instance, in George Homans' *Human Group* are general formulae which in their simplest form run 'if x then a', i.e.

[1] 'Making the Environment Respond to Basic Emotional Needs', *Psychiatry*, May 1952, XV, pp. 179–88.

in certain circumstances such and such a thing will happen. These are necessary formulae but they do not tell us what circumstances and what happenings are definitely inappropriate to the fundamental nature of man; they do not determine which x's and a's are definitely inimical to the smooth cultural transmutation of man's growth-cohesion conflict. On the other hand, the sociological norm, or rather abnorm, lists those x's and a's which foster the conditions of abnormal adjustment in individuals. A similar situation obtains in physiology where one formula may refer to correlations and sequences whilst another may relate these correlations and sequences to the norm of health or the abnorm of ill-health. In medicine all physiological laws are automatically—though sometimes only implicitly— evaluated in terms of their relevance to health or ill-health. In medicine we have an example of the positive-normative synthesis of physiology. But, just as in medicine an etiology may be complicated by physical, chemical, social, economic, and other factors, so in sociology social causation cannot be explained by psychology alone. In other words, medicine is self-contained in that it suffices for the definition of a medical norm of health— or 'abnorm' of ill-health—yet again it is not self-contained in that it does not suffice for the definition of the whole of physiological causality (etiology). Similarly, the psychological abnorm is all-explanatory and sufficient for the diagnosis of social abnormality but when the question arises, 'why is this society or that institution abnormal?' the psychological account is insufficient and the sociological point of view comes into its own. Psychological laws are not convertible into sociological laws but psychological norms are convertible into sociological norms; and conversely, whereas sociological laws cannot be reduced to psychological laws without remainder, sociological norms can be reduced to psychological norms. This distinction of norms from laws will be easily understood if we remember that the structure and functioning of an abnormal society too conforms to the laws of sociology.

5. *The Need for Metaphysical Roots*

The reader may be helped to overcome his resistance to a psychologically determined synthesis in sociology by being made aware of an important difference between psychology and sociology. This is that there is no such thing as 'metasociology' whereas metapsychology is a legitimate sector of metaphysics. The metaphysical substratum of all sciences is one common soil from which they are nourished, though scientists will admit this only with various degrees of self-consciousness. In spite of the antimetaphysical war-cries of many scientists they could not last a day without their unconscious metaphysical preconceptions.[1] A synthesis of the sciences is dependent on their common metaphysical parentage and a science which cuts itself off from this mother soil must eventually wither away. Sociology can hope to remain vital only if it retains its psychological link with metaphysics. I endeavoured to lend substance to this abstract-sounding claim in the first and second chapters of this book where I tried to show that metaphysical conceptions were by no means remote from the practicalities of everyday psychological problems. It was demonstrated there that the abnorm is one form of disbalance whilst disbalance in general is an ultimately essential quality of all that exists.

At any rate, no science can achieve synthesis unaided out of its own specializations. This is true even of physics and far more so of sociology. In sociology a wealth of as yet unassimilated material has been piled up, but the demand for its synthesis is spurred on only partly by a feeling of disorientation amidst this mass of detail and plethora of theoretical fragments. This demand is also inspired by another need which sociologists are reluctant to avow openly. They say that the sociologist is, after all, a scientist whose task terminates with the analysis and portraiture of facts and that concern with facts only is a necessary limitation of all sciences. With most of the life sciences however, and with sociology in particular, there is a difficulty. The very interest in the subject matter and the very dedication to its exploration would be impossible for a sociologist without a correspondingly profound concern with the anomalous and painful in social life. The sociologist, like other human beings, is inclined to forget his beginnings. Immersed in the often fascinat-

---

[1] Another of J. W. N. Sullivan's perspicacious observations may lend further emphasis to this, '. . . the truly significant change in modern science is not to be found in its increased powers to aid man's progress, but in the change in its metaphysical foundations' (op. cit., p. 196).

ing intricacies of his problems he will soon plead intellectual curiosity as his sole or, at least, dominant motive. And thus distracted by the labouring of detail and of limited abstractions he loses sight of the single-mindedness which impelled him towards inquiry at the outset. It is not that his work is trivial and synthesis is alone significant—this is emphatically not the moral of my argument. But it is imperative at this juncture that the social scientist should find a *raison d'être* more directly relevant to the total human situation than the analysis of social facts relative to time and place and unrelated to the metaphysics of life. Synthesis consists in transcending this relativism by anchoring all observations to ultimate principles. Without this commitment sociology is at best a 'policy science'—to use H. D. Lasswell's term—a science instrumental strictly to the realization of the arbitrary values of the moment. With synthesis sociology becomes consciously, openly, and deliberately a science of values. This is not to say that sociology will determine values— no science can do that, for values are unalterably inherent in human existence and are part of man's bio-psychological nature. In the ultimate resort, no science *creates* values, it only discovers, specifies, and defines them.

To escape from the disillusioning insight that substantive first principles cannot be found in sociology, sociologists continue to eschew the *a priori* lead and take refuge in conceptual theory-making on the one hand or monographic studies of detail on the other. It would be most unjustifiable to discourage either of these two pursuits while pleading for the practice of a third. Sociological synthesis presupposes both of these endeavours. At the same time this is a commonplace which conveniently conceals the limitations of these two methods of study. In physics the interpretations of all phenomena are integrated into a basic system of hypotheses concerning the ultimate nature of matter and energy. A similar trend is clearly the case with the other sciences including biology and psychology. In all these the systems of basic hypotheses are unashamedly metaphysical though the empirical façade is broader and less transparent in physics than it is in psychology. As we proceed along the line of sciences from physics to psychology the element of the empirical shrinks and the scope of the metaphysical increases. Now, there is nothing novel in these observations nor even surprising in the facts to which they refer; this progression is a permanent feature of the hierarchy of sciences. It is perhaps less apparent that this hierarchy entails a rule of decreasing empiricism which cannot be contravened without interesting consequences. For instance, a synthesis in psychology, such as the one offered by the psycho-analytic theory, is rooted in a less quantitative empiricism than the one so far achieved in biology; but should any psychological synthesis aspire to a more quantitative empiricism than what has been possible in biology it would soon find itself disorganized and in a blind alley. No science can imitate the empiricism of the discipline which precedes it without creating confusion. To ensure therefore that a too ambitious empiricism does not sidetrack the development of a science the latter's precise position in the general metaphysical framework must be defined. A psychological synthesis, for instance, is not going to be undermined by subsequent biological discoveries if the metaphysical basis of this synthesis is the same as the metaphysical basis upon which the biological, chemical, and physical syntheses are built. In other words, just as no synthesis in, say, biology is possible on the basis of strictly biological empiricism, similarly none is possible in sociology on the basis of strictly sociological empiricism. I contend that sociology has failed to integrate our knowledge of social life because it has paid little attention to this rule. Empiricism in sociology has been allowed to dictate attempts at synthesis, sometimes irrespective of the metatheoretical first principles in psychology, biology, chemistry, and physics. It is probable that this sudden break-away of sociology is a reaction against the aprioristic sociologies from Plato to Marx, yet its lamentable consequence today is that sociologists are most reluctant to consider a total substantive hypothesis even when its explanatory value may be high.

Contemporary sociological attempts at 'cumulating' empirical parts into meaningful wholes constitute a break from the hierarchy of sciences. In trying to effect a synthesis in an autarchic fashion sociology has assumed more confidence than is its due. This confidence is further boosted by the show of precision in measuring, weighing, scoring, and counting social phenomena. The usual objections against the quantitative and statistical etiquette are that they cramp our imagination and resourcefulness in reflection. Of course, one often feels that the unwritten and ominous rule 'measure what you can, not what you will' has already degenerated into 'reflect only on what you can measure'. While I have no intention to disparage quantitative methods in social science I feel it necessary to say that these methods in social science encourage the mistaken view that we can do without metaphysical first principles in sociology.

By outlining the principal limitations of this study I may be better placed to claim for it the credit of a modest contribution. In the first place no norm has been defined. Instead of this I tried to show that the 'normal-abnormal' dimension in adjustment *can* be defined. The second limitation is that the critical (zero) point in this dimension had to be left to an operational decision. Nevertheless any charge of arbitrariness against this operational solution is met by the following arguments, firstly, that there is agreement on the dimension; secondly, that there is agreement on the *specific direction* of the abnormal end of this dimension; thirdly, that the operational zero point would be such as to be fixed as far away as possible from the extremes of that specific direction without raising it extravagantly high above the statistical abnorm of the healthiest known societies; fourthly, that there is nothing disheartening in the upward changeableness of this operational limit or spurious in its 'progressivist' implications; a commitment to the doctrine of progress is not a philosophical decision but a bio-psychological imperative; and finally, agreement on the dimension alone—irrespective of the fickleness of the operational limit—is sufficient for the most fundamental moral philosophical decisions. Whereas for individual diagnosis the precision of the operational limit is frequently essential, for general ethical orientation, applied sociology, and social action, the acceptance of the dimension is decisive. For this reason, extrapolation, far from weakening the significance of the abnorm, consolidates its position.

Let no one complain that this is too flimsy a structure upon which to build a synthesis of sociology. There is no use pretending that we have a choice in this matter: we must act on the little certainties, the big certainties will never come. At any rate, time is not on our side.

BIBLIOGRAPHY OF THE 'ABNORM'

(It would be unnecessary to add to the several existing bibliographies on metapsychology, on the psychology of art and politics, on psychological and sociological method, and so on. The many admirable and comprehensive texts on these subjects are well supplied with reading lists. There is, however, among these treated in this volume one subject, indeed my cardinal topic, the concept of the normal and of the abnormal which, to my knowledge, has not yet been adequately furnished with a bibliography. As an attempt to remedy this situation I offer the following list. It comprises most of the sources from which reflection can be further nourished on such subjects as 'normality', 'health', 'abnormality', 'disease', 'adjustment', and so on. I should appreciate it if omissions from this list were brought to my notice so that I may eventually be able to compile a comprehensive bibliography on this subject.—P. H.)

BALINT, Michael, 'The Final Goal of Psychoanalytic Treatment', *International Journal of Psychoanalysis*, 1937, XVII, pp. 206–16.

BENEDICT, Ruth, 'Anthropology and the Abnormal', *Journal of General Psychology*, Jan. 1934, X, No. 1, pp. 59–82.

BINGER, Carl, 'What is Maturity?' *Harper's Magazine*, May 1951, Vol. 202, No. 1212, pp. 70–8.

CANTOR, Nathaniel, 'What is a Normal Mind?' *American Journal of Orthopsychiatry*, Oct. 1941, XI, pp. 676–83.

DALY KING, C., 'The Meaning of Normal', *Yale Journal of Biology and Medicine*, Jan. 1945, XVIII, pp. 493–501.

DURKHEIM, E., *The Rules of Sociological Method*, University of Chicago Press, Chicago, 1938.

DURKHEIM, E., *Suicide*, Routledge & Kegan Paul, London, 1954.

EDWARDS, A. S., 'A Theoretical and Clinical Study of So-Called Normality', *The Journal of Abnormal and Social Psychology*, Jan.–March 1934, XXVIII, No. 4, pp. 366–76.

FOLEY, J. P., 'The Criterion of Abnormality', *Journal of Abnormal and Social Psychology*, 1935, XXX, pp. 279–90.

FREUD, Sigmund, 'Analysis Terminable and Interminable', *Collected Papers*, 1952, V., Hogarth Press, London, pp. 316–57.

FROMM, Erich, *The Sane Society*, Routledge & Kegan Paul, London, 1956.

GILLETTE, J. M., 'An Examination of Criteria for the Determination of Normal Society', *American Sociological Review*, Aug. 1937, II, No. 4, pp. 501–7.

GLOVER, Edward, 'Medico-Psychological Aspects of Normality', *The British Journal of Psychology*, General Section, Oct. 1932, XXIII, pp. 152–66.

HACKER, F. T., 'The Concept of Normality and Its Practical Significance', *American Journal of Orthopsychiatry*, Jan. 1945, XV, pp. 47–64.

HARDING, D. W., *Social Psychology and Individual Values*, Hutchinson, London, 1953.

HARTMANN, Heinz, 'Psychoanalysis and the Concept of Health', *The International Journal of Psychoanalysis*, July–Oct. 1939, XX, parts 3–4, pp. 308–21.

HINSHAW, R. P., 'The Concept of Adjustment and the Problem of Norms', *Psychological Review*, May 1942, XLIX, No. 3, pp. 287–92.

HOLLITSCHER, W., 'On the Concept of Psychological Health and Illness', *The International Journal of Psychoanalysis*, 1943, XXIV, pp. 125–40.

JONES, Ernest, 'The Concept of a Normal Mind', *The International Journal of Psychoanalysis*, 1942, XXIII, pp. 1–8.

KUBIE, Lawrence S., 'The Fundamental Nature of the Distinction Between Normality and Neurosis', *The Psychoanalytical Quarterly*, 1954, XXIII, No. 2, pp. 167–204.

LEWIS, Aubrey, 'Health as a Social Concept', *The British Journal of Sociology*, June 1953, IV, No. 2, pp. 109–24.

LINDNER, Robert, *Prescription for Rebellion*, Gollancz, London, 1953.

LUNDBERG, G. A., *Foundations of Sociology*, MacMillan, New York, 1939.

OVERSTREET, H. A., *The Mature Mind*, Gollancz, London, 1950.

REDLICH, F. C., 'The Concept of Normality', *American Journal of Psychotherapy*, July 1952, VI, No. 3, pp. 551–76.

REIDER, Norman, 'The Concept of Normality', *Psychoanalytical Quarterly*, 1950, XIX, pp. 43–51.

ROMANO, John (Ed.), *Adaptation*, Cornell University Press, Ithaca, New York, 1949.

RYLE, John A., 'The Meaning of Normal', *The Lancet*, 4 Jan. 1947, Vol. 252.

SARBIN, T. R., 'Adjustment in Psychology', *Character and Personality*, Sept. 1939–June 1940, VIII.

SCHMIEDEBERG, Melitta, 'After the Analysis . . .', *The Psychoanalytical Quarterly*, 1938, VII, pp. 122–44.

SCHNEERSOHN, F., 'Zur Grundlegung einer Völker- und Massenpsychopathologie (Soziopsychopathologie)', *Ethos*, 1925–6, I.

SENN, Milton J. E., *Symposium on the Healthy Personality*, Josiah Macy Jr. Foundation, New York, 1950.

SKAGGS, E. B., 'The Meaning of the Term "Abnormality" in Psychology', *Journal of Abnormal and Social Psychology*, 1933, XXVIII, pp. 113–18.

SMITH, M. Brewster, 'Optima of Mental Health', *Psychiatry*, 1950, XIII, No. 4, pp. 502–10.

WEGROCKI, H. J., 'A Critique of the Cultural and Statistical Concepts of Abnormality', *Journal of Abnormal and Social Psychology*, 1939, XXXIV, pp. 166–78.

WILE, I. S., 'What Constitutes Abnormality?' *American Journal of Orthopsychiatry*, 1940, X, pp. 216–28.

WOLFF, Werner, *The Threshold of the Abnormal*, Medical Publications, London, 1952.

INDEX OF NAMES

INDEX OF SUBJECTS

Founded by KARL MANNHEIM
Late Professor of Education in the University of London

Edited by W. J. H. SPROTT
Professor of Philosophy in the University of Nottingham

The International Library

of

Sociology and Social

Reconstruction

ROUTLEDGE & KEGAN PAUL

BROADWAY HOUSE, CARTER LANE, LONDON, E.C.4

SOCIOLOGY OF EDUCATION

Mission of the University
JOSÉ ORTEGA Y GASSET. Translated and introduced by Howard
Lee Nostrand   *Second Impression.* 12s. 6d.

Total Education
A Plea for Synthesis
M. L. JACKS, *Director of the Institute of Education, Oxford*
                                                Fourth Impression. 15s.

Education in Transition
A Sociological Analysis of the Impact of the War on English Education
H. C. DENT, *Late Editor of the "Times Educational Supplement"*
                                                Fifth Impression. 16s.

The Social Psychology of Education
An Introduction and Guide to its Study
C. M. FLEMING, *Reader in Education, Institute of Education, London*
                                                Eighth Impression. 10s.

Education and Society in Modern Germany
R. H. SAMUEL, *Professor of Germanic Languages, Melbourne,* and
R. HINTON THOMAS, *Lecturer in German, Birmingham*   16s.

The Museum
Its History and Its Tasks in Education
ALMA S. WITTLIN   *Illustrated.* 28s.

The Educational Thought and Influence of Matthew Arnold
W. F. CONNELL, *Senior Lecturer in Education, Sydney.* With an Introduction by Sir Fred Clarke   23s.

Comparative Education
A Study of Educational Factors and Traditions
NICHOLAS HANS, *Reader in Education, Institute of Education, London*
                                                Fourth Impression. 23s.

New Trends in Education in the 18th Century
NICHOLAS HANS   21s.

2

From School to University
A Study, with special reference to University Entrance
R. R. DALE, *Lecturer in Education, University College, Swansea*   21*s.*

Education and Society
An Introduction to the Sociology of Education
A. K. C. OTTAWAY, *Lecturer in Education, Leeds.* With an Introduction by W. O. Lester Smith   *Second Impression.* 18*s.*

German Youth : Bond or Free
HOWARD BECKER, *Associate Professor in Primary Education, Akron*
18*s.*

Parity and Prestige in English Secondary Education
OLIVE BANKS, *Lecturer in Sociology, Liverpool*   25*s.*

Helvetius
His Life and Place in the History of Educational Thought
IAN CUMMING, *Senior Lecturer in Education, Auckland University College*
25*s.*

Adolescence
Its Social Psychology: With an Introduction to recent findings from the fields of Anthropology, Physiology, Medicine, Psychometrics and Sociometry
C. M. FLEMING, *Reader in Education, Institute of Education, London*
Fourth Impression. 18*s.*

Studies in the Social Psychology of Adolescence
J. E. RICHARDSON, J. F. FORRESTER, J. K. SHUKLA and P. J. HIGGINBOTHAM
Edited by C. M. FLEMING   23*s.*

SOCIOLOGY OF RELIGION

Sociology of Religion
JOACHIM WACH, *Professor of the History of Religions, Chicago*   30*s.*

The Economic Order and Religion
FRANK KNIGHT, *Professor of Social Science, Chicago,* and
THORNTON W. MERRIAM   18*s.*

SOCIOLOGY OF ART AND LITERATURE

Chekhov and His Russia: A Sociological Study
W. H. BRUFORD, *Schröder Professor of German, Cambridge*   18s.

The Sociology of Literary Taste
LEVIN L. SCHÜCKING   *Third Impression.* 9s. 6d.

Men of Letters and the English Public in the 18th Century, 1660-1744, Dryden, Addison, Pope
ALEXANDRE BELJAME, Edited with an Introduction and Notes by Bonamy Dobrée. Translated by E. O. Lorimer   28s.

SOCIOLOGICAL APPROACH TO THE STUDY OF HISTORY

The Aftermath of the Napoleonic Wars
The Concert of Europe—An Experiment
H. G. SCHENK, *Lecturer in Political Economics, Fellow of Exeter College, Oxford*   *Illustrated.* 18s.

Military Organization and Society
STANISLAW ANDRZEJEWSKI, *Simon Fellow, Manchester.* Foreword by A. Radcliffe-Brown   21s.

SOCIOLOGY OF LAW

Sociology of Law
GEORGES GURVITCH, *Professor of Sociology, Sorbonne.* With an Introduction by Roscoe Pound   *Second Impression.* 21s.

The Institutions of Private Law and their Social Functions
KARL RENNER. Edited with an Introduction and Notes by O. Kahn-Freund   28s.

Legal Aid
ROBERT EGERTON. With an Introduction by D. L. Goodhart   *Second Impression.* 12s. 6d.

Soviet Legal Theory: Its Social Background and Development
RUDOLF SCHLESINGER, *Lecturer in Soviet Social and Economic Institutions, Glasgow*   *Second Edition.* 28s.

CRIMINOLOGY

Juvenile Delinquency in an English Middletown
HERMANN MANNHEIM, *Reader in Criminology, London School of Economics*   14s.

Criminal Justice and Social Reconstruction
HERMANN MANNHEIM   *Second Impression.* 20s.

Group Problems in Crime and Punishment
HERMANN MANNHEIM   28s.

The Psycho-Analytical Approach to Juvenile Delinquency: Theory, Case Studies, Treatment
KATE FRIEDLANDER, *Late Hon. Psychiatrist, Institute for the Scientific Treatment of Delinquency*   *Fourth Impression.* 23s.

The English Prison and Borstal Systems
LIONEL FOX, K.C.B., M.C., *Chairman of the Prison Commission for England and Wales*   32s.

Crime and the Services
JOHN SPENCER, *Director of the British Social Project, Bristol University*
28s.

Delinquent Boys: The Culture of the Gang
ALBERT K. COHEN, *Assistant Professor of Sociology, Indiana*
In preparation

THE SOCIAL SERVICES

Social Service and Mental Health
An Essay on Psychiatric Social Workers
M. ASHDOWN and S. C. BROWN   18s.

The Social Services of Modern England
M. PENELOPE HALL, *Lecturer in Social Science, Liverpool*
Third Edition (Revised). 28s.

Lunacy, Law and Conscience, 1744-1845
The Social History of the Care of the Insane
KATHLEEN JONES, *Lecturer in Social Administration, Manchester* 21s.

British Social Work in the 19th Century
A. F. YOUNG and E. T. ASHTON   *In preparation*

SOCIOLOGY AND POLITICS

Social-Economic Movements

An Historical and Comparative Survey of Socialism, Communism, Co-operation, Utopianism; and Other Systems of Reform and Reconstruction

H. W. LAIDLER, *Executive Director, League for Industrial Democracy*
Second Impression. Illustrated. 37s. 6d.

The Analysis of Political Behaviour: An Empirical Approach

HAROLD D. LASSWELL, *Professor of Law, Yale. Third Impression.* 23s.

Dictatorship and Political Police

The Technique of Control by Fear

E. K. BRAMSTEDT
20s.

Nationality in History and Politics

A Psychology and Sociology of National Sentiment and Nationalism

FRIEDRICK HERTZ *Third Impression.* 30s.

The Logic of Liberty: Reflections and Rejoinders

MICHAEL POLANYI, F.R.S., *Professor of Social Studies, Manchester*
18s.

Power and Society

A Framework for Political Inquiry

HAROLD D. LASSWELL, *Professor of Law, Yale*, and
A. KAPLAN, *Professor of Liberal Studies, Indiana*
25s.

The Political Element in the Development of Economic Theory

GUNNAR MYRDAL, *Professor of Economics, Stockholm. Executive Secretary, United Nations Economic Commission for Europe.* Translated from the German by Paul Streeten
25s.

Higher Civil Servants in Britain

From 1870 to the Present Day

R. K. KELSALL, *Senior Research Officer, London School of Economics*
25s.

Democracy and Dictatorship: Their Psychology and Patterns of Life
Z. BARBU, *Lecturer in Social Psychology, Glasgow*   28s.

How People Vote: A Study of Electoral Behaviour in Greenwich
MARK BENNEY, A. P. GRAY, and R. H. PEAR
In preparation

FOREIGN AFFAIRS, THEIR SOCIAL, POLITICAL & ECONOMIC FOUNDATIONS

Patterns of Peacemaking
DAVID THOMSON, *Research Fellow, Sidney Sussex College, Cambridge,* E. MEYER and ASA BRIGGS, *Fellow of Worcester College, Oxford*   25s.

French Canada in Transition
EVERETT C. HUGHES, *Professor of Sociology, Chicago*   16s.

State and Economics in the Middle East
A Society in Transition
A. BONNÉ, *Professor of Economics. Director, Economic Research Institute, Hebrew University, Jerusalem*   *Second Edition (Revised).*   40s.

The Economic Development of the Middle East
An Outline of Planned Reconstruction
A. BONNÉ   *Third Impression.* 16s.

The Danube Basin and the German Economic Sphere
ANTONIN BASCH   18s.

Peasant Renaissance in Yugoslavia, 1900-1950
A Study of the Development of Yugoslav Peasant Society as Affected by Education
RUTH TROUTON   28s.

Transitional Economic Systems
The Polish-Czech Example
DOROTHY W. DOUGLAS   25s.

Political Thought in France from the Revolution to the Fourth Republic
J. P. MAYER
14s.

Central European Democracy and its Background
Economic and Political Group Organization
RUDOLF SCHLESINGER
30s.

ECONOMIC PLANNING

Private Corporations and their Control
A. B. LEVY
Two Volumes. 70s. *the set*

The Shops of Britain
A Study of Retail Distribution
HERMANN LEVY
Second Impression. 21s.

SOCIOLOGY OF THE FAMILY AND ALLIED TOPICS

The Family and Democratic Society
J. K. FOLSOM, *Professor of Economics, Vassar College*
35s.

Nation and Family
The Swedish Experiment in Democratic Family and Population Policy
ALVA MYRDAL, *Director of the Dept. of Social Sciences, UNESCO*
Second Impression. 28s.

The Deprived and the Privileged
Personality Development in English Society
B. M. SPINLEY, *Educational Psychologist, Sheffield Child Guidance Clinic* 20s.

Prosperity and Parenthood
J. A. BANKS, *Assistant Lecturer in Sociology, Liverpool*
21s.

Family, Socialization and Interaction Process
TALCOTT PARSONS, *Chairman of the Department of Social Relations, Harvard,* and ROBERT F. BALES, *Lecturer in Sociology, Harvard*
In preparation

The Home and Social Status
DENNIS CHAPMAN   119 *tables, diagrams and plates, 35s.*

Women's Two Roles
ALVA MYRDAL and VIOLA KLEIN   *In preparation*

TOWN AND COUNTRY PLANNING.
HUMAN ECOLOGY

The Social Background of a Plan: A Study of Middlesbrough
Edited by RUTH GLASS. With Maps and Plans   42s.

City, Region and Regionalism
A Geographical Contribution to Human Ecology
ROBERT E. DICKINSON. With Maps and Plans
Second Impression. 25s.

The West European City: A Study in Urban Geography
ROBERT E. DICKINSON. With Maps and Plans   42s.

Revolution of Environment
E. A. GUTKIND   *Illustrated.* 32s.

The Journey to Work
Its Significance for Industrial and Community Life
K. LIEPMANN, *Research Fellow in Economics, Bristol.* With a Foreword
by Sir Alexander Carr-Saunders   *Second Impression* 16s.

Stevenage: A Sociological Study of a New Town
HAROLD ORLANS   30s.

The Genesis of Modern British Town Planning
A Study in Economic and Social History of the Nineteenth and Twentieth
Centuries
W. ASHWORTH, *Lecturer in Economic History, London School of Economics*
21s.

SOCIOLOGICAL STUDIES OF MODERN COMMUNITIES

Negroes in Britain
A Study of Racial Relations in English Society
K. L. LITTLE, *Reader in Anthropology, Edinburgh*   25*s.*

Co-operative Living in Palestine
HENRIK F. INFIELD. With a Foreword by General
Sir Arthur Wauchope   *Illustrated.* 12*s.* 6*d.*

Co-operative Communities at Work
HENRIK F. INFIELD   18*s.*

Colour Prejudice in Britain
A Study of West Indian Workers in Liverpool, 1941-1951
ANTHONY H. RICHMOND, *Lecturer in Social Theory, Edinburgh*   18*s.*

Social Mobility in Britain
Edited by DAVID V. GLASS, *Professor of Sociology, London School of Economics*   36*s.*

The Absorption of Immigrants
S. N. EISENSTADT, *Head of the Department of Sociology, Hebrew University, Jerusalem*   25*s.*

Studies in Class Structure
G. D. H. COLE, *Chichele Professor of Social and Political Theory, Oxford*   21*s.*

The Study of Groups
JOSEPHINE KLEIN, *Lecturer in Social Studies, Birmingham*
In preparation

SOCIOLOGY OF INDUSTRY

Mobility in the Labour Market
MARGOT JEFFERYS, *Lecturer, London School of Hygiene and Tropical Medicine*   15*s.*

Patterns of Industrial Bureaucracy
ALVIN W. GOULDNER, *Professor of Sociology, Illinois*   21*s*.

Wildcat Strike
A Study of an Unofficial Strike
ALVIN W. GOULDNER   16*s*.

ANTHROPOLOGY & RURAL SOCIOLOGY

The Sociology of Colonies: An Introduction to the Study of Race Contact
RENÉ MAUNIER, *Member of the French Academy of Colonial Sciences.*
Translated from the French by E. O. Lorimer *Two volumes.* 63*s. the set*

A Chinese Village: Taitou, Shantung Province
MARTIN C. YANG   23*s*.

A Japanese Village: Suye Mura
JOHN F. EMBREE, *Associate Professor of Anthropology, California.* With
an Introduction by A. R. Radcliffe-Brown   *Illustrated.* 21*s*.

The Golden Wing: A Sociological Study of Chinese Familism
YUEH-HWA LIN, *Professor of Social Anthropology, Yenching.* Introduction by Raymond Firth   18*s*.

Earthbound China: A Study of Rural Economy in Yunnan
HSIAO-TUNG FEI, *Professor of Sociology, National Yunnan,* and
CHIH-I CHANG, *Lecturer in Sociology, National Yunnan Illustrated.* 20*s*.

Under the Ancestors' Shadow: Chinese Culture and Personality
FRANCIS L. K. HSU, *Professor of Anthropology, College of Liberal Arts,
North Western University*   *Illustrated.* 21*s*.

The Mende of Sierra Leone
A West African People in Transition
K. L. LITTLE   28*s*.

Transformation Scene: The Changing Culture of a New Guinea Village

H. IAN HOGBIN, *Reader in Anthropology, Sydney*   *Illustrated.*   30s.

Indians of the Andes: Aymaras and Quechuas

HAROLD OSBORNE   *Illustrated.*   25s.

Religion, Science and Human Crises

A Study of China in Transition and Its Implications for the West
FRANCIS L. K. HSU   14s.

Colour and Culture in South Africa

A Study of the Status of the Cape Coloured People within the Social Structure of the Union of South Africa
SHEILA PATTERSON   30s.

The Family Herds

P. H. GULLIVER, *Government Sociologist, Tanganyika*   *Illustrated.*   25s.

Growing Up in an Egyptian Village

HAMED AMMAR, *Lecturer in the Sociology of Education, Heliopolis University, Cairo*   28s.

Indian Village

S. C. DUBE, *Professor of Sociology, Osmania University, Hyderabad*   25s.

Gosforth: The Sociology of an English Village

W. M. WILLIAMS, *Lecturer in Geography, University College, North Staffs.*   *In preparation*

The Negro Family in British Guiana: Family Structure and Social Status in the Villages

RAYMOND SMITH, *Research Fellow, Institute of Social and Economic Research, University College of West Indies*   *In preparation*

The History of a Soviet Collective Farm

FEDOR BELOV

In preparation